SEATTLE IN BLACK AND WHITE

Seattle in Black and White

THE CONGRESS OF RACIAL EQUALITY
AND THE FIGHT FOR EQUAL OPPORTUNITY

Joan Singler

Jean Durning

Bettylou Valentine

Maid Adams

V ETHEL WILLIS WHITE BOOKS

University of Washington Press · Seattle and London

This book is published with the assistance of a grant from the V Ethel Willis White Endowed Fund, established through the generosity of Deehan Wyman, Virginia Wyman, and the Wyman Youth Trust.

Publication is also supported by a grant from 4Culture.

University of Washington Press, PO Box 50096, Seattle, WA 98145, USA
www.washington.edu/uwpress

Library of Congress Cataloging-in-Publication Data
Seattle in Black and white : the Congress of Racial Equality and the fight
for equal opportunity / Joan Singler . . . [et al.].
p. cm. — (V Ethel Willis White book)
Includes bibliographical references and index.
ISBN 978-0-295-99084-2 (hardback : alk. paper)
1. African Americans—Washington (State)—Seattle—History—20th century.
2. African Americans—Civil rights—Washington (State)—Seattle—History—
20th century. 3. Civil rights movements—Washington (State)—Seattle—
History—20th century. 4. Congress of Racial Equality—History. 5. Seattle
(Wash.)—Race relations—History—20th century. I. Singler, Joan.
F899.S49N464 2011   323.1196'0730797772—dc22   2010035649

CONTENTS

PREFACE

The civil rights movement of the 1960s was militant, was nationwide, and was shaped by innumerable leaders. It was an uprising of citizens insisting that American democracy should finally live up to its ideals. Yet only during Black History Month do public media and schools take much note of the dynamic changes wrought in the civil rights era. And then, the media tend to portray the civil rights movement as a "great leader" event, with Dr. Martin Luther King Jr. receiving the credit and the South being the arena. Others refer to "Martin and Malcolm." These were extraordinary leaders, of course, as were others who may have faded from public memory, including Ella Baker, James Farmer, Fannie Lou Hamer, Dorothy Height, A. Philip Randolph, and Roy Wilkins. These and countless other leaders inspired thousands across the nation who rose up in action.[1]

As they stood up for their rights in the 1950s and 1960s, African Americans in the South suffered ruthless suppression. The brutality, portrayed on television, shocked viewers everywhere. We, far in the Northwest, were inspired to champion their rights both in the South and at home. Joan and Ed Singler and a handful of others established a chapter of CORE—the Congress of Racial Equality—and hundreds of us joined.

CORE, founded in Chicago in 1942 by James Farmer and other Christian pacifists, adopted Gandhi's philosophy of noncooperation with evil and pioneered many of the nonviolent direct action techniques of the civil rights movement. It was one of four national organizations that led the movement, with the NAACP (National Association for the Advancement of Colored People), Martin Luther King's Southern Christian Leadership Conference (SCLC), and the Student Nonviolent Coordinating Committee (SNCC). According to a definitive history, "CORE, more than any other organization, was responsible for the massive outpouring of direct action against housing, employment and educational discrimination in the North."[2] Seattle paralleled scores of cities across the nation in the 1960s. With dozens of energetic leaders and hundreds of members, Seattle CORE was a powerful force for positive change and had a strong impact on life in the city. It confronted the local "establishment" to open opportunities in employment, in housing, and in public schools. Most people knew about CORE then, but fifty years later both the name and Seattle's movement are nearly invisible. No other northern cities, as far as we know, have been the subject of participant memoirs of 1960s civil rights experience.[3] This book, we hope, will let twenty-first-century readers see and feel the efforts and accomplishments of civil rights activists of the 1960s.

The seeds of this book were planted when, at Walt Hundley's memorial service in 2002, it became clear that memories of events were failing and that a number of Seattle CORE activists were dying. Bettylou Valentine and Joan Singler recognized the necessity of recording Seattle civil rights activities and events as recalled by the participants themselves. To collect memories they mailed out a questionnaire to all former CORE activists whose addresses they could find, and they started research in the University of Washington library archives. Unfortunately, limited response to the questionnaire left the project in limbo. After the death of Don Matson, more resources became accessible when boxes of Seattle CORE files from Don's basement went to Joan and Ed Singler. Maid Adams joined the project, though with some trepidation over the amount of work required. At about the same time, Jean Durning, volunteering at Martin Luther King Jr. Elementary School, was inspired to write about Seattle civil rights efforts. She saw how little information on the local movement was available for school celebrations of Dr. King's birthday or Black History Month. Remembering the questionnaire, Jean phoned Joan Singler and the book was under way.

The authors are all early Seattle CORE members and all served as officers, committee heads, or project leaders. We each had moved to Seattle as young adults, but our backgrounds varied. Bettylou Valentine grew up in a mixed-race family in Pittsburgh. Maid Adams grew up in a blue-collar family, playing with children of color during her childhood in Southern California. Jean Durning, from a white town in Massachusetts, spent a college semester as an exchange student at Fisk University. Joan Singler was introduced to activism when she worked as a shop steward for office workers employed at Teamsters Union headquarters in Detroit. By college, all four of us were aware of—and shocked by—the many injustices suffered by African Americans. We all grew up in the shadow of World War II and were influenced by what one historian has called "the wartime rhetoric of democracy."[4] Like CORE members everywhere we subscribed to what another scholar called "the official 'American creed' of human equality."[5] We were idealistic. The pledge of allegiance was our sacred vow—to strive for Liberty and Justice for All.

We four women were active in leadership roles in Seattle CORE, building on our previous community experience. Joan Singler, one of the founders of the Seattle chapter, was a leader in open-housing campaigns. Jean Durning became a negotiator on employment and organized some dramatic CORE demonstrations. Bettylou Valentine, active against housing discrimination, became CORE's most conscientious secretary. Maid Adams (then called Jean Adams), cochair of the Negotiations Committee and a Freedom School coprincipal, was the only one of us still active in Seattle CORE when it became exclusively black in 1968. We all became friends through Seattle CORE. Like other CORE members, we earnestly believed that our goal of a just and integrated society would be achieved in our lifetime.

Like all CORE projects, this book is a cooperative undertaking. In addition to the memories of the four authors, two dozen former Seattle CORE members contributed their thoughts and recollections. Unfortunately, many members have died, particularly African American men (see appendix 3)—sadly exemplifying the statistics that black men on average have life spans shorter than those of white men and of women, both black and white. We feel an urgency to share our memories before all participants in the momentous efforts of the movement are forgotten. The times were intense and left us with many clear, specific memories. Some of these memories, we're gratified to find, closely match stories in 1960s newspaper clippings.

This book is both a researched history and a joint memoir. Joan Singler did extensive research and initial drafting for chapters 1, 2, 4, 5, 6, 7, 8, and part of chapter 9. Bettylou Valentine drafted the introduction, part of chapter 9, the openings of most chapters, and the epilogue. Jean Durning researched and drafted chapter 3, part of chapter 9, this preface, the bibliography, and the acknowledgments and did considerable editing. Maid Adams drafted chapter 10 and parts of other chapters. Although individuals wrote first drafts of specific chapters, the book is truly written by all of us. Research, reminiscences, discussion, rewriting, and editing from all four were contributed throughout the book, and the content benefited substantially from the attention of four minds. Our process also emphasizes an important CORE principle—collective work plus a collective consciousness. Forty-plus years after the events, we remain a cohesive voice.

The spirit that infused CORE members still inspires us. After the party to celebrate Seattle CORE's twenty-fifth anniversary, former CORE members went to protest apartheid by picketing the home of the South African consul. In 2004 several former CORE members, including two of the authors, traveled to Florida to participate in the Election Protection Coalition to guard the hard-won right to vote, particularly of African American voters. On October 3, 2004, reporting on our trip to Florida, *Seattle Times* columnist Jerry Large wrote: "A lot of people talk about what they did in the '60s when they were young, but for these people being involved wasn't a youthful lark. It's at their core." CORE is indeed still at our core.

ACKNOWLEDGMENTS

We are indebted to Don Matson and his family for saving boxes of CORE files. These include posters, fliers, clippings, buttons, bumper-strips, and a pennant, as well as negotiation reports, research studies, and a nearly complete set of *Corelators*. His family is donating these papers to the Special Collections Division of the University of Washington Libraries.

Many Seattle CORE "alumni" and others active in the movement responded to Joan Singler, Bettylou Valentine, and/or another author in personal interviews. We thank each of them: Sue Davidson, Ellen Fawcett, Elaine Hayes, Barney Hilliard, Felisa Hundley, Gordon Jackins, Sadikifu Akina-James (Ernestine Rogers), retired judge Charles V. Johnson, Norman O. Johnson, Wallace Johnson, James and Marjorie Kimbrough, Ivan King, John David Lamb and Mary Lamb, Bill Lynch, Dick Morrill, Esther Hall Mumford, Cara Newoman, Folayan Oni-Robertson (Barbara Davis), Dr. Infanta Spence-Lewis, and retired judge Robert Winsor. Yvonne Chotzen, Loren Chotzen, and Benjamin Chotzen shared information about their mother, Carla Chotzen. Several former CORE members gave their time generously in telephone interviews: Raymond Cooper, Gilbert Esparza, Reverend Mance Jackson, Millie Russell, Carole Dianne Smith, Marion West, and Ray Williams. We thank them and others, including Harold (Hal) Newman, for informative email communications. We appreciate the help of Folayan Oni-Robertson in consulting with Maid Adams regarding the final year of

Seattle CORE. This book could hardly have been written without the cooperation and the memories of each.

Trevor Griffey, project coordinator of the Seattle Civil Rights and Labor Project, made innumerable helpful suggestions toward publication of this book. He arranged for a video interview of three of the authors, referred us to Brian Purnell and sent us Purnell's dissertation, guided Joan Singler through the pursuit of our FBI files, and encouraged us throughout our process. We also thank Dr. James N. Gregory, Harry Bridges Professor of Labor Studies and director of the University of Washington's Seattle Civil Rights and Labor Project, for his support.

We particularly appreciate Sue Davidson's willingness to allow us to use "Seattle's Freedom Patrol" (written when she was Sue D. Gottfried), which is reprinted here as appendix 1 by permission from *The Progressive*, 409 E. Main St, Madison, WI 53703, www.progressive.org. We thank Ed Singler, David Lamb, Adele Peterson, Ahren Stroming, Karen J. Ferguson, W. J. Rorabaugh, and Mary Henry, who read the manuscript in draft. Their many suggestions have been helpful. The ongoing encouragement of teacher Mrs. Joyce MacDonald and others in Central District schools inspired Jean Durning to keep plugging away. Carrol Sutcliffe kindly volunteered her computer and transcribed Val Valentine's DEEDS report. Walter Bodle was most generous in photographing CORE memorabilia and the four of us. We appreciate Mary Henry for directing us to James Washington Jr.'s files and for her entries at www.BlackPast.org and www.HistoryLink.org. We thank Naomi Pascal, former editor at the University of Washington Press, who encouraged us with her time and advice. Horizon House provided spaces for author meetings and gave other assistance. We also thank Blake Holiday for his help. We are deeply appreciative of our editors at the University of Washington Press, Marianne Keddington-Lang, Mary Ribesky, and others, who have seen us through the publication process with enthusiasm and forbearing.

Carla Rickerson, head of Public Services for Special Collections at the University of Washington Libraries, now retired, and Eleanor Toews, archivist for the Seattle Public Schools, assisted throughout our research. Tim Detweiler at The James and Janie Washington Foundation helped, with enthusiasm. Numerous librarians in the Seattle Public Library's history department, business department, and Seattle Room helped track down elusive details. Historian Lorraine McConaghy of the Museum of History and Industry encouraged us and taped our reminiscences, and head librarian Carolyn Marr persisted in searching MOHAI's collection of *Seattle Post-Intelligencer* photos, even though our favorite picture from the P-I could not be found. We thank them all.

Thanks also stretch back to the 1960s. Ernalee and Jerry Thonn are in the category "we couldn't have done it without you" for the countless hours they put in baby/toddler sitting for at least five years, enabling Joan and Ed Singler to spend those hours uninterruptedly on CORE.

All four authors owe a deep debt of gratitude to Marvin Durning and Ed Singler for their long-suffering help and support during the years it has taken for this concept to become the printed book in your hands.

SEATTLE IN BLACK AND WHITE

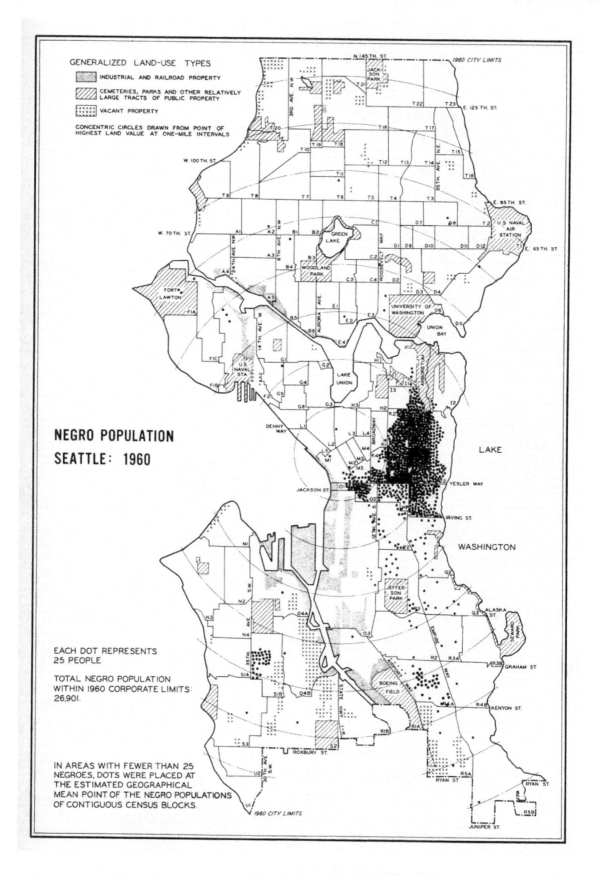

GENERALIZED LAND-USE TYPES

INDUSTRIAL AND RAILROAD PROPERTY

CEMETERIES, PARKS AND OTHER RELATIVELY LARGE TRACTS OF PUBLIC PROPERTY

VACANT PROPERTY

CONCENTRIC CIRCLES DRAWN FROM POINT OF HIGHEST LAND VALUE AT ONE-MILE INTERVALS

NEGRO POPULATION
SEATTLE: 1960

EACH DOT REPRESENTS
25 PEOPLE

TOTAL NEGRO POPULATION
WITHIN 1960 CORPORATE LIMITS:
26,901.

IN AREAS WITH FEWER THAN 25
NEGROES, DOTS WERE PLACED AT
THE ESTIMATED GEOGRAPHICAL
MEAN POINT OF THE NEGRO POPULATIONS
OF CONTIGUOUS CENSUS BLOCKS.

INTRODUCTION

T his is a history of the Seattle chapter of the Congress of Racial Equality (CORE), the projects undertaken, and the people who made it happen. CORE became a way of life for many members, who spent time every day for weeks, months, and years working on various campaigns to end discrimination and segregation in the Seattle area. With support from the National Association for the Advancement of Colored People (NAACP) and clergy of both black and white churches, CORE brought about some crucial changes in Seattle—important steps in American's stride toward "a more perfect Union."

Seattle in Black and White is a participant history of a significant period (1961–68) following the explosive postwar growth of a Northwest city. It is also a participant history of a major social movement of the twentieth century: the attempt to end discrimination and work toward a just, equal, and integrated society. We four authors have a joint, cumulative history of almost two hundred years of citizenship and activism in Seattle. In these meaningful lives, our work in Seattle CORE represents our greatest contribution to democracy. Even our subsequent decades in the anti–Vietnam

(Facing page) Concentration of African American population in Seattle, 1960. (From Calvin F. Schmid and Wayne W. McVey, Growth and Distribution of Minority Races in Seattle, Washington, by permission of Seattle Public Schools, and reproduced courtesy of The Seattle Public Library, Seattle Room)

War movement, feminism, farmworkers' struggles, education, the environment, youth and family, aging issues, and a myriad of community projects cannot match our intense efforts in the civil rights movement.

This book does not aim to be a theoretical or academic exercise. Instead, it is grounded in personal experience. We hope to reach ordinary readers—newcomers to the Northwest, long-established families, people whose parents and grandparents experienced the 1960s in Seattle, young people for whom the 1960s seem ancient history. For all these potential readers we hope to inform them about the 1960s or to reawaken memories and to set the record straight from the perspective of participants.

To begin, it is important to sketch in the background. In the early 1960s, technology had not yet provided mobile phones or answering machines, bar codes and scanners, ATM machines, personal computers, or the resources of the Internet. Prices were less than one-seventh of those in 2009. And, in a startling difference from the present, "Negro" was the *only* reputable word to refer to African Americans.

WHAT'S IN A NAME?

People fighting for respect had labored for decades to get "Negro" used instead of slang or derogatory names and insisted that—for respectability—"Negro" must be capitalized. In the early 1900s when the National Association for the Advancement of Colored People was established, "colored people" was one of the least pejorative ways to describe former slaves and freedmen. Later "Negro," from the Spanish and Portuguese, derived respectability from its association with the since-discredited identification of the world's people into three major "racial" groups—Negroid, Caucasoid, and Mongoloid. Thus, the word provided a certain scientific propriety. Now, race as a scientific idea is known to be meaningless. Race as a social category, even after the election of an African American president, remains a major issue in our society.

Gaining respect and acceptance from the larger society were important issues for the black community in the 1950s and early 1960s. And in CORE, being perceived as "respectable" was considered essential if we were to be persuasive in our struggle against discrimination. As the sixties proceeded, our physical energy went into negotiations and demonstrations for jobs, housing, schools, and voting rights. Intellectual energy went into self-definition and self-presentation. Should Negroes be defined by origin, as were other hyphenated Americans? Should we be African-Americans despite our attenuated connection with Africa? Was Afro-American a broader and better way to describe ourselves? Then in mid-decade Stokely Carmichael and H. Rap Brown proclaimed Black Power, and the rhetoric of the movement changed dramatically. In 1965, CORE's Twenty-Second Annual National Convention was titled "The Black Ghetto: An Awakening Giant."

For this book the authors will often use the word of the time—Negro—to immerse the reader in the era before Seattle CORE's later years, when the language started to change. (The change was inconsistent; the *Corelator* and other documents use all the above terms throughout CORE's remaining existence.) Thus, this book's introduction to 1960s Seattle will use the term "Negro." The later chapters, as recalled participant history, will use the terms most people now feel comfortable using. Quotations, of course, will use the speaker's term, be it "colored," "Negro," or "African-American." When writing from our current perspective we will use "black," "Afro-American," or "African American." No matter the words, our goal in the ongoing struggle is a society that will truly look to the content of our character.

SEATTLE, 1960

Decades ago Seattle was very different from today in terms of the size of the population, its distribution throughout the city, and its wealth. In 1960, if you were one of the city's white residents, you could live your entire life without seeing—or at least without interacting with—a Negro person. This reality was not only a result of numbers (26,900 blacks in a total population of 557,000, or one in twenty)[1] but because discrimination was built into the city at all levels, including housing, employment, education, and other aspects of life. Negroes lived almost exclusively in four central Seattle census tracts, then usually called the "Central Area," now the "Central District," or the CD.

If white Seattle citizens took a bus or a taxi downtown to shop in 1960, they were not transported by a Negro bus driver or taxi driver. White citizens were not waited on by Negro clerks, and their purchases were not delivered by Negro truck drivers. There were no Negro bank tellers and only one Negro firefighter in the entire city. Negro and white children, with rare exception, did not go to school together. A 1970s book describes this reality as whites showing "a wall of vast indifference."[2]

Some of us were not indifferent. We and the Central Area residents who had joined the fledgling CORE knew the need not only to help Seattleites see reality but to urge them to care. Caring about fairness and equal treatment fit easily within Christian and Jewish creeds. The need for fairness also received a warm but limited welcome among university professionals and students, and of course, it was felt on a daily basis by the victims of the inequality. The next step beyond seeing and caring was recognizing the need for action and change. CORE provided a blueprint for this change that called for fact-finding, negotiation, and nonviolent direct action.

CORE's commitment and activities on behalf of change encompassed many areas, including working for employment opportunities, open-housing options, and school integration. Although the following material is organized into these separate areas, it is important, even crucial, for the reader to understand that all this activity often occurred simultaneously. Energy was high, just as the barriers were high. The authors, CORE officers, and most of the organization worked on more than one project at a time in addition to regular employment, childbearing and rearing, going to school, and pursuing the other activities of normal life. To get a sense of this exciting, frenetic, and also rewarding action, we invite the reader to visit http://depts.washington.edu/civilr/CORE_timeline.htm, which offers a summary of the organization's activities taken from their newsletter, the *Corelator*.

CORE IN ACTION

Employment was crucial to supply the bread and butter of daily life. Negroes in "indifferent" Seattle were largely limited to employment in menial tasks such as dishwashing, janitorial work, odd jobs, and the like. Negro women worked as house-cleaners, babysitters, and domestic help at a time when women generally did not work outside the home. We in

CORE recognized the urgent need for employment opportunities at a living wage.

Seattle CORE's first action project targeted supermarkets for a number of reasons. Supermarket employment discrimination was a daily in-your-face reminder of inequality. Grocery stores were located among and financially dependent on the very people who were not accepted as employees. As local representatives of national chains, they reflected national racism and reinforced it locally. In addition, if we succeeded in combating discrimination in a single store, we potentially could affect an entire chain regionally and eventually nationally. An action project could have leverage because CORE members, their neighbors, and almost all Central Area residents shopped for food on a daily or weekly basis.

The Seattle branch of the NAACP had negotiated with Safeway in 1947 but achieved no sustained change. CORE's 1961 negotiations and demonstrations accomplished breakthroughs at Safeway and then other chains. In hindsight it still seems strange that supermarkets resisted so adamantly. A&P, for example, would hire only a token number of Negroes until CORE and four hundred volunteers in multiple shifts had picketed the chain for months. Dozens of volunteers even showed up in the Thanksgiving picket line at A&P five days after President Kennedy had been assassinated. In the following pages we describe CORE's employment activity in detail. We all took part in picketing on a regular basis for months, rain or shine. We joined with others—the Urban League, the NAACP, and churches—to recruit and train potential employees. All these activities required discipline and commitment. Change came slowly, but we opened up hundreds of jobs not previously available to Negroes.

Housing was another challenge. In 1960s Seattle, if you were white you could live in any neighborhood of the city—the north end, West Seattle, Wallingford, Ravenna, Queen Anne, Seward Park, or any other area you could afford. There were some class and ethnic exceptions; for example, Jewish people were often discriminated against. There was also discrimination against other people of color, including Native Americans, Filipino Americans, Chinese Americans, and those Japanese Americans who had returned to the city after World War II internment. Yet aside from "Chinatown" the Negro population was the most restricted to a housing ghetto.

In general, Negroes were limited to living in an area bounded by Madison Street on the north, Dearborn or Irving on the south, the downtown on the west, and Thirty-Fourth Avenue on the east. This area did not expand even though the Negro population grew by 70 percent during and after World War II. Whites reserved the area on the east slopes of the Madrona and Mount Baker neighborhoods down to Lake Washington. Thirty-Fourth Avenue, along the crest of a hill, was the dividing line. This commonly accepted demarcation led many to refer to the eastern/lakeside area as the "sunrise side of the mountain" and the (Negro) Central Area as the "sunset side of the hill."

This housing segregation did not just "happen." It was a conscious process backed by covenants where buyers and sellers signed contracts to discriminate. Owners were forbidden to sell homes to Negroes and other "undesirables." Courts sometimes ruled against such covenants, but housing remained segregated. In 1964 an overwhelming majority of Seattle citizens voted two to one *against* a city-sponsored housing antidiscrimination law.

Some individuals resisted discrimination on the housing front in a number of ways—by selling to Negroes (which provoked resistance, harassment, cross burning, and even destruction of property in some white neighborhoods), by working for the passage of new housing legislation, and, in a unique case, by founding a company. Harmony Homes, Inc. built houses specifically to sell to minorities. This may have made Seattle different from any other city in the country. Sid Gerber was the founder, with Jim Kimbrough, of Harmony Homes and was a friend and supporter of CORE. He died in a tragic airplane accident in May 1965 along with Wing Luke, the first person of color on the Seattle City Council. No Negro had yet been elected to the city council. As the book illustrates, Seattle CORE worked with all those opposed to housing discrimination, including Harmony Homes, the Fair Housing Listing Service, the Urban League, Christian Friends for Racial Equality, and the Anti-Defamation League. CORE's biggest direct action project was against Picture Floor Plans, a large local real estate company of the time. Our demonstrations led to CORE's first police harassment—regular photographing of individual peaceful picketers and recording of their license plate numbers. We might have felt intimidated, but no arrests resulted.

We four were personally involved in seeking and advocating for integrated housing in the 1960s. We were active in negotiations with realtors and with the city, working with other housing groups and later in picketing on behalf of any person's right to live in any place the buyer or renter could afford. We describe these activities, drawing on numerous files, newspaper articles, records of meetings with government authorities, and a court case to retell our story. Seattle CORE's housing activities even attracted the attention of the *Huntley-Brinkley Report*, NBC's national news program. We detail CORE's testing to determine that discrimination existed. The results of these investigations were submitted to the Seattle City Council in support of passing an open housing ordinance.

The shameful history of Seattle government delay over open housing begins with the Civic Unity Committee (CUC), which was established in 1944 in reaction to race riots in the East. Forming a committee to do further study was a common way to seem to do something. A dozen years later, in 1956, the CUC created the Greater Seattle Housing Council to begin to address an open-housing policy; its program committee was chaired by a representative of the Seattle Real Estate Board. In 1961 when the NAACP urged the city council to pass an antidiscrimination ordinance, the council did nothing. Later, Mayor Clinton appointed the Human Rights Commission, which recommended an ordinance. The city council chose not to adopt the legislation immediately but rather placed the ordinance on the ballot for a citywide vote. In March 1964 Negro citizens learned that 66 percent of their fellow citizens were opposed to having Negroes live in their neighborhoods. Then in April 1968 Martin Luther King was assassinated. The city council passed an open-housing ordinance fifteen *days* after the King tragedy and almost fifteen *years* after they were first urged to do so!

Realtors, financial advisers, and history agree that housing is a major part of any American's personal wealth. Home ownership provides stability and increasing value and funds for education and for retirement. A lengthy history of discrimination in one's ability to acquire this source of wealth affects not only the current owner/generation but also future generations. In the long term the Negro community's financial status has suffered seriously from this discrimination.

Housing discrimination in the 1960s and preceding decades had an immediate effect on educational opportunities. In 1964, a full decade after the Supreme Court urged "all deliberate speed" in its school integration decision, *Brown v. Board of Education*, Seattle public schools were still segregated, in large part because neighborhoods were segregated.

In 1964 Seattle CORE established its Education Committee. Charles (Val) Valentine produced a report analyzing segregation in Seattle schools. Using this report, Seattle CORE recommended a five-point program and began negotiations with the Seattle School Board. A year earlier the NAACP had begun talking with the school board and in 1964 proposed a program of "educational clusters." A year later (1965) the Urban League submitted its Triad Plan to the Seattle School Board. The board turned down CORE's recommendations, the NAACP "educational clusters" plan, and the Urban League's Triad Plan with the comment that "the public schools do not exist for the purpose of imposing broad social reform upon the people." All the civil rights forces in Seattle were unable to make the school board see, care, or act.

Late in 1965 CORE became convinced that dramatic action was needed to educate and activate people citywide on school segregation. The idea of a school boycott was born. By 1965 two of us had moved away due to employment demands, and one of us, although still in Seattle, was overwhelmed with three small children and multiple obligations. The fourth author, Jean (Maid) Adams, became a major player in the schools project.

The school boycott committee organized to educate the public and to provide an alternative, integrated educational experience, called Freedom Schools. This became CORE's major education project. Committee volunteers established a curriculum, recruited and trained teachers, secured safe places suitable for hundreds of children, and coordinated the myriad activities required. The public and the press deemed the school boycott to be the most newsworthy activity in Seattle CORE history. Local newspapers printed lengthy criticisms, debates, and letters to the editor, both positive and negative. Philosophy, morality, and law became topics of daily discourse in the press—de facto segregation versus legal segregation and citizens' responsibility to a "higher authority" or "greater good." All these were background to Seattle CORE's work on the school boycott. In our chapters on schools we describe in full detail CORE's efforts, problems, and solutions. We talk about the parents, students, and professionals involved and describe the cross section of Seattle's musical, artistic, and religious leaders who became volunteer teachers.

In addition to action projects, the book addresses philosophy and moral/legal issues that motivated us as individuals and as a group. We, each of us, wanted respect and acceptance for ourselves, our neighbors, and our friends. We wanted an integrated society. To help people see, care, and act was a means to these ends. Looking back now, we can smile, even laugh, that we sometimes looked for respect in minor things like image. We asked women to wear dresses, not slacks, when participating in CORE activities such as picketing and sitting-in. We actually wore hats and gloves. On one level our message was "we're just like you, respect us, accept us." We wanted to be integrated into society at the same time that we were trying to change that society.

Seattle CORE faded away in 1968 with the rising emphasis on black self-determination. But our efforts produced change, including in ways we had not anticipated. Nationally, one result of the civil rights movement was the entry of many more blacks into government service. Thomas Sugrue points out: "Beginning in the 1970s, thousands of blacks were elected to office in northern cities, an unprecedented shift in the color of local and national politics. By 1996, . . . unprecedented numbers of blacks served [as mayors and] on city councils, school boards, in local and federal courts, and in statewide offices. The surge in black political power may have been the most enduring consequence of the civil rights revolution."[3] And so it was, as well, in Seattle and King County.

CORE in Seattle 1961–68 represented a particular stage in the development and growth of the civil rights movement and toward respect and acceptance for all people. Respect and acceptance remain valid goals. Fortunately, those fighting for respect have widened the discussion and now say, "Accept us as we are, not as you want us to be." To the extent that we the people do learn from history, the authors of *Seattle in Black and White* hope that our efforts in the 1960s and our work on this book will help all of us to see, care, and act in the future. We urge the reader to participate in Seattle's and society's continuing attempts to build a more just society of equal opportunity, mutual responsibility, and respect.

PART I **Beginnings**

1 • THE FORMATION OF SEATTLE CORE

A s the nation, in the late 1950s and early 1960s, watched nightly TV coverage of the struggle for civil rights in the South, we saw the vicious treatment of black people who asserted their rights as Americans. We saw people walking in Montgomery, Alabama, for a year in 1955–56 until they could get fair seating on the buses. We saw bayonets drawn against black high school students in Little Rock, Arkansas, in September 1957. We saw black college students denied service at the Woolworth lunch counter in Greensboro, North Carolina, in February 1960. Inspired by their example, disciplined students in seventy-eight cities sat-in at legally segregated lunch counters. Students endured assaults by angry whites who ground mustard into their hair or put lighted cigarettes down their backs. In May 1961 in the first wave of Freedom Riders, John Lewis (now a member of Congress) and Albert Bigelow were badly beaten as they left the bus in Rock Hill, South Carolina. In Anniston, Alabama, NBC and CBS showed vivid film clips of the burning of the same Freedom Riders' Greyhound bus. Its occupants, both whites and Negroes, were assaulted with sticks and bats. We saw the vicious and violent attack by a Ku Klux Klan mob of two hundred against passengers who were simply testing their legal right to integrated service in the Trailways bus station in Birmingham, Alabama.

Shocking events happened almost every day. Who could stand idly by? Even in the northwest corner of America we heard the call for action and a plea to join the Freedom Riders, to fill the jails, to work to end the violence and to end segregation.

One evening in May 1961 four white strangers met by chance after a performance of Lorraine Hansberry's play *Raisin in the Sun* at the Cirque Playhouse in the Madrona neighborhood of Seattle. Ken Rose, Ray Cooper, and Joan and Ed Singler were drawn together to talk about the moving performance. They were stirred by the play's message of both the destruction of human dignity and the hope for the future. After the show they went backstage to talk with the actors, including Norman Johnson, who had performed the role of George Murchison. The conversation led from discussing the play to sharing deep concerns about the violence in Alabama and Mississippi and the segregation experienced in Seattle. They were fast becoming friends. The thoughts and passionate feelings that surfaced in that conversation made them aware that something had to be done. They agreed that they needed to meet soon.

Ken Rose was an articulate nineteen-year-old student of political theory at the University of Washington and an active member of the Liberal Religious Youth at the University Unitarian Church. His friend Ray Cooper, two years out of high school, lived in the University District. Ray realized that he could not sit idly by engaging in coffee house discussions about art while people were being brutalized in the South. Ed and Joan Singler were in their late twenties. Ed, from Detroit and the son of union organizers, had many encounters with discrimination while traveling with his best friend from law school, who was black and lived in an integrated neighborhood. Joan, whose parents were community volunteers, was aware of how much just one or two committed people could accomplish. She was also active in the unions. She had recently returned from Pasco, Washington, where she had been appalled at what looked to her like a southern ghetto. Norman Johnson, a draftsman for Boeing, frequently experienced police harassment as he traveled to his job assignment at the Applied Physics Lab in a "white" part of town, being stopped and questioned, especially after dark or if he was carrying his black gym bag.

These five people from diverse backgrounds and experience were drawn together by a commitment to correcting racial injustice. They met a few days after the play at Norm Johnson's home on Superior Avenue in the Leschi neighborhood. That evening Norm Johnson, Ken Rose, Ray Cooper,

Joan and Ed Singler, along with Carl Jordan, one of Norm's roommates who joined the conversation, took the first step in answering CORE's call for national action. Ray, in spite of concerns for his personal safety—how many more Freedom Riders would be beaten?—had decided to join others responding to urgent requests by National CORE to participate in the Freedom Rides to Mississippi. What he needed now was financial help. Ray's willingness to join any activity taking place in Mississippi came as a shock to Bob Anderson, Norm's other roommate. Having grown up in Naches, Mississippi, Bob knew all too well the conditions and intimidation that black people had to face every day just to live. "Why," he asked "would anyone go there voluntarily and put themselves at risk of bodily harm?"[1] Ray listened to Bob's comments but was not deterred, nor were the rest of us in the group, who committed ourselves to raising the money to send Ray to Mississippi. If we had understood how lawlessly the Klan and white supremacy groups operated in Mississippi, sometimes with the cooperation of a sheriff, we might have been more cautious.

Nationally, CORE was at the forefront of volunteer militant action against discrimination. Since the little group's first commitment involved sending Ray off to be a CORE Freedom Rider, the obvious way to organize in Seattle was to join the Congress of Racial Equality. In June 1961 the Seattle chapter of CORE was born.

PRIOR CIVIL RIGHTS EFFORTS IN SEATTLE

Although it is true that the founding of Seattle CORE was the result of a chance meeting of five people, the immediate infusion of a cadre of people who were already seasoned supporters of civil rights soon filled the ranks of dedicated CORE members and contributed greatly to our early successes.

In 1957 Don Matson, Walt Hundley, Ivan King, Ray Williams, and others had tried to form a CORE group in Seattle but were not able to rally enough supporters to establish a chapter or take on an action project.[2] Many of them were members of Church of the People, where socialist ideals and people of color were welcome. With a congregation that included many interracial couples, the church experienced as much discrimination, if not more, than individual blacks. As sometimes happens in intense groups, the congregation split over differences of religious and political ideology, and these CORE pioneers moved on to become members of the University Unitarian Church.[3]

Don Matson, an invaluable white member of Seattle CORE, brought his organizing skills and leadership in the Unitarians for Social Justice to bear on his activism in CORE. Unitarians for Social Justice organized a subcommittee devoted to integration. Small in number but extremely active and led by Don Matson, the committee included Doris Eason, Jean Jones, Mary Barton, and John Cornethan.[4] By July 1961 all these people, plus other members of the congregation, were either active members of CORE or supported CORE projects.

So with the help and support of the Unitarians' Integration Committee, the Unitarians' Liberal Religious Youth, university staff and faculty responding to notices placed on campus, and members of the black community, CORE took off. Ray Williams, an African American, became the first chairman of Seattle CORE.

FREEDOM RIDERS

Before Seattle CORE held its first organizing meeting, Seattle's Freedom Rider was on his way south. Contributions paid for his airline ticket, and Ray Cooper flew to Los Angeles, where there was an established CORE chapter. On July 12, 1961, along with other young people, Ray then headed east to New Orleans for training. Most of those in the civil rights movement used Gandhian nonviolent passive resistance as a discipline and a response to violence and hatred. Volunteers participating in the Freedom Rides accepted nonviolence as a tactic, accepted the possibility that they might be physically attacked, and practiced not striking back.

Once their training was complete the Freedom Riders boarded a Greyhound bus headed to Jackson, Mississippi, to challenge the segregated facilities at the interstate bus station. When Ray Cooper and his fellow Freedom Riders stepped off the bus in Jackson, they were immediately arrested and sent to Hinds County Jail. Earlier Freedom Riders had already filled the county jail, so Ray and the riders with him were then sent to prison at Parchman Farm Penitentiary in Parchman, Mississippi. Ray spent forty-seven days, and lost twenty pounds, in what he describes as "Hell's Kitchen" before being arraigned and given a court date in March 1962. After his release from prison Ray spent some days meeting the black residents of Jackson before he boarded another bus to return to New Orleans. The return trip seemed equally dangerous for the Freedom Riders. The Mississippi State Patrol and members of the Ku Klux Klan (KKK) followed the bus and intimidated the returning Freedom Riders.[5]

That fall Ray returned to Seattle to be an active member of Seattle CORE. He remembers leaving a small, mostly white group of civil rights activists and returning in just a few months to find a fully integrated chapter of CORE. In 1963 he was one of twenty-one young people who sat-in at the Seattle City Council chambers, protesting city officials' inaction on the issue of segregated housing.

Shortly after Ray left Seattle for the South, Widjonarko Tjokroadismarto, an exchange student from Indonesia and a graduate student at the university, participated in the Freedom Rides. As reported in the August 3, 1961, issue of the University of Washington *Daily*, his motivation was "to stay for a few weeks in Jackson to study segregation problems in the South." (Having never been to the South, his plan for a two-week stay was somewhat naïve and at odds with what the Jackson City officials had in mind for Freedom Riders.) Widjo, as he was known on campus, was the son of an Indonesian diplomat. Because of diplomatic immunity his plan never got off the ground. When he arrived at the bus station in Jackson with a group of Freedom Riders from New York, two detectives forcibly removed him from the bus station's Negro waiting room. The *Daily* went on to report, "Widjo said he gave up plans to file suit against the detectives." What he did do, however, was to speak out about his experiences at several showings of the film *Freedom Ride* sponsored by Seattle CORE.

A third person from Seattle, Jon Schaefer, raised in the all-white gated community of Broadmoor, answered the call for national engagement in the struggle for civil rights and joined the Freedom Riders. A member of CORE, Jon was sponsored by the Unitarians for Social Justice and given some financial help by Seattle CORE. Schaefer became part of a Freedom Ride and received the same "Southern reception and hospitality" and served the same jail time as Ray Cooper did. Jon, however, stayed in the South and became involved in Freedom Highways, a project protesting discrimination at Holiday Inns and Howard Johnson's Restaurants along U.S. highways in the South. His protest took place at a Howard Johnson Restaurant in North Carolina. Jon, a Caucasian, and four Negro young women waited but were never admitted into the restaurant, so they sat-in in the doorway. For refusing to leave they were arrested and each served a thirty-day prison term, for Jon his second incarceration. Finally, after Jon's release, he was asked to join the staff of National CORE and worked as a field secretary in the North and East.[6]

SEATTLE CORE TAKES OFF

How to change "segregated Seattle" and raise bail money for Ray Cooper and Jon Schaefer became Seattle CORE's challenge. To reach other people outraged about the injustice and violence in the South we sent out a three-cent-postcard announcement of an organizing meeting. This notice listed our purpose "to plan direct action projects in Seattle" and "to send Freedom Riders to the South." We assumed that those who received the mailing knew about CORE and the Freedom Rides taking place in the South. If they did not, perhaps they would come anyway. The meeting was scheduled for July 14, 1961, at the YMCA at Twenty-Third and East Olive. Our mailing list (perhaps based on Christian Friends for Racial Equality members) was quite small, so we placed ads in the black newspaper, *The Facts*, and in the student newspaper at the University of Washington, *The Daily*. We also posted notices in black churches, which led to a number of black parishioners becoming early members of CORE. Ministers and parishioners of many congregations became very involved and proved to be among the strongest supporters of Seattle CORE.

Ken Rose, CORE's organizing secretary, placed a notice for the July 14 CORE organizing meeting at the University Unitarian Church and at other sites on the campus of the University of Washington. The notices on campus attracted faculty and staff, including Si Ottenberg, of the Anthropology Department, and his wife, Phoebe; Larry Northwood, of the School of Social Work, and his wife, Olga; and Richard Morrill, of the Geography Department, and his wife, Margie, who were also Unitarians. They all became active members of CORE. From those who attended that first meeting on July 14, a cadre of people emerged who were committed to ending discrimination in

C.O.R.E.

Congress On Racial Equality

CENTRAL MEETING — Friday,   July 14, 1961

YMCA — 23rd and E. Olive.

PURPOSE: To plan direct action projects
           in Seattle

           To send "Freedom Riders" to the
           South

Seattle and spent intense weeks, months, and years trying to attain this goal.[7]

After the July 14 meeting we approached the NAACP and the Baptist Ministers Alliance to request their cooperation and support. Although the NAACP was recognized as the organization working on behalf of African Americans nationwide, its major thrust at this time was initiating lawsuits and providing legal counsel for the many demonstrators being jailed in the South. CORE would use more direct action. Locally, the NAACP had attempted to change segregated housing patterns and discriminatory hiring practices, negotiating with Safeway in the late 1940s for a few jobs for Negroes and proposing a city open-housing ordinance in 1961 with no success. To support student lunch counter sit-ins in the South, the Seattle NAACP organized picketing at the downtown Woolworth. Joan and Ed Singler and Maid Adams participated in this protest. Joan remembers experiencing hostility and bigotry in almost-all-white downtown Seattle. A simple picket sign "Equal Service" provoked angry white shoppers into name-calling and shouting, "Communist, go back to Russia!"

The past president of the Seattle NAACP, Philip Burton, and Ed Singler were friends from the 1950s, when they had both spoken out against the hysteria of the McCarthy era. For the nascent CORE, Phil arranged for Ed to speak at an August meeting of the local NAACP board. Given the daily brutal confrontations in the South, it was not difficult for Phil to get CORE's presentation on the board's agenda. The Seattle NAACP board then included

Chapter President Charles V. Johnson, Legal Counsel Philip Burton, Secretary E. June Smith (all African Americans), and Sidney Gerber (white). Johnson, who had been among the first black Law School students at the University of Washington, later became the NAACP's northwest regional president, a member of the national NAACP board, and a King County Superior Court judge. Phil Burton had petitioned the city in 1961 and would file a lawsuit against school district segregation in 1963. Phil had his own personal confrontation with bigotry in 1951 when he and his wife bought a house in Bothell, a Seattle suburb. Phil recalled believing that "once people began to know each other the housing problem would be resolved, [but] we did not correctly gauge the hostility we found in the white community of the North."[8] E. June Smith, a businesswoman, later became the president of the Seattle NAACP. The NAACP office was in the basement of her house on Pine Street near Twenty-Third, and it became the staging area for CORE's first leaflet distribution and the assembly area for our picketing of Safeway. Sid Gerber, past president of the Washington State Board against Discrimination, was a man of action who donated time and dollars to get CORE's projects off the ground. These people were all well respected in Seattle's black community.[9]

Ed Singler's presentation to the board was a broad outline of CORE's dual plans: support for the struggle going on in the South by supporting the Freedom Riders and a direct action campaign in the area of employment in Seattle. After a short discussion the board approved our request for the use of NAACP mailing lists and its lists of other groups, including churches and social clubs. Sid Gerber reached in his pocket and contributed money. With the mailing lists in hand we sent out a call for activists to rally support for the Freedom Riders and to develop a Selective Buying Campaign in efforts to end discrimination in Seattle. By early September 1961 we had forty-five members.[10]

Those of us in Seattle CORE did not view the NAACP as primarily committed to direct action; however, throughout the period from 1961 to 1967, CORE's approach and the resulting direct action projects were embraced by many NAACP members, Wallace Johnson, Dr. Earl Miller, and James Washington Jr. among them. They and other members, including Bettylou Valentine, who had been on the NAACP national board, would go on to participate as leaders and committee chairs in Seattle CORE.

Another member of the black community and a transplant from New Orleans, Walt Hubbard, offered important support for CORE projects. As president of the United Garment Workers Local 17, he provided a platform for CORE representatives Ed Singler and Wallace Johnson to explain the Safeway boycott. Walt, a cofounder of the Seattle chapter of the Catholic Interracial Council (CIC), worked with Father John Lynch, of St. James Cathedral, and the Most Reverend Thomas A. Connolly, archbishop of Seattle.[11] As CORE's direct action projects spread from the Central Area to the city's all-white neighborhoods, these Catholic leaders did not back away from the public controversy created by our demonstrations. They were staunch supporters of our efforts to end discrimination. "The Archbishop of Seattle is committed on all fronts to the successful realization of Human and Civil Rights for all our citizens," he wrote, and further, "We view this commitment as a moral obligation, and we cannot rest until the goal in question has been achieved."[12] In September 1964 Project Equality, launched by the National Catholic Conference for Interracial Justice and adopted in Seattle with the full support of the archbishop, recognized that "the economic power of the church itself by reason of its hiring, purchasing and investment policies, can be harnessed as a massive influence on the employment policies of suppliers, builders, unions, bankers and insurance companies."[13]

Both Father Lynch and Archbishop Connolly inspired a number of Catholics to become active members of CORE, including Fred and Mary Provo, Sarah Lynch, her daughter Daisy Boyetta, and her granddaughter Infanta Spence, tireless workers all. Father Lynch, a white member of the Central Area Civil Rights Committee, was often seen walking shoulder to shoulder with representatives of black churches and civil rights leaders in the front line of marches and demonstrations.

SEATTLE CORE BECOMES OFFICIAL

Before we received official recognition from National CORE, we had sponsored two Freedom Riders and carried out successful nonviolent direction action campaigns against discriminatory hiring at Safeway and other supermarket chains. Immediately after our success with Safeway, Seattle CORE was visited by CORE's West Coast field secretary, Genevieve

Hughes. She asked us to document what we had done, so she could carry that information to other CORE chapters. Other boycotts up and down the West Coast would be possible, as Safeway had stores from Seattle to San Diego, and California already had numerous CORE chapters.[14]

Meanwhile, our chairman, Ray Williams, with a full-time job, a large family to care for, and membership on several advisory boards, decided he could not continue as chair of CORE and resigned in October 1961. Vice chairman Ed Singler filled the post until the next election of officers. Our application for recognition as a CORE chapter was pending, subject to writing our constitution and bylaws. In November 1961, sitting at the Singlers' kitchen table and following a sample from National CORE, Wallace Johnson, Tim Martin, John Cornethan, Norm Johnson, and Joan and Ed Singler did just that. At the December membership meeting active members ratified Seattle CORE's constitution and bylaws.[15] Next we started our newsletter, the *Corelator*, to provide a monthly report of all CORE activities and pending decisions.[16] By February 1962 we were recognized as an official chapter of the Congress of Racial Equality.

That same February, CORE secretary Joan Singler was selected to join more than a hundred representatives at the national CORE convention in Covington, Kentucky. The diverse and racially mixed group of activists came from the South, the East, the Midwest, and, for the first time, the West Coast. Joan wished we all could have listened to the people she met, who, she recalls, "risk their jobs, their educations, their safety, just by being members of CORE." Most inspiring, James Farmer, the dynamic and passionate national leader of CORE, stirred everyone at the convention.[17] Farmer, who had participated in the Freedom Rides, appealed to the chapter representatives to help raise money. Funds were desperately needed for legal fees and for the salaries of field secretaries who were being sent out to train and support the newly formed chapters and new direct action projects. The Freedom Rides had ended in the fall of 1961, but CORE was about to undertake new projects: Freedom Highways, ending de facto segregation in schools, and a huge voter registration campaign—all filled with risks, jail time, and, as it turned out, the deaths of dozens of civil rights workers.

Seattle CORE worked to answer the national plea for funds. We raised money for national and our own expenses through a raffle for a free day at the Seattle World's Fair and tickets to a public basketball game played by well-known disc jockeys (long before Seattle had—or lost—its NBA team).[18] Without being asked, Sid Gerber made a major contribution and provided the bail for Ray Cooper. He was generous with "seed" money for printing, postage, and the first CORE "Freedom Now" button, which we sold to raise more income.[19] Members paid $2.00 annual dues and some contributed more. A Boeing mathematician, Ed O'Keefe, made significant contributions of $10 or even $25 a month to support Seattle CORE (about $75 and $187 in today's dollars). Ongoing fundraisers throughout CORE's history paid for our costs as well as supporting projects in the South. With little advance notice we quickly put together a financially successful, major theatrical production and fundraiser by sponsoring an evening with Dick Gregory and Dizzy Gillespie at the Moore Theater.

Button produced by Seattle CORE as fundraiser, using seed money from Sid Gerber. (CORE, Matson Collection)

BUILDING THE MEMBERSHIP

People learned of CORE from various sources. First impressions are important, so it is no surprise that the effective, successful boycott campaign against Safeway helped to increase our ranks. The black community learned about the Safeway boycott through fliers, posters, and word of mouth even though major media did not cover it. On Wednesday afternoons Tim Martin (Harold T. Martin), a technical illustrator for Boeing, hosted the *Seattle CORE* program on KZAM radio, "the voice of the Negro Community," giving us another platform to urge activists to get involved and an opportunity to urge contributions to the efforts in the South. National television coverage inspired others to join CORE, as it showed graphic scenes of terrible physical abuse suffered by southern children and adults walking in peaceful demonstrations. In September 1962 the intensity of opposition to James Meredith's enrolling as the first Negro at the University of Mississippi stunned all of us. Seattleites and the rest of the world were horrified at the rioting mob that killed two bystanders and injured 160 U.S. marshals.

Membership in Seattle CORE grew rapidly, despite the rigorous process involved in becoming an active member. First a person went through orientation and training in nonviolence. Training took place at monthly orientation meetings and was considered essential preparation for all CORE direct action projects. After orientation, training, and committing to CORE's

CORE's goal is an integrated society where each member is judged solely on the basis of individual worth. We believe that a lasting resolution of problems of racial discrimination can best be obtained through a spirit of goodwill. This spirit must be organized in action programs directed to specific problems.

ED Singler
is an active member of the
Congress of Racial Equality
in SEATTLE
Don Matson TREAS.

JUNE	JULY	AUG	SEPT	OCT	NOV
DEC	JAN	FEB	MAR	APR	MAY

1962-63

Membership card for active member Ed Singler, with CORE's goal as inspired by Gandhi on reverse. (CORE, Matson Collection)

"Rules for Action," an applicant paid $2.00 yearly dues. Then there was a one-month probation period before that person was voted into the chapter by two-thirds of the active members. Active members had voting rights and could run for office. To become an associate CORE member, a supporter simply agreed to abide by the "Rules for Action" and paid only $1.00 dues per year.[20] We all tried to contribute more if we could afford it.

Membership grew until, by December 1962, just a year after Seattle CORE became an official chapter, we had nearly one hundred active members and numerous projects. CORE needed to be better organized. Chairman Reverend Henry Hall (like all chairmen who followed, he was African American) proposed and the membership established six committees. Two committees oversaw Seattle CORE's first major projects: the Employment Committee led by Carl Taylor, Wallace Johnson, and Jean Adams, and a Negotiations Committee then under the leadership of Reverend Mance Jackson and Jean Durning. Other committees were Fund Raising, led by Bill Lynch, Norm Johnson, and Joyce Rowe; Voter Registration, led by John Cornethan and George LaNore; and Membership, led by Willie Crawford and Daisy Boyetta. Except for the Public Relations Committee, which was chaired by Ed Singler, all committees were chaired or cochaired by African Americans.[21] Don Matson was responsible for the orientation sessions and printed the monthly *Corelator*.

CORE by that time had decided to focus on employment opportunities and had investigated various employers. The next priority was negotiating with employers. The Negotiations Committee included representatives from CORE, the NAACP, Baptist Ministers Alliance, and the Methodist Episcopal Ministers Alliance. Often individual negotiators were members of several organizations and might represent one group one time and another group at a later appearance. Negotiating teams included house-wives, lawyers, ministers, teachers, retirees, doctors, and students. No matter who was speaking, the negotiators' message was clear—it was time to change hiring practices to include black employees.

By early 1963 the need to be heard as "one voice" led to the formation of the Central Area Civil Rights Committee (CACRC), which, with slight varia-tions in its name, functioned throughout the civil rights era. As Charles V. Johnson recalls, CACRC originated as friendly get-togethers among black community leaders Walt Hundley, Edwin Pratt, Meredith Matthews, and himself.[22] It soon expanded into a broader group of community leaders car-rying the message of civil rights. The CACRC included ministers of the major black churches and leaders of CORE, the NAACP, and the Urban League, with Reverend Mance Jackson as the first chair and public spokesman. In time, prominent religious leaders Rabbi Raphael L. Levine, of Temple de Hirsch; Reverend Peter Raible, of the University Unitarian Church; Reverend Lemuel Petersen, representing the Greater Seattle Council of Churches; and Father John Lynch, of St. James Cathedral became members of the CACRC. They spoke as one voice but also as individuals and were frequently quoted in the news media on civil rights issues. In late summer 1963, Mance Jack-son moved to Atlanta, and Reverend John Adams, minister of the First AME Church, became chairman and the public voice of CACRC.[23]

THE FREEDOM RIDE FILM

Seattle CORE, according to Field Secretary Genevieve Hughes, had a reputation as a well-organized chapter, and Seattle was selected as one of twenty-five cities in the country to premiere the documentary film *Free-dom Ride* on Lincoln's birthday, 1962. "Heroic Freedom Rides set stage for the stepped up pace of battle for civil rights," the February *Corelator* quoted *Ebony*, in announcing Seattle's premiere at the First AME Church. On Feb-ruary 12 a huge turnout, mostly black, filled the sanctuary. After the min-ister offered a prayer, Ed Singler introduced the film, with its powerful visual message of travelers who faced hatred and brutality in their attempt to break "the color line." The Freedom Riders, both white and black, were shown fleeing a burning bus and being severely beaten as they tried to "freedom ride"

TUESDAY
FEBRUARY 27
8:00 P.M.
UNIVERSITY
UNITARIAN
CHURCH
sponsored by
UNITARIANS for
SOCIAL
JUSTICE

Comments by

Dr. Costigan

and

Freedom Riders: Tickets $1.00
Ray Cooper
Widjo Tuokoadisumaric
  A Documentary Film

PROMOTIONAL DEPARTMENT
BOX 305   NEW YORK 27, NEW YORK

Film Sponsor: Social Action Commission,
            A.M.E. Church
Dr. Frederick James, Consultant Director

Flier announcing a showing of the film Freedom Ride, with Statue of Liberty torch holding burning bus. (CORE, Matson Collection)

escape. The audience gasped and groaned, shocked at the scenes of violence. Many people had tears in their eyes. It was hard to believe this actually happened in this country. After the film Ray Cooper told his story, answered questions from the audience, and made a pitch for contributions. Some people joined CORE on the spot. Others donated to support National CORE projects or to send Ray Cooper back to Jackson, Mississippi, for his trial, raising about one-third of the $1,500 needed "to keep Ray free." Substantial support was provided by sixty-eight patrons of the film premiere, including many black professionals, white lawyers and university professors, and local businesses such as Annie's Beauty Shop, the Cirque Playhouse, Brown and Hightower Gas Station, and Dave Shaw Realty.[24]

The University Unitarian Church sponsored the film two weeks after the First AME showing. Introductory comments were made by Seattle's most distinguished advocate for human rights, the erudite and popular University of Washington history professor Dr. Giovanni Costigan. Both Ray Cooper and Widjo Tjokroadismarto described their experiences.[25] Again we gained members and donations.

Other speakers were needed to help introduce Freedom Ride to new audiences. CORE established a Speakers Bureau chaired by Georgia Martin and ran training sessions on how to become an "instant public speaker." Those who completed the training took turns with Ray Cooper in addressing audiences when the movie was screened. The film was seen by fairly large audiences in the greater Seattle area, predominantly in churches, both black and white, and on college campuses. Requests came from all over the state, including Tacoma, Bell-

1.5 Buttons designed and produced by National CORE and sold by the Seattle chapter. (CORE, Matson Collection)

ingham, Vashon Island, Yakima, Cheney, and the Tri-Cities of Richland, Pasco, and Kennewick. A small black community in Pasco suffered severe segregation and discrimination in jobs, housing, and schools. Showing the film there served as the catalyst for a new chapter that formed in the Tri-Cities under the guidance of Charles Talbot and Beverly Fox.

THE CORE OFFICE

We needed more help, we needed people, and we needed money. In 1964 Seattle CORE took on the additional responsibility of staffing and paying $30 a month rent for an office up a rickety flight of stairs in a dilapidated old building at Twenty-Second and Union (no longer standing) that had not seen paint for years. Had the building been located in any other neighborhood, we were sure it never would have passed the city fire code. We had the entire second story with its odd-shaped rooms and broken linoleum floors. Volunteers were upstairs staffing the office six days a week from 9 a.m. until 5 p.m. and often many hours after that. We equipped the corner office with donated mismatched furniture and used the large open space for work parties to build signs, put out mailings, and coordinate the many door-to-door leaflet projects. Having a telephone there helped us to reach the community and, more important, provided a way for the community to contact us. How could we pay the rent? "Reach deeper" was our message to members as a pledge drive was launched, and CORE activists were asked to donate $1.00, $2.00, $5.00, or, if possible, $10.00 a month to pay our bills. CORE was truly part of the community now.

The CORE office, a meeting point for activities coordinated among civil rights groups, here with Ann Holiday, Ed Pratt, and Randolph Carter setting out for a Freedom Patrol, July 24, 1965 (see Appendix 1). Miller/Post-Intelligencer photograph.

HOW IT USED TO BE

Bettylou Valentine

I don't use email. I don't text or Twitter. Yet in the 1960s I was an expert in the technology of the day. I had the support of large numbers of people who took part in the physical work using specialized machinery to produce CORE's meeting minutes, leaflets, investigative reports, and the *Corelator*.

To send out a mailing was time-consuming and involved many steps. Mimeographing was the main way of producing duplicate copies for distribution. The relevant work team or committee would write the text. Joan Singler or I or another good typist would type it onto a mimeograph stencil—a gelatin-like page that the sharp metal typewriter keys (with the ribbon removed) would cut through. We had to patch any errors with dabs of gelatin-like goop and retype. Then we traveled to use a rented mimeograph machine at the A. B. Dick Co. on Aurora Avenue or the Unitarians' machine in Don Matson's basement. There the stencil would be attached around the drum of the mimeograph machine, gooey black ink inserted into the drum, blank paper stacked in the feeder tray, and someone would turn the crank hundreds of times to squeeze ink through the letter-shaped slits in the mimeo stencil onto paper for the hundreds of copies we needed. It wasn't clean work.

Copies in hand, we would organize a mailing party at a member's kitchen table or later at the CORE office, and volunteers would fold, seal, address, and stamp—hundreds of times. Newsletters could be simply folded, stapled or taped shut, addressed, stamped, and mailed. A letter with an enclosure would have to be put into an envelope first. Stamps and envelopes were licked, and most addresses written by hand. Then someone would carry the boxes of letters to a post office to be mailed. I remember many late-night trips to the Lander Street postal station, the only post office that was open after-hours.

PART II Employment

2 · SEATTLE CORE'S EMPLOYMENT ACTION

O h, Seattle doesn't have problems. It doesn't have racial problems. That's just the South,'" according to what Dr. James N. Gregory calls "annoying local mythology." On the contrary, says Professor Gregory, "If it's a nice place, . . . it's because people fought like hell to make things better."[1]

Seattle CORE in the 1960s "fought like hell." Our challenge was where to start. In 1961 all aspects of life for African Americans in Seattle were affected by segregated practices. As in other parts of the North, segregation was not set by laws or the "white only" signs seen in the South, but discrimination was practiced in Seattle with similar intensity. Police harassment and brutality were commonplace. Job opportunities were very limited. A few African Americans worked in government positions, such as the post office, and at the University of Washington and Boeing, but a great many were employed in what were considered menial positions: maids, janitors, dishwashers, and so forth. Few minorities were hired for any business or manufacturing jobs. There were no black delivery or truck drivers, no black clerks in the department stores, hotels, or banks. The fire department had one black firefighter. With most of the black population restricted to living in the Central Area, segregated housing that caused de facto segregated schools was a huge problem that needed to be addressed.

With so much to be done the question was where to begin. Housing? Police brutality? Schools? Seattle CORE finally agreed that ending dis-

CORE

Rules for **ACTION**

CONGRESS **O**F **R**ACIAL **E**QUALITY
38 Park Row, New York 38, New York

Cover of leaflet from National CORE, "CORE Rules for Action." (CORE, Matson Collection)

crimination in the workplace would be the place to start. We would begin with retail enterprises, because we could affect those businesses through their customers, using tools we knew—boycotts and picket lines.

National CORE, founded on the principles of nonviolence and passive resistance, established "Rules for Action" setting forth very specific rules of behavior and procedures that had to be followed by any group identified as a CORE chapter. We were required to maintain our dignity at all times, appearing "respectable" so that our demands would be taken seriously and worthy of response and corrective action. First, the chapter had to "*investigate* the facts carefully to determine whether or not racial injustice existed." Second, CORE would try to *negotiate* a solution. Only if negotiations failed, *demonstrations* to correct the injustice took the form of nonviolent direct action, avoiding "malice and hatred toward any group or individual."[2]

EMPLOYMENT DISCRIMINATION: THE INVESTIGATION

Seattle CORE narrowed down the field to banks, department stores, and grocery store chains, places where every member of the black community did business, supporting these companies with their dollars, but where they were never hired. Although employment discrimination seemed obvious, CORE's "Rules for Action" required that the first step was to get the facts. CORE members set about surveying businesses.

Assignments were given out, and members went to businesses and

counted employees, noting if any employees were Negroes. CORE member John Cornethan, a tall, polite, reliable, and dedicated man, simply stood at the employees' entrance to the J. C. Penney's store at Second and Pike with a note pad and counted every employee who walked through the door. He noted the minorities, if there were any, then walked into the store to find out the position they held. Sometimes he would simply ask other employees where the Negro or colored person worked. From the information gathered from surveys taken by John and many others, an obvious target emerged. The supermarket chains, we thought, had the worst record.[3]

Safeway Supermarkets, with three stores in the Central Area that had an 80 percent customer base from the black community, had very few black employees. Safeway had negotiated with the NAACP some years earlier and made promises to include Negroes in their workforce. Instead of increasing the number of black employees, however, store managers were now laying off the very group of people they had promised to hire. To make things worse, Safeway had never promoted one black employee to any of the better-paying jobs in their stores, such as department managers. In our continuing investigation of Safeway Stores, including the three stores in the Central Area, we found that no African Americans worked outside Seattle's Central Area. Of the more than 1,700 Safeway employees in King County, only 6 were black.[4]

On a hot day in late August 1961 CORE and NAACP members handed out five thousand leaflets door-to-door in the Central Area. For door-to-door leafleting, project leaders selected areas based on census data depicted on Dick Morrill's hand-drawn map. Then they marked free gas station maps of Seattle with assigned blocks in blue pencil and boundary streets named on the margins. The walking maps were used for leaflet distribution for many different campaigns.[5]

Our leaflets reminded the reader: "Don't Shop Where You Can't Work! You are one of the thousands of non-whites who, each week, spend the largest part of their earnings in grocery stores, where, because of your color, you cannot work. You have been doing this year after year, even when you have been unemployed. Quit buying discrimination." We wanted to make people aware that a boycott—a Selective Buying Campaign—might be necessary and to remind them, "don't buy where you see the freedom

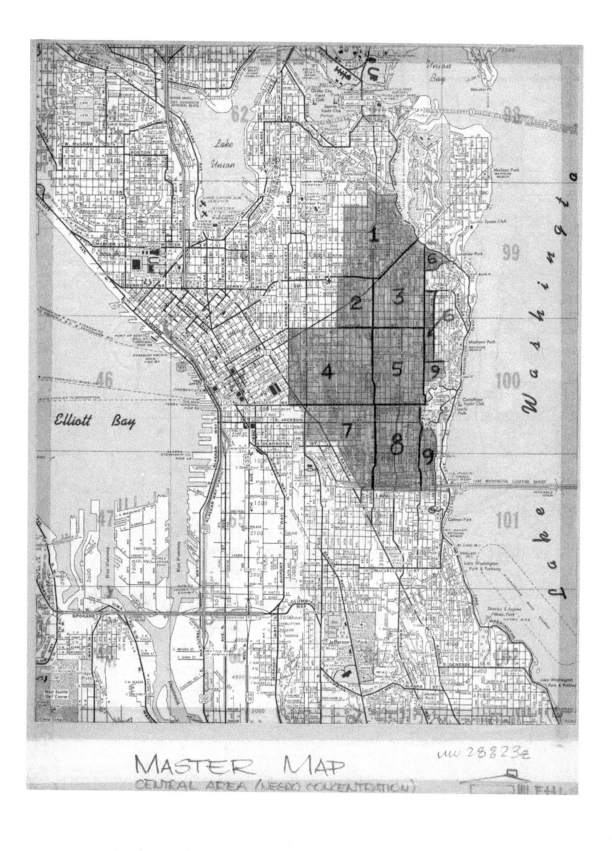

MASTER MAP
CENTRAL AREA (NEGRO CONCENTRATION)

uw 28823z

line." At this point Safeway was the *intended* but not *named* target. In addition to building awareness for a possible boycott, CORE wanted to appeal to those looking for work. At the bottom of the leaflet was a coupon to be completed and mailed to CORE that said, "I am available for supermarket work immediately."[6] We intended to make sure that we knew people were applying for work at Safeway. Over eighty of these coupons were returned to CORE at a post office box we had established.

Immediately, CORE's vice chairman, Wallace Johnson, who was completing the requirements for his master's degree in business administration, created a training program for those who were looking for work. As an African American he was a role model to encourage candidates. Wallace put together practice sessions that included a simulated employee interview. He developed math tests similar to those taken by a grocery store cashier, so that, for example, if frozen french fries were on sale at four packages for 89 cents, the clerk could figure what to charge for one package. Wallace explained recently, "Understanding schemes of multi-pricing, making change and balancing the cash drawer were critical to completing the test."[7] Wallace asked those who planned to apply for jobs to report back and let him know if they were hired. Despite the fact that there was no direct bus service to Safeway's employment office, which was in Bellevue, many Negroes did apply and *no one* was hired. The results of our training sessions proved to CORE that there were a number of qualified people ready to start work immediately.

NEGOTIATIONS

On September 20, 1961, a negotiating team of Wallace Johnson, representing CORE, Benjamin McAdoo, representing the NACCP, and Reverend Samuel McKinney, of Mount Zion Baptist Church on behalf of the Baptist Ministers Alliance, met with manager Robert E. Lee from Safeway. Negotiators followed all the principles of respectful dialogue, thoroughness, and firmness that CORE used thereafter in our many negotiations with

(Facing page) Free gas station "Master Map" with zones marked for nine volunteer teams to distribute leaflets door-to-door. (Special Collections Division, UW28823z, University of Washington Libraries)

DON'T SHOP WHERE YOU CAN'T WORK!

YOU are one of the thousands of non-whites who, each week, spend the largest part of their earnings in grocery stores, where, because of your color, you cannot work. You have been doing this year after year, even when you have been unemployed.

IT'S TIME TO QUIT BUYING DISCRIMINATION

The National Association for the Advancement of Colored People and the Seattle Committee on Racial Equality (C.O.R.E.) are determined that racial discrimination in chain grocery hiring practices must be ended. They are moving to launch a Selective Buying Campaign that demands:

1) Hiring and promotion on the basis of merit only — color cannot determine ability.

2) An end to the practice of hiring one or two non-whites only, and then only in non-white areas.

This campaign requires the unity and cooperation of the entire Negro community. As a member of the community you can and must **refuse** to shop where you cannot work. If you, or someone you know is available for super-market work, or available to be trained for super-market work, fill in the coupon in the bottom of the page and mail it — without delay — to C.O.R.E, P. O. Box 299, Seattle. Join the FREEDOM LINE that will march at the stores that discriminate. Help make others aware of this campaign: spread the word.

"DON'T BUY WHERE YOU SEE THE FREEDOM LINE"

Help launch this campaign: call the N.A.A.C.P. office, EA 4-6600 and indicate when will you be available and what you can do.

Further information about the campaign will be available through the community churches and social organizations.

I am available for super-market work immediately.

Name _____ Age _____

Address _____

City _____ Phone _____

I do _____ do not _____ need training for this work.

MAIL IMMEDIATELY TO:

C.O.R.E.
P.O. Box 299, Seattle, Wash.

Flier urging Central Area residents to support CORE's first direct action and to apply for super-market jobs. (CORE, Matson Collection)

Seattle employers. The negotiating team shared the information we had gathered on Safeway employees—African Americans were employed in only three of the thirty-eight stores in Seattle, all in the Central Area. Safeway gave the following rationale for not having more black employees:

- they hired only people who lived close to the store,
- they were replacing women cashiers with men,
- they could not find qualified people, and
- they were not hiring at this time.[8]

By October 15 none of the black applicants who CORE knew were qualified had been hired. CORE did one more test to provide evidence that Safeway's claims to our negotiators were bogus—we sent interview teams to twenty-five of the thirty-eight Safeway stores in the Seattle area. Two CORE members from the University of Washington's Department of Sociology, Beth and John Huttman, created a detailed questionnaire to use for interviewing Safeway store managers. The twenty-five stores were surveyed within forty-eight hours of each other. People who conducted the interviews identified themselves, not as members of CORE, but simply as people engaged in an "employment survey." We always spoke with the store manager. We asked about new hires, where their employees lived, what numbers of employees were minorities, and how many men and women worked in the store. Safeway stores were only open until 7:00 or 9:00 p.m., so it was not difficult for CORE members working in shifts to count the people who worked in the stores and easily check the store manager's information.

Answers to our survey confirmed what we suspected. There was no preference given to hiring men over women. Many employees lived long distances from the stores where they worked—for example, an employee working in Fremont lived in West Seattle and a person working at the University District store lived in Renton. Although one store manager identified a "Persian" employee as a minority, we found no black employees in any store outside the Central Area. Of the 581 employees in these twenty-five stores, only 6 were black. Most importantly, we verified that within thirty days after our first contact with Safeway, thirty-one new jobs had been filled, and not one of them by a minority. As soon as the Safeway surveys were completed, the interviewers called the results in to Beth and John Huttman, who tabulated the data.[9] It was obvious that Safeway had lied to the negotiators to cover up their discriminatory hiring practices.

Employees of Safeway were members of the Retail Clerks Union. A number of labor union members active in CORE urged us to contact the union and request their support. CORE sent representatives to speak to both the Retail Clerks Union and also the King County Labor Council, but we did not receive their help or support.[10]

CORE tried once more to reach Mr. Robert E. Lee, our contact at Safeway, but we were told he was out of town. Mr. Lee apparently did not think this issue important enough to assign another staff person to talk or meet with us. We sent a letter to the management explaining our position, another example of our sense of responsibility in dealing with employers.

DEMONSTRATIONS

The "Rules for Action" had been followed. We had investigated and we had negotiated. It was now time to demonstrate through nonviolent direct action. We set the date for the Selective Buying Campaign for Friday and Saturday, October 27 and 28, 1961.

To alert customers, we needed signs to place in Central Area store windows. James Washington Jr. was an acclaimed artist sculpting beautiful works in stone, but despite his prestige he came to paint signs designed by a teenaged artist. He arrived at the sign-making session in his monogrammed artist smock carrying paintbrushes and proceeded to fill in the letters outlined by a Lincoln High School student, Fred Jacobson. Our signs urged, "don't cross the freedom line" and "don't shop where you can't work." We placed a notice of the picket line in the NAACP newsletter and sent a mailing to CORE's members and friends—fewer than a hundred at this point. We sent out news releases announcing the boycott to the television and radio stations and newspapers two days prior to the event. The weekend before the demonstration Baptist ministers focused on the boycott in their Sunday sermons. Don Matson spent evenings after work running the mimeograph machine in his basement to produce leaflets to be handed out on the picket line.

On the evening of October 26 about forty people attended the CORE meeting at the East Cherry YWCA and made a commitment to picket the next day. Picket captains, including Bill Lynch, Reverend Henry Hall, and Norm Johnson, volunteered and completed a training session on how to conduct and control a demonstration. To preserve the element of surprise, we gave no advance notice as to which of the three Safeway Stores would be picketed.

On the morning of October 27 demonstrators met at the NAACP office, located in the basement of E. June Smith's house, about three blocks from the Safeway store at Twenty-Third and Union. Across the street from the store was a real estate office owned by a black realtor, who offered it as a rest station for the demonstrators. It also provided a phone if we needed to contact the NAACP office. Once the picket line assembled at Twenty-Third and Union, the Seattle Police arrived. The police gave instructions that pickets could not block the entrance to the parking lot, a rule we were well aware of and observed throughout the demonstration. Each shift had a designated picket captain assigned to be leader of the line and spokesperson for the boycott. Each participant in the picket line was required to read and agree to the Picket Rules—specific instructions defining behavior and appearance:

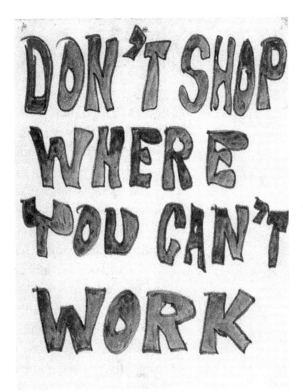

Poster painted by James Washington Jr. and Fred Jacobson in preparation for boycott of Safeway. (CORE, Matson Collection)

- Do not respond to jeers and insulting remarks—ignore these.
- Those participating in the demonstrations will dress neatly. Women no slacks please.
- Pick up any leaflets that are thrown on the ground.

And finally,

- This is a non-violent demonstration . . . If at anytime you feel that you can no longer remain non-violent, you will report to the picket captain and excuse yourself from the line immediately.[11]

Above all, we wanted to look and act respectable. (The Bay Area chapter of CORE went one step further. Their instructions to participants in a demonstration stated, "Ladies should refrain from wearing slacks . . . young men should wear neckties and be well shaven.")[12]

On Friday, October 27, shoppers arriving at Safeway were approached by picketers, given a leaflet, and urged to shop elsewhere. On the picket line were a number of people who lived in the area, who convinced their friends and neighbors to honor the picket line and to find another grocery store that day. It was an easy request to honor since there was a Tradewell supermarket directly across the street. (We would negotiate with Tradewell another day.) The picket line remained in front of the Safeway from early morning until closing time. As people marched and carried picket signs, other volunteers supported the boycott through an organized phone campaign. Several Central Area churches had organized to spread the message of the boycott by telephone. Sixty-five volunteers each phoned five people on the first and second day of the boycott.[13] Once a person got our message, we asked him or her to call three friends and ask those three friends to call three more friends and so on. Very few people crossed the line, and the store was almost empty.

News of the boycott traveled fast. On Saturday, October 28, additional members of the black community who had not been part of CORE showed up to join the picket line. Because of the large turnout that day, a second picket line was formed at the Safeway Store at Twenty-Third and Jackson (the current site of the Welch Plaza complex).[14]

Unexpected help arrived when the Teamsters Union truck drivers, as a matter of general union policy (but perhaps not in support of hiring blacks), refused to cross the picket lines. They would not make deliveries to the stores. Perishable items such as milk had to be moved to other stores by private car. The Selective Buying Campaign worked, as the black community honored the "Freedom Line." Grocery store clerks had little to do those two days. We were overjoyed with the success of the boycott. We could not have sent a stronger message to Safeway that their policy of excluding black employees would no longer be tolerated.

No response came from Safeway, however, so we made plans to picket again the following weekend. Two days after picketing, on October 30, CORE's secretary delivered a six-pound baby girl. On that same day Safeway tried unsuccessfully to reach a representative of our negotiating team. The next day, October 31, Reverend Henry Hall, the pastor of Washington Park Baptist Church, was called and asked if the negotiators would meet with Safeway immediately. They met that afternoon, with Ed Singler and Wallace Johnson representing CORE, Hascal Humes representing the NAACP, and Reverend Hall and Reverend McKinney representing the Baptist ministers. Robert E. Lee was replaced as a negotiator. Instead, Safeway was represented by the Northwest regional director, Mr. MacRae; the manager of Safeway's Central District, Mr. Wringer; and the head of personnel, Mr. Drilling. At that meeting, Safeway agreed not only to hire black workers but also to open a branch employment office at the Safeway store at Twenty-Third and Union to hire and train recruits.[15]

CORE, the NAACP, and the black churches urged people to apply for positions. Ed Pratt, executive director of the Urban League, directed his agency to send people who were looking for work. Safeway hired four male and one female cashiers immediately and others within a short period of time. Soon thereafter a black cashier at a Safeway was threatened with termination because of an alleged cash shortage. Wallace Johnson and a few other CORE members went to the store to observe the changing of cashier shifts and review store management practices. They noted that four people handled the same cash drawer in one business day without cashing out, which allowed the manager to accuse the new hire. CORE negotiators made some recommendations to Safeway on how to change their procedures so that each cashier's report could be verified and secured. It turned out that the store manager was responsible for the cash shortages. The accused cashier kept her position.[16]

Follow-up negotiations continued. In January 1962 CORE was represented by Bill Lynch. Within sixteen months Safeway had twenty-eight black employees, with many of these employees working outside the Central Area. A very good start, we thought.[17]

OTHER GROCERY CHAINS

The success of the Selective Buying Campaign that targeted Safeway led to a number of minorities being hired by other supermarket chains. Simply by sending a negotiating team to meet with corporate leaders of supermarket chains, CORE obtained jobs for African Americans. The negotiators' message was clear: hire black employees or be the target of a demonstration and boycott. Tradewell hired five blacks, including one truck driver, a first. Thriftway had one new black employee. A&P, which had a number of stores in Seattle and four hundred employees here, hired one black office worker and two store clerks.[18]

Lucky and Foodland stores, however, did not respond. Did they not understand the economic impact of a Selective Buying Campaign? With thirteen Lucky or Foodland supermarkets in the Seattle area, CORE focused on the new store due to open in November at East Union and Empire Way (later renamed Martin Luther King Jr. Way). The Madrona neighborhood, where this new Lucky's was being constructed, straddled a ridge with one side a black neighborhood and the other side mainly white. Most black neighbors agreed with the "Don't shop where you can't work" slogan, and most whites in the neighborhood supported equal opportunity. Both sides of the hill would support a boycott of a new store that did not hire enough African Americans in family-wage jobs.

Negotiations with Lucky's started in May 1962 and continued until November, with no changes in the company's hiring practices. The company felt it had done the right thing by hiring five black employees (two of them box boys) for the new Lucky store in the Central Area. Our goal was to increase the number of blacks employed and to have these new hires placed in stores outside the Central Area. Negotiators made our objectives clear, but it often took direct action before employers would understand and change. We had delivered this message to Lucky's in May and again on October 30 but saw no improvements made or even promised until CORE's Selective Buying Campaign started in November.[19]

November was the beginning of Seattle's cold wet season, when the weather only varied between "rain" and "showers," and the penetrating chill seemed colder than the thermometer showed. Seattle CORE became so proficient at making picket signs to outlast the rain that Tim and Gordon Jackins, brothers and Ballard High School students, gave a workshop on constructing waterproof signs at the regional CORE conference in Berkeley, California, in spring 1963. Fortunately for our Lucky's campaign, active CORE members Odie and Willie Crawford's modest house was a block uphill from the store, and they were happy to offer it as picketing headquarters. Demonstrators gathered in their small, comfortable living room for instructions fifteen minutes before picketing on Friday evening, then collected our signs and umbrellas from the front porch and tramped down to the store. More important, the Crawfords let us warm up with a cup of coffee after a couple of hours marching in the drizzle, before we returned to the picket line. We remained in front of Lucky's until closing time.

Sign painted by James Washington Jr. and Fred Jacobson, used in campaign against Lucky Stores and other supermarket chains. (CORE, Matson Collection)

Another group returned on Saturday morning to picket the store, but as we began the store manager came out and told the picket captain that Lucky's hiring policy would change. He indicated that he had not recognized how strongly the community felt about better-paid jobs for Negro workers. In less than twenty-four hours our picket line had produced the results we had requested but had been denied in seven months of negotiations. The number of Negro employees at Lucky's increased within a month from five to eleven, with some people placed in stores outside the Central Area and the hiring of the first Negro meat cutter, who was admitted to the Meat Cutters Union. Within the next ten months Lucky's increased that total to fourteen Negro employees, including a part-time pharmacist, a produce man in West Seattle, and a meat cutter in Kent.[20]

IMPROVING OUR SYSTEM

By August 1963, Seattle CORE was negotiating with eight different firms on fair employment, investigating housing discrimination, supporting the March on Washington, plus a host of other projects. To deal with these pressing issues and frequent new crises, the membership voted to create an Emergency Committee. This group of fifteen (five officers and ten active members elected at large) met every Tuesday to handle urgent matters that could not wait for monthly membership meetings or information via the *Corelator*. Previously, negotiations for Negro employment had been conducted with a few firms, mainly by CORE officers. The only record of what had taken place consisted of verbal reports to the membership that the CORE secretary wrote up to include in the monthly *Corelator*. This somewhat unsystematic approach worked because of the small number of people involved, all of whom worked closely together. CORE wanted to increase the number of companies and spread this workload. In September 1963 Chairman Reggie Alleyne reestablished a formal negotiation committee to "receive and evaluate reports, establish priorities and maintain records." He appointed an interracial team, Walter Hundley and Jean Adams, as committee cochairs.

Walt Hundley had come to Seattle as associate minister for the Church of the People but later turned to graduate study in the University of Washington School of Social Work. A class assignment sent him to CORE meetings to "record interactions between members." He stayed on in active roles, eventually serving as chairman of Seattle CORE.[21] Jean Adams, a white stay-at-home mother, had joined CORE on the advice of Wing Luke, whom she met through Jean Durning early in 1962. Soon to be elected the first person of color on the Seattle City Council, Wing Luke recommended CORE to her as the most effective civil rights group in Seattle.

Walt Hundley and Jean Adams implemented Chairman Alleyne's directives, putting policies in writing for the first time. The negotiating team should consist of three to four people, each with an individual role but jointly responsible for determining in advance the purpose of the negotiation. Team members must familiarize themselves with the hiring practices of this specific business and agree on what the firm would be asked to do.

Negotiators were to meet only with top managers and decision makers. The spokesperson for the team was always a black man; a note taker was responsible for accurately recording facts, figures, and agreements from the session; a third person was to support and add to points made by the spokesperson; and a fourth person might bring expertise in an area such as unions. CORE would never ask that anyone be fired to achieve integration. We expected that hiring would involve all branches, all categories of work, and all areas of the firm. Emphasis was on full-time jobs for the principal wage earner of a family. We expected a firm's intention to hire black employees to be communicated to inside and outside personnel, including the use of the new phrase "Equal Opportunity Employer" in its employment ads. The basic goal of negotiations was to change a firm's hiring practices from discrimination against minorities to fair employment based on ability, without regard to race, creed, or color.

Negotiating teams made no decisions regarding boycotts or other direct action. All information was brought to the executive committee and the membership for such critical decisions. Direct action was initiated only after numerous negotiation attempts, repeated requests, and a fair warning that if change did not occur, then action was possible.

Walt and Jean established a training program complete with role playing to equip people for becoming effective negotiators. Jean maintained the records and became the nerve center for the multitude of detailed reports (in triplicate) required of the negotiating teams, which involved many hours of phoning. Walt carried out the training sessions, assisted by Jean. He was often the lead spokesperson on one of the negotiating teams.

By 1964, more than thirty trained and active negotiators enabled CORE to negotiate with twelve to fifteen firms within a short period of time. As CORE's employment campaign continued, the list of companies we contacted included all the other supermarket chains, the major department stores, bakeries, Carnation and Darigold Dairies, and Washington Natural Gas Company. Later the list grew to include Bartell Drug Stores, Clark's Restaurant, Crown Zellerbach Paper Company, Fisher Flouring Mill, Greyhound Bus Lines, Manning's Coffee Cafes, Pay 'n Save Corporation, Rainier Brewery, the taxicab companies, and Western International (later Westin) Hotels.[22]

BAKERIES, DAIRIES, DRUG STORES

Sometimes opening up jobs at companies that had few or no black employees took only a short while. The manager at Wonder Bread convinced negotiators James Washington Jr., John Cornethan, Jean Durning, and Don Matson that he was trying to increase black employees but having little success. This was partly because of "hiring hall" contracts with the Bakers Union. For a single truck driver's position, instead of the usual word-of-mouth, they had put an ad in the paper. The responding line of applicants stretched around the block at Eighteenth and Main—but only two were black. At their first meeting on August 23, 1963, the CORE negotiators suggested how Wonder Bread's outreach could be more effective—contact the Urban League, NAACP, CORE, and Central Area churches for possible employees, advertise in *The Facts*, and list their company as an equal opportunity employer. With these tools, the bakery soon hired additional African Americans, including its first truck driver, increasing their total to 12 among the company's 295 employees. Wonder Bread was a division of Continental Bakeries, and we hoped this success would also influence the smaller Continental branch here, Hostess Cakes.[23]

Some employers initially responded well to our negotiations but without our constant vigilance made no further progress in hiring blacks. In August 1964 when CORE negotiators John Cornethan, Charles Oliver, and Mona Howard contacted the other large bakery, Langendorf, all three African Americans employed there were janitors. By November the company had added a receptionist, a part-time warehouseman, and the first black driver-salesman for a bread company. But two years later, in October 1965, Langendorf still had only six black employees. The negotiators returned and demanded that two more driver-salesmen be hired in the next two months.

Other companies required repeated visits. Walt Hundley, Marion West, Phoebe Ottenberg, and Reverend Donald Clinton's attempts to negotiate with Darigold turned into one continual delay after another. Its managers stated that they wanted Darigold to be considered an equal opportunity employer but were not willing to state such a startling new idea in local newspaper ads. By 1964, however, Darigold had agreed to use "Equal

Opportunity" on its billboards and bus advertising—a major step forward—and "expected to hire some Negroes in winter."[24]

A new twist on negotiations occurred when Mayor Dorm Braman interceded on behalf of Lamont Bean, the corporate CEO of Pay 'n Save Drug Stores, and Frank Ruano, the developer of a shopping center being built at Twenty-Second and East Madison. Very likely this meeting was set in response to CORE's action taken on February 11, 1965. The membership voted that Seattle CORE focus all its attention on a direct action project against the three parts of the large corporation headed by Lamont Bean—Pay 'n Save Drugs, Ernst Hardware, and Malmo Nurseries. The mayor arranged to have a meeting on March 5, 1965, at his offices on the twelfth floor of the Municipal Building. Representatives from community agencies and civil rights organizations included Walt Hundley for CORE, James Washington Jr. for the NAACP, Phil Hayasaka, chair of the Human Rights Commission, Ed Pratt on behalf of the Urban League, plus building contractor Johnny Allen, and businessman John Eichelberger. Bean's and Ruano's purpose in meeting us was to obtain a written agreement that "Negroes would not boycott or picket a proposed Pay 'n Save store in this new shopping center." The group told Bean that those at the meeting could not give such a pledge on behalf of the organizations they represented. Bean stated that he was willing to train Negroes to work in the store at Twenty-Second and Madison but could not give assurances that Pay 'n Save would integrate its other stores. The two sides had widely different perspectives.[25] Negotiations continued. Within a month, CORE's negotiators reported in the April 1965 *Corelator* that Pay 'n Save "has doubled its number of Negro employees, and will add more by the end of April. They also agreed to the principle of integrating those employees among their many stores in the Seattle area. So far we have not had to use direct action, and it is our hope that the plan will be implemented fully." Pay 'n Save did open a store as the lead tenant in Ruano's small shopping center, and we did not demonstrate.

Some companies, such as A&P and Tradewell Stores, made initial commitments to correct discriminatory practices and hired two or three black employees. They showed no intention, however, of following through on their promises of many more hires.

Top portion of flier urging
boycott of A&P, which
kept postponing its hiring
of minority employees.
(CORE, Matson
Collection)

Top portion of flier urging boycott of A&P, which kept postponing its hiring of minority employees. (CORE, Matson Collection)

THE A&P CAMPAIGN: THE LONG HAUL AND SHOP-IN

When negotiators Tim Martin, Father Lynch, Walt Hundley, and Bettylou Valentine first met with the manager for A&P, Ray Sheehan, in early 1962, there were no African Americans working in any of their stores, including the one in the Central Area. The initial 1962 agreement with A&P resulted in three blacks being hired in a total workforce of four hundred employees. For a year CORE's negotiating team continued to press A&P to follow through on their promise of additional black hires. But the negotiators reported no progress—just excuses—and recommended to the membership that we boycott A&P. The membership agreed and designated the store at Thirteenth and Union, which had the largest percentage of black customers (about 50 percent), as the first target.[26]

The *Corelator* gives the account, month by month, of what happened after that. In March 1963, more than a year after meeting with negotiators and little change in their hiring practices, we staged a demonstration against A&P. Immediately A&P hired another two black employees. Then another six months went by without any additional minorities being hired. The general superintendent for the Seattle unit of A&P, Ray Sheehan, followed through on his commitment to hire more blacks only when demonstrators appeared in front of the stores.

CORE felt that there was only one course of action open to us. The picket line was reinstated at the Thirteenth and Union store in September 1963. On the picket line CORE members worked hard to convince prospective shoppers to honor the boycott. Since we knew that the percentage of A&P shoppers who were black was smaller than the percentage at Safeway, every customer we could keep out of the A&P was a victory. At one point a black woman apologized and said that she needed to go into the A&P to cash a check. To discourage her from entering the store, Bob Winsor, an attorney on the picket line, pulled out his wallet and handed her a $20.00 bill in exchange for a personal check from a woman he did not know. That was a lot of money (equal to $150 now). Grateful, she stayed out of the store.[27]

The direct action project tested our endurance and commitment. The picket line involved six to ten people walking each shift with picket signs and handing out leaflets every Friday, Saturday, and Sunday, rain or (occasionally) shine. The weekend was divided into shifts: two shifts Friday afternoons and evenings, four shifts on Saturdays between 9 a.m. and 9 p.m., three shifts on Sundays between 10 a.m. and 7 p.m. Nine three-hour shifts each weekend for forty-five long days added up to 405 hours of picketing from September to December 1963. Active members and supporters from all over Seattle joined the picket line or participated in our phone campaign to recruit demonstrators. A list provided by Dave and Mary Lamb recorded over four hundred who stayed engaged in this effort for over three months. In addition, on the November 11 holiday, CORE members went door-to-door with leaflets explaining why we were asking for the communities' participation in boycotting A&P.

Regulars on the picket line became friends, whether shivering together in winter rain or singing. Mary Lamb recently recalled, "I am embarrassed that I do not remember his name, but I certainly remember the Pullman porter who walked on our picket line whenever he was in Seattle. I often walked with him because we were both fairly short, and it was common to walk with a person of the other color and to talk about experiences. He called on the day that President Jack Kennedy was shot and we wept

together on the telephone."[28] Many in CORE shared Mary's grief at the loss of our president. Dave Lamb made an impassioned plea to call off the demonstrations for a week or so at this time of national mourning. But CORE members voted to continue the picket line. Sixty-two people turned out to demonstrate on November 23, 24, and 25, asking shoppers to join "Operation Turkey" and reduce the number of Thanksgiving turkeys on Seattle residents' tables purchased at A&P.[29]

By this time CORE had a mailing list of twelve hundred that included active members and those sympathetic to civil rights concerns in Seattle.[30] For this reason CORE was able to take the message of the A&P boycott to other parts of the city, and from September through December 1963 over four hundred individuals participated in our picket lines. A picket line at the A&P store in the University District was maintained by the newly formed Civil Rights Action Group (CRAG). CRAG was a University of Washington campus civil rights group, which included Esther Hall, Bettylou and Val Valentine, Paul Dietrichson, Si and Phoebe Ottenberg, and Diane and Gordon Bissett. A membership list for CRAG names 222 students, staff, and faculty members.[31]

Other A&P stores were chosen in parts of the city that we believed would not welcome demonstrators. In 1963 Broadway on Capitol Hill was a very different scene than it is today and at that time included several upscale shops and designer furniture stores. Many white citizens disapproved of the disruption caused by signs and leaflets or picketers reminding them that they lived in a segregated city. Our presence calling for an integrated workforce at their favorite supermarket upset many people. In Mississippi, blacks were being beaten or killed for registering to vote; but Seattle, likewise, did not think blacks deserved the same rights as whites. Hostile shoppers, who considered us nothing but radical agitators, tried to ignore us or tore up our leaflets. Others resorted to verbal attacks, threw water on picketers, and in one case physically attacked a demonstrator. Someone threw raw eggs at picketers at the Capitol Hill store. Our demonstrators not only maintained their dignity, we even cleaned up the broken eggs.

Despite our efforts to appear as upright, respectable citizens, the news media often photographed some person who might send a different message. Work pants were not acceptable on women; fur coats were. But when Louise Crowley showed up to picket in men's workpants or coveralls, it was she, not Joan Miracle with her picket sign and her full-length mink coat, who was shown on television representing CORE.

The *Corelator* reported that the A&P demonstrations of 1963 caused the stores to lose approximately $4,000.00 a week. This campaign was expensive not only for A&P but also for CORE, which spent over $400 on this one project. We did, however, end up with a renewed commitment (we thought) from A&P and a new picket line song written by Dave Lamb, a music teacher and composer.[32] The words of many verses of his song said it all.

> The A&P says we've got no problem here.
> There's one Negro in our store,
> Who could ask for any more?
> At the A&P, 'cause there's no problem here.

Singing always helped to relieve the tension and lift the spirits of the people who walked that picket line for forty-five endless days. Picketers found a welcome respite at John Adams's First AME Church, located a couple of blocks from the Thirteenth and Union A&P. The church became a place to dry off, have a cup of hot coffee, and get warm on those cold

rainy Seattle weekends when picketing became a way of life for so many in Seattle CORE.

After months, the business disruption caused by the continuous picketing at Thirteenth and Union and other A&P stores led management to agree to fulfill its original hiring commitment. In December the picketing and boycott were called off. The afternoon paper, the *Seattle Times*, announced on December 20, 1963, "Food Chain, CORE Reach Job Accord." The article reported, "R. T. Sheehan general superintendent of A&P . . . and Tim Martin . . . of CORE called the agreement a major advance toward equal job opportunities." The *Times* continued, "They said in a joint statement: the understanding between A&P and CORE assures that jobs and advancement will continue to be available to the qualified person, regardless of race, color or creed." This was the first time a company issued a press release and the first time a company was on record publicly as committing to signing an agreement with Seattle CORE.

Once more CORE waited for A&P to carry out its promise to increase the number of blacks in its workforce and provide the same opportunities for advancement to blacks that were afforded to white employees. Again it was a token gesture. In two years of serious negotiations, A&P had hired a total of nine blacks. Frustration in the CORE membership was growing. A new tactic had to be used. By March 1964, in preparation for the next level of demonstrations, we distributed fliers door to door that asserted: "A&P has NEVER hired Negroes without pressure . . . Well qualified applicants have been turned away . . . DON'T SHOP AT A&P. TOKEN HIRING IS NOT ENOUGH."

CORE then organized and trained people for a "shop-in." We would disrupt normal functions at a store by completely taking over all the shopping carts, and we anticipated that shoppers and store employees would become frustrated and even hostile. Could we expect more than water and eggs to be tossed at us? This direct action project required intensive training. Trainers conducted role-playing sessions so we could act out our responses in anticipation of possible aggression from store clerks and customers. Our goal was to train enough people to occupy all checkout lines for hours. CORE shoppers were instructed to fill their carts and were reminded, "No perishable items, or frozen food, pay for anything you break, always be courteous."

By March 1964 we were ready. The shop-in began as large numbers of CORE members took shopping carts, walked up and down the aisles, and filled each cart to the top with nonperishable grocery items. (Don Matson specialized in collecting the smallest cans or jars he could find—baby food and many varieties of anchovies and olives.) We then proceeded to the checkout counter, where the cashier would push the cash register keys hundreds of times to ring up all the items. The CORE shoppers then would inform the cashier that they did not want the groceries and would not shop at A&P again because of its discriminatory hiring practices. Store clerks had no time to restock the items from our carts. The front of the

Carts filled by "shop-in" demonstrators lining a wall of the A&P in the University District, March 22, 1964. (Seattle Times original photo has been lost; clipping from Special Collections Division, UW 28886z, University of Washington Libraries)

store soon became cluttered with shopping carts filled with groceries, and long lines at the checkout stands frustrated the few regular shoppers who were able to secure a cart. Simultaneously, CORE maintained a picket line outside the store, giving leaflets explaining our action to prospective shoppers. Although the shop-in sounds like a straightforward action, most CORE members were nervous, uncertain of other people's reactions, and unaccustomed to facing anger.[33]

David Lamb, CORE's major sign maker, who had been in charge of the picketing in 1963, was in charge of the shop-in at the A&P at Thirteenth and Union. David still recalls that day clearly and remembers the frustration of the A&P cashier. Shopper after shopper had been through his check stand and then refused the sale. Since David was the last shopper to leave the store, the cashier seemed to think he was not part of the CORE group. Looking for a sympathetic ear, he remarked to David, "All those crazy people are trying to tell us how to run our business." When David explained that he did not approve of discrimination either and walked out after having had all his groceries rung up, the clerk's remark and his look of disbelief and frustration became embedded in David's memory.[34]

Similar scenes also occurred at three other A&P stores—Broadway, Rainier and Empire, and, led by CRAG, the University District. The shop-in was the last demonstration CORE carried out against A&P. Due to the loss of business and customers at the Thirteenth and Union store and the disruption of the shop-ins, A&P finally hired black employees in each of their fifteen stores. Yet Ray Sheehan was still rationalizing. In September 1964, according to the *Argus*, "He indicated no concessions were made to end the shop-in. 'It was a matter of convincing CORE that we were conscientious in hiring people, not whites or colored.'"[35]

TRADEWELL, TOO

As it turned out, A&P became the training ground for the next shop-in, which occurred three months later in July 1964. CORE negotiators James Washington Jr., Ray Jones, and Judy Esparza revisited the agreement that Tradewell had promised to fulfill on numerous occasions. They found no progress. Only two full-time cashiers, listed by Tradewell as being on a trial basis, and two additional box boys had been hired since 1962. They recommended that CORE should engage in a direct action project.

The membership voted to stage a shop-in at two large Tradewell stores in the all-white neighborhoods of Laurelhurst and Wedgewood. Trainers who schooled shop-in participants emphasized nonviolence as a tactic and a way to deal with possible hostile behavior by some of Tradewell's customers. Knowing that we had to make a major impact on the stores' business, CORE trained over one hundred people as shoppers. Despite the training, once the first shop-in began, it was *not* easy to remain calm when interacting with angry and frustrated people. Maid Adams still remembers the cold, piercing blue eyes of a Tradewell cashier, infuriated with her for refusing to pay. He was intimidating, but she knew she was right. It was

DON'T SHOP AT TRADEWELL
DON'T BUY DISCRIMINATION

SEATTLE CORE HAS BEEN
NEGOTIATING WITH TRADEWELL
FOR OVER 2 YEARS!
CORE KNOWS OF QUALIFIED
NEGRO APPLICANTS WHO HAVE
APPLIED AT TRADEWELL AND
HAVE NOT BEEN HIRED WHEN
OPENINGS WERE AVAILABLE

TRADEWELL'S EMPLOYMENT RECORD
260 FULL TIME EMPLOYEES IN STORES
ONLY 6 NEGRO CLERKS
115 FULL TIME IN OFFICE AND WAREHOUSE
ONLY 2 NEGROES IN THE WAREHOUSE
NO NEGRO TRUCK DRIVERS
NO NEGROES IN THE OFFICE
18 GREATER SEATTLE AREA STORES
NEGRO EMPLOYEES RESTRICTED TO 2 CENTRAL
AREA STORES

TOKEN HIRING IS NOT ENOUGH
SUPPORT EQUAL JOB OPPORTUNITY

Seattle Congress of Racial Equality (CORE) - Box 299 - Seattle, Wa. - EA 5-5496

important to remind ourselves that the change we hoped to bring about
was long overdue. Again the shop-in was effective and the stores became
filled with shopping carts full of nonperishable items we refused to buy
because of the hiring policy. Not only had we filled carts with items that
needed to be restocked, but there were no shopping carts for their regular
customers. Those outside on the picket line handed out leaflets explaining,
"Seattle CORE has been negotiating with Tradewell for over two years . . .
CORE knows of qualified Negro applicants who have applied at Tradewell
and have not been hired when openings were available." They emphasized,
"Token Hiring is Not Enough, Support Equal Job Opportunity." The leaflet
pointed out Tradewell's failure to live up to its agreement. The message on
our picket signs asked for customer support. But customers were aggra-
vated and hostile, and the police were called to the Laurelhurst store. The
officers simply checked out the scene—there was no violence and no one
was arrested. After we completed the shop-in, filling every cart at Laurelhurst, the group moved to the Wedgewood Tradewell at NE Eighty-Fifth
and Thirty-Fifth NE. Tired but committed to getting our message out, many

in the group ended the day by forming a picket line in front of the Tradewell at Twenty-Third and Union. Finally, another victory—Tradewell changed its policy and ten blacks were hired within the next week.

REDLINING BY CARNATION

In addition to supermarkets, our struggle for equal employment included the local division of a nationwide company, Carnation Milk. The first negotiating team met with the manager, Mr. Henry C. Weber, in September 1963. At the first meeting, CORE learned that in a workforce of 375 employees only one was black, a custodian. During the next nine months just one more black was hired. Because most of CORE's energy was being directed at segregated housing, the follow-up negotiating team did not meet with Weber again until May 1964. This negotiation team, chaired by Reggie Alleyne, made it clear that CORE was aware that openings were filled by acquaintances of current employees, who were white. Without a system to alert the general public of job openings, blacks would never get hired. Reggie pointed out that "the unusual circumstances of the American Negro's exclusion from the main stream of employment" made it necessary for Carnation to change its approach to hiring.[36]

In addition, the chairman of CORE, Tim Martin, sent a letter to President Johnson's Committee on Equal Employment Opportunity in Washington, D.C. Tim documented the poor performance of Carnation and asked that it be investigated for noncompliance with the rules of its government contract. Tim stated that the situation at Carnation had reached the breaking point. The President's Committee on Equal Employment Opportunity requested the Defense Supply Agency to conduct a special compliance review of Carnation's employment practices and report back within sixty days.[37] Seattle CORE was about to alert National CORE and the West Coast CORE chapters and suggest a national boycott. At this time there were twenty-six CORE chapters on the West Coast alone, among more than a hundred chapters nationwide. But the Defense Supply Agency's review must have been pressure enough.

Carnation finally hired its first black office worker, Esther Hall, who was a member of Seattle CRAG. (Esther later wrote several books about the history of African Americans in the state of Washington, including *Seattle's Black Victorians, 1865–1901*, *Seven Stars and Orion*, and *Calabash*.) Esther remembers trying to set up milk delivery service for a person who lived in the Central District. A Carnation staff person told her that Carnation drivers made no deliveries in that area. Another employee showed her a map of the milk delivery routes. A red line had been drawn around the Central District—no service given in this area.[38]

While Seattle CORE dealt with employers in Seattle, Congress debated—and endlessly filibustered—the civil rights legislation that finally passed in 1964. At a Senate hearing in July 1963, Governor Ross Barnett of Mississippi identified civil rights demonstrations as "part of a world Communist conspiracy to divide and conquer from within." Senator Strom Thurmond of South Carolina agreed that Communists were behind the protests. Governor Barnett testified further, "If New York wants to integrate and end up with a mongrel race, that's New York's business. If Mississippi or Alabama or Georgia want to . . . maintain the purity and integrity of both races, that's our business."[39] We Seattleites thought ourselves superior to such sentiments; few people here stated bigoted views so bluntly. But the biased opinions of many whites resulted in widespread injustice.

THE PHONE TREE

Joan Singler

There were times when I was not only picketing or sitting-in but trying to motivate others to do the same. I was a "lieutenant" who reported to Elizabeth Patton, who as chair of the Phone Tree Committee did an incredible job of speeding communication within CORE.

As in most volunteer organizations, there was no paid staff. The success or failure of CORE's many activities, whether we were planning a demonstration, picketing the Seattle School Board, or recruiting people for an all-night vigil, depended on turning out people to support the event. How to reach these members became the challenge. Yes, an appeal would appear in the *Corelator*, but that newsletter was only printed once a month and there was no way to obtain a count of those willing to get involved without actually making a call. Many times we had to rally the membership and friends on very short notice. As a phoner I remember how important it was to convey with some passion and emotion the dire need for people to commit to an event.

Today, with email, it takes but a few moments to send and receive many messages. In the early 1960s, without cell phones, Blackberries, call-waiting, or even answering machines, the Phone Tree workers had to put in hours just to talk to someone on their phone list. Numerous callbacks were made after getting busy signals or to find someone at home.

And so as a phone tree volunteer I called my list of callers, who called their list of callers, who called their list of volunteers—a good job for those with some limitation or small children who were not free to demonstrate but had the time, patience, and passion to pick up the phone and call.

3 · EMPLOYMENT DOWNTOWN

While still continuing intensive efforts on jobs in supermarkets, on opening housing outside the Central Area, and on support for our Freedom Riders and other fundraising, by spring 1962 CORE was ready to confront employment discrimination downtown. The Bon Marché (later Macy's), J. C. Penney, Nordstrom, Frederick and Nelson, Best's, Rhodes, and MacDougall's—stores that defined Seattle's retail commercial identity—entered the 1960s with virtually no black employees, except for cleaning staff and plantation-themed waitresses. In April 1962 CORE volunteers started a second survey of department stores. Civil rights groups in Seattle cooperated on most activities; negotiations with employers included the NAACP and religious representatives. But it was CORE, following its national principles, that did the initial investigations, carefully documenting numbers and characteristics of employees and numbers of recent hires. We developed responses to employers' excuses for why their employees were almost exclusively white. Typical statements were "We don't discriminate." "We don't have applicants." "People aren't qualified." "We're not hiring now." "You send us some people and we'll consider them."[1]

In May 1962, its data collected on department store employment, CORE was ready to negotiate with its first store, J. C. Penney, whose downtown store was on Second Avenue at Pike. Soon thereafter we met with managers of the locally owned Rhodes Department Store at Second and Union.

To strengthen our position, CORE and other civil rights organizations jointly issued a call for job applicants who would coordinate with the negotiation effort. The negotiating team met repeatedly over the summer with both Penney's and Rhodes, but by September there were no visible results. CORE began organizing for a Selective Buying Campaign like that used with the grocery chains and training volunteers for nonviolent picketing in a downtown "Freedom Line." When negotiators informed store managers of these plans, the stores suddenly responded. Penney's hired two African Americans that same day, began a management training program that would include blacks, and promised to advertise in Central Area press and radio. Rhodes hired two blacks in sales, two as sales trainees, and four in a new telephone orders department; it too agreed to advertise job openings in the Central Area. By late December 1962, J. C. Penney had hired Seattle CORE chairman Reverend Henry Hall as a management trainee for a position in San Francisco and Mr. Barney Hilliard as a management trainee in downtown Seattle. Negotiations continued with Penney's, under the leadership of Tim Martin. In May the *Corelator* announced that Penney's had hired thirteen employees in one month, nine of them black. We learned on May 21 that Penney's had hired management trainees in stores near the university and in Renton in addition to downtown.[2]

THE BON

The next target of the department store campaign was much larger—the Bon Marché, familiarly called the Bon (much later, Macy's). As Ed Singler recalls, CORE's initial survey in the summer of 1961 showed the Bon had no African Americans as sales or office staff. Its only black employees were cleaning staff and "colored" waitresses in the "plantation theme" restaurant. On December 1, 1962, eight CORE members (Blanche Reece, Wiley Allen, Dianne Moore, Joan Miracle, Willie Crawford, Carl Taylor, Joyce Rowe, and Jean Adams) did another survey. Floor by floor, repeated morning and afternoon, they noted all employees in public view. They counted ten African Americans employed as salespeople (full- or part-time), fifteen as waitresses (fourteen of them in the Corner House), and five matrons in public or employee restrooms. Months of negotiations followed but

Barney Hilliard, first African American management trainee at Seattle J. C. Penney, in men's wear department, with his supervisor, Robert Gillis, October 1963. (Photo from Barney Hilliard, reproduced by permission of DeGolyer Library, J. C. Penney Company records, 1902–2004, collection A204.0007, Southern Methodist University, Dallas, Texas)

accomplished almost nothing. By late February 1963 the Bon apparently had fewer black salespeople than at CORE's December survey—three full-time and two part-time salespeople out of a sales force of more than four hundred downtown plus eighty-one full-time employees in the Northgate store. In the last three weeks of that February, sixty-seven African Americans applied for jobs. The store hired ten new employees, none of them black. On February 28, 1963, Reverend Mance Jackson, for CORE, Dr. Earl Miller, representing the NAACP, and other negotiators met with the Bon Marché for the third time in three months but made no progress. The March *Corelator* reported, "Things got so bad that the negotiators indicated to the Bon that they would not return unless there was some concrete evidence of change in the Bon's attitude toward hiring black employees . . . Sounds like an old refrain from a familiar song." Decades later Reverend

Jackson recalled the Bon Marché manager as utterly uninterested in talking to negotiators, even belligerent.[3]

CORE had followed its procedures: had investigated the facts and tested them, had negotiated and would continue to do so. It was time for nonviolent direct action. It would take a major campaign to affect the largest department store in downtown Seattle. CORE would solicit as much support as possible for a boycott—by letter, by leaflets distributed door-to-door and at places where potential supporters gathered, and by announcements from pulpits. To picket a store that filled an entire city block, we had to train many more picket captains and picketers. CORE started organizing.

Jean Durning remembers that early in April 1963, when her second baby was about two weeks old, CORE asked her to run the campaign to integrate the Bon. Reverend Jackson would be the public face of the effort; it was important for an African American to be the leader, though a white woman could be the organizer behind the scenes. But Reverend Jackson had a full-time job in addition to his duties as pastor of his church and his various efforts for CORE and the Methodist Episcopal Ministers Alliance. Other CORE leaders had major obligations with respect to fair housing, the A&P and other supermarkets, the James Baldwin fundraising lecture, and support for protests in the South. "Even though I had a brand-new baby," she recalls, "I was the only logical candidate. I was still recovering. I was too busy. But the task needed to be done. I agreed."

Someone suggested we should get customers to turn in their charge cards. This innovative idea was exactly suited to CORE's strengths. The minority community increasingly agreed with "Don't shop where you can't work." In addition, white liberals all over the city, appalled by news of bigotry and violence in the South, supported Seattle CORE's efforts, and we could reach many through white churches. Thousands of people had charge accounts at the Bon, and we were sure we could convince many to cancel their accounts. So we composed a letter (dated May 10, 1963), mimeographed thousands of copies, addressed, sealed, and stamped envelopes, and took them to the post office. The letter, signed by Seattle CORE chairman Reginald Alleyne, went out to all "fair-minded people" whose addresses we could find. We also sent the letter to many clergy, church social action groups, and all the Central Area fraternal, social, and civic groups. A cover note asked leaders to spread the message to their members. The letter invoked images of men with fire hoses and police dogs attacking Negroes the preceding week in Birmingham, Alabama, cited the lack of job opportunities there and here, and asked, "Will you help us in the fight for equality?" After describing the history of our negotiations with the Bon, the letter continued, "We ask you and your friends not to shop at the Bon Marché and to cancel your charge account with a note explaining your reasons."[4] Pledge cards returned to CORE helped us keep track of our support. We were gratified at how many responses came in.

CORE's Bon Marché committee met often to coordinate the campaign. Jean Durning remembers leading planning sessions of eight or ten people seated around her living room with her infant propped on the floor beside her. Before one meeting, distinguished sculptor James Washington Jr., his hands shaping an oval in the air as he spoke, commented that he would like "a nice piece of granite" to carve the compact figure of the baby—a mental image Jean still treasures. At regular monthly CORE meetings we informed members of details and urged them to volunteer. Maid Adams remembers almost an entire meeting devoted to an account of the Bon negotiations, with all members completely absorbed and participating in decisions. The May 1963 *Corelator* reminded members and friends, "If you do not have a charge account, simply write a note telling them you will no longer shop at their store until you can see a drastic change in their hiring policy."

CORE had picketed grocery stores and would picket the Bon. But we wanted something more newsworthy. This time, we would borrow an action widely used in the South. To dramatize the start of picketing, we would hold a large march downtown to the Bon Marché. Following rules of nonviolence would be crucial, so trained CORE members would lead and monitor the demonstration. We set Saturday, June 15, 1963, as the date for this Freedom March. The committee solicited participants from CORE and the NAACP. We contacted churches, both black and white, and many promised their support. Reverend Mance Jackson invited ministers of about eighteen Central Area churches to a meeting on June 3 at Goodwill Baptist Church to share ideas and plan "for leading your people in this struggle for human dignity." To inform Central Area residents, fifty volunteers working out of Reverend Jackson's own church, Bethel CME at Twenty-Third Avenue and Spruce (now Curry Temple), distributed thousands of leaflets door-to-door inviting everyone to "Join the Freedom Marchers." The leaflet urged citizens to protest racial discrimination in employment by joining this march. "Walk downtown to the Bon Marche, a glaring example of discrimination in Seattle, whom we will picket on this day to demonstrate to the public their discriminatory hiring practices . . . to change these practices and to dramatize to the rest of the community that racial discrimination in Seattle will no longer be tolerated." Leaflets were also handed out week after week at the downtown Bon. Our leafleteers were harassed by the police at its Northgate store. We sent our news release to newspapers, including the aeromechanics paper.[5]

A number of white ministers supported the demonstration, even though some opposed this method of "bringing happier relations between the races." Pastor Everett J. Jensen, president of the Greater Seattle Council of Churches, wrote of "deep unrest and frustration with unequal opportunities . . . throughout our metropolitan community, which many Caucasians join in deploring . . . We believe that the Negro ministers and the officers of CORE and NAACP leading this movement are responsible and moderate people. They represent the best in American idealism and the finest in the Jewish-Christian tradition. They deserve our support."[6]

All marchers would have to pledge to remain nonviolent. But most would not have been trained in nonviolent response the way active CORE members had. The numbers would be much greater than those previously trained for picketing other stores, so we would need to train monitors, who would walk beside every few rows of marchers. With so many CORE stalwarts like Ed Banks, Major John Cannon, Tommie Lamb, and Willie Crawford, we assumed we could cover that. Someone lettered "CORE" on armbands to identify the monitors. Signs were silk-screened and stapled to sticks. Organizers contacted the police and agreed that the marchers would observe traffic signals. We planned a rally at Mount Zion Baptist Church at 9:30 the morning of the march to inspire the participants.

In a letter to her grandfather on June 8, Jean Durning wrote, "Penney's . . . now has 23 Negroes employed in sales & office positions . . . the Bon Marché management has been quite uncooperative until this week. Now under the threat of a widespread boycott starting next Saturday they have begun hiring."[7]

Also on June 8, 1963, exactly a week before the scheduled march and picketing, CORE chairman Reggie Alleyne wrote to the Bon Marché management that the civil rights negotiators would meet again only if the Bon was represented by its board chairman, president, and managing director, so all its commitments would be credible. At a "final" negotiation session the afternoon of Tuesday, June 11, the Bon was represented by five officers plus their attorney, and the civil rights movement was represented by Reverend Mance Jackson for Central Area ministers, Dr. Earl Miller for the NAACP, and Ethel Lightfoot and Joan Singler for CORE. Three observers also attended: Reverend Lemuel Petersen for the Greater Seattle Council of Churches, Rabbi Norman Hirsh for Temple Beth Am, and Ken MacDonald for the Washington State Board against Discrimination. The Bon Marché, to avoid "Seattle put on the TV as having a race problem," conceded they could hire more Negroes "if they had a little more time"—an excuse used constantly, North and South, in response to civil rights pressure. CORE, the NAACP, and the ministers had identified appropriate positions for fifty-four full-time hires. The store manager found that these numbers were not unreasonable and said he would attempt to meet these demands but felt that it would be impossible to do so by Friday. He also mentioned potential problems with their unions, to which Joan Singler, an experienced union activist, responded that we would talk to the unions about any problems. The Bon was anxious that the demonstration be postponed and asked for "an additional six or seven days to try to fill the demands." The civil rights representatives were willing to consider minor adjustments in our demands, but the march had too much momentum to be deferred, and as Reverend Jackson pointed out, the Bon Marché had "had over a year to do something."[8]

The Bon did hire more blacks that week. At the rally preceding the march the morning of June 15, CORE and the NAACP distributed a flier announcing, "There will be no picket at the Bon Marche today, since yesterday they informed CORE & NAACP negotiators . . . in the past week Negroes were hired in these jobs at the downtown store—11 full time in sales, 5 part time in sales, 5 full time in the office, 5 part time in the warehouse, 1 member of the College Board," plus at Northgate one part-time and seven full-time salespeople.[9] The Freedom March stayed on schedule, but its focus was broadened to a general protest against job and housing discrimination in Seattle.

Later on, huge marches became more common, especially in opposition

to the Vietnam War, but in 1963 Seattle was not accustomed to large protest marches. On Saturday morning, June 15, the organizers were thrilled to
see the overflow crowd that gathered at Mount Zion Baptist Church before
the march. Civil rights tragedy was occurring frequently across the nation;
at Mount Zion that morning the congregation prayed for Medgar Evers,
the NAACP field secretary who had just been assassinated in Mississippi.
Reverend Jackson exhorted the crowd, "This is an occasion of historical
importance to Seattle . . . we declare war on one of America's greatest ene-
mies—discrimination, segregation and racial bigotry . . . We will have to
sacrifice and suffer." He urged everyone to participate in future demonstrations to "Integrate Seattle!"[10] Speakers reminded the marchers to follow the
principles of nonviolent direct action. As at every event, the crowd crossed
arms, held hands, and swayed as they sang verse after verse of "We Shall
Overcome."

The throng, about one-third white, filed out of the sanctuary and formed
a column. Six abreast, led by Reverend Mance Jackson and other Seattle
civil rights leaders, everyone walked up Madison Street and crossed to Pine.
Monitors reminded marchers to walk silently and with dignity, ignoring
any hecklers. As those toward the end of the procession reached the crest of
the hill and looked forward, down across the freeway overpass, they gasped
at the size of the column ahead—block after block of people marching for
freedom and justice. Surely, we thought, full equality would be accomplished in only a few years.[11] CORE's parade monitors counted the sections
of marchers, multiplied by the number of rows in each section, and concluded we had nearly 1,200 people marching for Freedom. As the march
passed the Bon's upscale competitor, Frederick and Nelson, its managers
stood at their main doorway watching with extremely sober faces.

Instead of picketing around the Bon, the march concluded in a downtown rally, with speaker after speaker calling for an end to discrimination
in employment and housing. Chairman Reggie Alleyne decried de facto
segregated schools, caused by housing restrictions. Several community
ministers spoke. Reggie Alleyne later wrote, "As witnessed by the loud and
frequent cheering, the crowd was singularly responsive." The Seattle Post-
Intelligencer reported, "In addition to fiery oratory, the rallies were punctu-
ated by prayers and the singing of such hymns as 'We're Marching for Freedom.'" People were urged to attend the city council meeting two days later,

Seattle's first civil rights march: guided by monitors, including Tim Martin (front left, wearing armband), nearly 1,200 demonstrators setting out from Mount Zion Baptist Church, June 15, 1963. (Seattle Times original photo has been lost; copy courtesy of Dr. Quintard Taylor)

when the mayor would announce a new Human Rights Commission. Reverend John Adams declared, "We will let the mayor know we don't approve his timetable . . . We don't want any more study groups—we want action now!"[12] Someone led the call-and-response shout: "What do we want?" "Freedom." "When do we want it?" "Now!" The rally concluded with nearly twelve hundred people crossing arms to hold hands with their neighbors for ringing choruses of "We Shall Overcome."

For almost the first time in Seattle CORE's efforts, news reporters and photographers were there to record the action. In the *Seattle Times* that afternoon, reporter Bob Lane wrote that there were 1,300 marchers. The Sunday *Seattle Post-Intelligencer* article was headlined "1,000 March in Rally." Reggie Alleyne's report to National CORE noted, "The demon-

stration should put to rest the longstanding and much believed myth that there is no discrimination in Seattle."[13]

Feeling triumphant, CORE officers, the organizing committee, and numerous monitors and friends then went across town, crowding into the Durnings' house at Thirty-Sixth and East Union to celebrate. We turned on the kitchen radio and heard the KING newscaster describe the Seattle demonstration against discrimination, saying that nearly nine hundred Negroes and whites had marched. We were incensed; how did they get so small a number? Tom Brose, irate, picked up the phone and called the news desk. "There were eleven hundred and eighty-seven people in the march, by actual head count!" he declaimed, not exactly stretching the truth, just inventing the detail. Ten minutes later, to our delight, KING announced that 1,187 people had marched for Freedom![14]

Ten days later a mailing party at the Durnings' house folded, addressed, and stamped letters to CORE members and all those who had pledged to cancel charge accounts, saying the boycott was suspended and people might reopen their charge accounts if they wished. The letter, authorized by Reverend Jackson and signed by CORE chairman Reggie Alleyne and

Long line of orderly marchers following civil rights leaders down Pine Street toward Westlake Mall, June 15, 1963. (Seattle Post-Intelligencer photograph)

NAACP president Charles Johnson, was a "good faith" effort to fulfill the civil rights leaders' commitment to the Bon's management in negotiations. Two young black CORE members, Infanta Spence and her friend, as Jean Durning recalls, worked on the mailing awhile before realizing that this letter called off the boycott—and stormed out. They felt the boycott was our best weapon and should be continued until the Bon hired enough blacks to really reflect the racial proportions of Seattle. They were right about our leverage, but civil rights leaders felt honor bound to our negotiators.

The Bon took its time in hiring blacks for living-wage positions, partly due to a number of grievances filed by union member employees. By January 1964 the Bon Marché, both downtown and at Northgate, had fifty-eight full-time and thirty-nine part-time black employees but fewer than half of them—twenty full-time and sixteen part-time—were in nonmenial and nonsegregated jobs. This was some improvement over the situation in June but was a long way from representing the relative proportions of Seattle's population. The Bon was still on the February 1964 agenda of CORE's Executive Committee.[15] We met regularly with its managers but progress was sluggish.

OTHER DOWNTOWN STORES

Two days after the big march, on June 17, 1963, civil rights negotiators led by James Washington Jr. held their first meeting with the Bon Marché's elegant competitor, Frederick and Nelson (usually called Frederick's). Frederick's president, Mr. Cornelius Bryce, wanted to be cooperative. Within days, in newspaper "help wanted" pages, it had placed tiny announcements, "All applicants for employment at Frederick & Nelson will be considered irrespective of race, creed, color or national origin." This ad was a first. At the follow-up meeting on July 3, we learned of African Americans recently hired and the impending appointment of a black girl to the prestigious high school fashion board. Frederick's president "expressed appreciation for the fine quality of referrals . . . very impressed with the caliber of persons hired for the sales positions . . . this had been a very educational experience for the personnel department." This comment was of major importance, after so many employers had told our negotiators, "We can't find qualified applicants." Of all CORE's efforts, changing the biased perceptions of personnel departments would have the longest-lasting value. Negotiations continued for five months, by which time Frederick's had hired thirty-six black employees, and CORE reported that working relations seemed to be good. But Frederick and Nelson would not hire African Americans for certain positions in prominent view, for example, no elevator operators. All these were young women who, wearing white gloves, welcomed customers and answered their questions; all were pretty young Caucasian brunettes and to Frederick's management "those girls are like our daughters," the fashionable face of the store. What a classic example of how culturally blind some "leading citizen" businessmen could be, dismissing every young black woman as not attractive or stylish![16]

A fashionable women's store, Best's Apparel, was located in the same part of downtown, at Fifth and Pine. Mrs. Sarah Lynch noted that its employees all seemed to be white. One day beautiful young Infanta Spence insisted on meeting with Best's president and urged him to hire her. His response, perhaps influenced by her assertive manner but, she was convinced, because of her color, was direct: "We don't hire your kind!"[17] Needless to say, CORE opened negotiations with Best's.

Nordstrom's was still a local shoe store in the early 1960s, with seven branch stores in addition to the large shoe store in downtown Seattle. By 1964 the Nordstrom family had bought Best's and later combined them, temporarily renaming their stores Nordstrom-Best. This began the gradual expansion of the chain to Nordstrom's nationwide status. Prior to an official visit from CORE's negotiating team, Sarah Lynch and her granddaughter Infanta Spence met with Elmer J. Nordstrom about the lack of black salespeople at his shoe store. Mrs. Lynch, a senior member of CORE who in the past had bought all the shoes for her five children at Nordstrom's, insisted that he hire black shoe salesmen. After a long meeting, Mr. Nordstrom agreed and hired—just one.[18]

Seattle CORE felt that the store's large workforce should include many more blacks and, under Tim Martin, began months of fruitless negotiation. Harold Newman recently recalled that he and Walt Hundley met Mr. Nordstrom at his store when "no blacks worked there except the shoe shine guy. Nordstrom said, 'I don't discriminate against them . . . I play basketball with them'!"[19] Nordstrom managers believed they could not find competent black salespeople, despite Tim's informing them that both Penney's and the Bon Marché had African Americans in shoe sales. CORE members voted to boycott Nordstrom's and planned a direct action campaign of picket lines and a "shoe-in" for May 16–21, 1964. The phone committee moved into action, a leaflet about Nordstrom's bad employment record was mimeographed, and fifty picket signs were printed. Ed Singler was appointed overall leader of the action, with Bettylou and Val Valentine assisting him; captains were chosen for each end of a line of thirty-six picketers, while twenty-eight demonstrators would participate in the shoe-in. The picket line was to be silent, with no musical instruments, singing, or chanting. CORE leaders composed telegrams that would be sent to the police and to Elmer Nordstrom, and a press conference was scheduled for Friday, May 15. Suddenly, on May 15 Mr. Nordstrom asked for a meeting. (Some CORE members suspected that the police department had a spy among our members who reported on CORE plans. For whatever reason, Mr. Nordstrom suddenly changed his stance on hiring minorities.) He had just hired two black women for the office and he offered a training program for twenty men for shoe sales, expecting that he would hire at least five of them by August 1. In response CORE suspended its direct action, and a shoe-in never took place. After training them, Nordstrom did hire five apprentice salespeople—three for downtown and two for its branch stores.[20]

Negotiation teams continued to meet with the Bon Marché, Frederick and Nelson, Best's, J. C. Penney, Rhodes, and MacDougall's. We also met with other types of firms, such as grocery stores, taxi companies, and Seattle First National Bank. In September 1964, the *Argus* reported on a survey of CORE action campaigns on employment. "Already a number of firms . . . have felt the sting of this relatively small (200 member) but militant organization." The reporter "found great reluctance to talk about negotiations with CORE and an equal desire '*not to have any more trouble*' . . . a testament that the . . . pressure tactics have considerable bite to them . . . '*It's hard to swallow, not running our own business*,' in the words of one manager." Tim Martin responded to the *Argus* that it was "a matter of redressing old wrongs. To run a business on a discriminatory basis is not a valid right."[21]

Interestingly, businesses that did cooperate found that with CORE's help it was not difficult to find qualified black workers and that this could actually be good for business.

DEEDS

Negotiating with grocery chains and department stores individually was tough, but even when employers responded positively, overall progress toward equal employment was painfully slow. The November 1964 *Corelator* noted, "If Negroes in America continue to gain jobs in the future at the same rate . . . it will take over 700 years for Negroes to secure jobs" proportional to their percentage of the U.S. population. We began to consider this problem at a CORE retreat in May 1964, with extensive discussion of our "piecemeal" approach so far. Members decided to undertake a new employment project on a much bigger scale—all of downtown. We named it "Drive for Equal Employment in Downtown Seattle," abbreviated DEEDS.

Investigation came first. University of Washington anthropologist and CORE member Dr. Charles "Val" Valentine, building on existing documentation plus surveys by thirty CORE volunteers, produced a seventy-five-page report on employment of blacks downtown, "DEEDS: Background and Basis," usually called the DEEDS Report. In addition to maps, charts, and government statistics, the report details its methodology and has an extensive bibliography. It cites the U.S. census that there were 8,000 positions in federal, state, and local government downtown, along with 55,000 jobs downtown in private firms: retail trade, restaurants, bars, hotels, entertainment, auto dealers, parking facilities, taxicabs, private offices, banks, insurance and other financial establishments, manufacturing, and all other private employment. For each category it identifies the number and percentage held by African Americans. Of these 63,000 jobs in downtown Seattle, blacks held only 2,160, or less than 3.5 percent.[22]

The census data was enhanced by CORE surveys, information gathered in our negotiations with employers, and statistics from the Washington State Board against Discrimination and other agencies. Unlike the census, these sources provided detail on types of positions held by blacks, based on large samples. Analysis of these details showed that African Americans were overwhelmingly in low-paid positions, with "scant hope of promotion and little or no contact with the public." For example, "In restaurants more than two thirds of the Negro employees are bus boys, dishwashers, or janitors . . . In [most] downtown hotels . . . virtually all the Negro workers are maids, porters, or shoeshine men."[23] The DEEDS Report concluded, "Negroes hold hardly more than 1% of all paid positions above the menial level with private downtown employers," and wages, for skilled and nonskilled together, probably were about 2 percent of total downtown payrolls. This disproportionate pattern persisted in spite of the fact that blacks were responsible for well over $12 million, or 5 percent, of all purchases downtown and in some retail stores as much as 30 percent. Lane Smith reported in the *Seattle Times* that "nobody has disputed CORE's figures that Negroes hold less than 2 per cent of retail-trade jobs, less than 3 per cent of office jobs [about half of whom were janitors], and only 1 per cent of the jobs in banking, insurance, real estate and related."[24] Appropriately, the DEEDS Report opened with a quotation from comedian Dick Gregory, "But the ad said 'Engineers.' And besides I've no experience as a janitor."

CORE's investigation indicated that normal turnover alone would provide thousands of job openings downtown. The DEEDS Report listed the numbers of people fired, retired, resigned, or laid off in specific employment sectors in one recent month alone and counted their replacements plus new hires. For example, ninety-nine people were newly hired in retail trade, sixty-three in manufacturing, and thirty in finance-related fields, among nine employment sectors the report identified.[25] In addition to normal turnover, recent history showed growth of 400 to 600 new downtown jobs annually, according to the major association of downtown Seattle businesses, which also predicted that job growth would increase to more than 1,000 new jobs per year in the near future.[26] Including both turnover and new positions, Valentine estimated conservatively that about 5,350 new people would be hired downtown in the coming year.

The DEEDS Report provided the basis for our campaign. Following a July 24 letter to downtown leaders, negotiation with business and public employers began with three meetings in August 1964. Tim Martin and Val Valentine represented CORE, Reverend John Adams and Charles Johnson represented the Central Area Committee on Civil Rights, while the Chamber of Commerce served as an umbrella group for downtown businesses. Meetings continued over several months. As in their negotiations with individual employers, the civil rights advocates urged that no person presently employed lose his job but that many of the new openings should be filled with minority workers.

CORE proposed that black employees in downtown Seattle be increased by 300 in thirty days and by 1,200 within a few months. Given the 5,350 or more new hires expected downtown during the year, these goals seemed reasonable. Negotiators specified ways that employers could find qualified applicants—through the Urban League job line, advertising in black and mainstream press and radio using the phrase "Equal Opportunity Employer," and contacts with civil rights organizations and black churches. Employment should involve department stores, specialty stores, movie theaters, law firms, city, county, and federal government jobs, banks, restaurants, hotels, small factories, and others. The Chamber stalled with promises of jobs, and proposed a "Jobs Fair" for October 17 but then postponed it indefinitely. They did open an "Equal Opportunity Center" in Washington Junior High, at Eighteenth and Jackson. CORE felt that the center offered only counseling, not real jobs.

Meanwhile, CORE had begun planning for direct action, in anticipation that it would become necessary. Starting in July 1964 CORE organized neighborhood meetings to inform the black community about DEEDS and asked for help in getting the word out. By September CORE had distributed fifteen thousand leaflets describing facts of black unemployment and proposed actions. The public Drive for Equal Employment in Downtown Seattle officially started with a "Jobs Rally" at the Mount Zion Baptist Church parking lot on Sunday afternoon, October 4, cosponsored by CORE, the NAACP, Catholic Interracial Council, Unitarians for Social Justice, Baptist Ministers Alliance, Seattle Urban League, Greater Seattle Council of Churches, and others. Nonviolent direct action—a CORE boycott of all downtown—was initiated after the Chamber canceled its October 17 Jobs Fair. That Saturday, October 17, leaflets were distributed all over the Central Area, partly with the help of nearly a hundred Methodist student volunteers. Unlike other CORE projects, this time the NAACP and the Urban League—although urging equal employment downtown and helping to recruit job applicants—did not support the boycott. The *Seattle Times*'s Lane Smith reported, "One civil-rights leader said CORE has a 'tiger by the tail.'" The article concluded that one leader "was critical of CORE's present tactics, but acknowledged CORE was facing up to the most basic issue in the Negro's struggle for equality—jobs."[27]

At 5:00 p.m. on Monday, October 19, one hundred activists started

JOBS FOR NEGROES NOW!

SUPPORT **DEEDS** NOW!!

DRIVE FOR EQUAL EMPLOYMENT DOWNTOWN SEATTLE

Seattle business and government leaders say jobs are the solution to racial problems---yet. . . .

- LESS THAN 2% OF RETAIL TRADE JOBS HELD BY NEGROES
- LESS THAN 3% OF AVAILABLE OFFICE JOBS HELD BY NE-GROES
- NEGROES HOLD ONLY 1% OF THE JOBS IN BANKING, INSURANCE, REAL ESTATE, ETC.
- NEGROES SPEND $12 MILLION DOWNTOWN ANNUALLY
- NEGROES ACCOUNT FOR 5% OF ALL SALES GENERALLY

**Seattle Needs Deeds . . .
Not Words**

"Jobs for Negroes Now" leaflets distributed to 15,000 homes urging boycott of downtown businesses. (CORE, Matson Collection)

picketing retail stores in downtown Seattle, the first of a great many days of roving picket lines. (Mondays were when stores stayed open in the evening and working people could shop. Stores were closed on Sundays.) CORE urged customers, "Refuse to Buy Discrimination!" After our picketing on October 24 and 26, Ernst Hardware Store hired its first African American, but we saw no other response. In addition to picketing on Saturday, October 31, and the Monday evening following, we did a mass distribution of a new explanatory leaflet on Sunday, November 1. For extra effect, a crowd of volunteers came downtown for leafleting and picketing on the day after Thanksgiving, the busiest shopping day of the year.[28]

To make the boycott of downtown effective, people were urged to shop or attend movies or restaurants in other neighborhoods: Northgate, Greenwood, University District, Renton, or White Center. Seattle CORE even ran an hourly "Freedom Bus" every Saturday from Twenty-Third and Union Street to the University District and Northgate, as there was no public crosstown bus service at this time. Members stuck "Don't Shop Downtown" signs in their lawns and on top of their cars. To spread the word we organized a great many neighborhood meetings. CORE sent a mailing with pledge cards to ten thousand households in the Central Area. The response, according to the December 1964 *Corelator*, was "beyond our wildest imagination." In addition to pledges that they would not shop downtown, "Many people want more information on CORE, want to become members and want to send money." The theme of Seattle CORE's Christmas party was

"Don't Shop Downtown," as the boycott ran through Christmas and on into 1965. Picket lines in the retail core continued for almost three months. Cooperating with CORE on DEEDS were the Unitarians for Social Justice, the Seattle Teachers Union, Christian Friends for Racial Equality, and the Ship Scalers Union.

The DEEDS project had a considerable financial impact on downtown; the January 1965 *Corelator* cited a Federal Reserve Bank report and announced, "Business was horrible." Many companies asked for help in finding employees, and the city set up a special recruiting team for the police and fire departments. The Chamber of Commerce estimated that one hundred to two hundred new jobs had been offered; CORE called it only a limited number, far below CORE's goal of twelve hundred new black employees. Despite media coverage, leafleting, yard signs, car top signs, and picket lines, we were falling short. The Seattle daily newspapers, in the words of the January *Corelator*, were spreading "intentional confusion." After the many weeks of picketing and without NAACP participation, it was hard to maintain the boycott. The December *Corelator* said we would evaluate the project at our next meeting. On January 12, 1965, after hearing a report on negotiations the previous day, we voted to suspend the downtown boycott.

Was CORE naïve in thinking it could accomplish so ambitious a goal as twelve hundred new hires in a few months? Val's analysis of the project was printed in the February 1965 *Corelator*. The response from the community, he noted, "produced much evidence that employment remains the civil rights issue which interests Seattle Negroes most." DEEDS had been an expensive campaign, both financially and in volunteer hours. Only the federal govern-

Announcement of Jobs Rally in preparation for boycott of downtown. (CORE, Matson Collection)

ment had met CORE's employment goals for the period. Was the Chamber of Commerce really able to represent private downtown employers or had we been talking to the wrong people? If DEEDS was too big a project for CORE, Val asked, "How else can we produce significant change toward equal opportunity and an integrated society?"

From our perspective decades later, CORE seems both naïve and audacious in undertaking such a giant goal. That we tried is a testimony to our enthusiasm, our commitment, and our frustration at the slow pace of achieving equal racial opportunity. But failures to accomplish enough through nonviolent persuasion helped feed African Americans' impatience, leading to the more militant demands of Black Power advocates at the end of the 1960s and in the 1970s.

4 · TAXI COMPANIES AND UNIONS

At Farwest and Graytop cab companies, every single driver was white. Concurrent with the Drive for Equal Employment in Downtown Seattle (DEEDS), Seattle CORE turned a spotlight on these all-white workforces. As early as October 1963, CORE had begun investigating the taxi companies. Jean Adams attempted to meet with representatives of each company to gather statistics on the number of employees, the various job categories, and the number of minorities employed (see table 4.1). She then reported this information to the general membership. Yellow Cab was eager to talk with Jean, as their workforce of four hundred employees included thirty-five black drivers. Yellow Cab had started integrating its workforce in 1962. Graytop met with CORE and gave out information on their workforce but had to admit they had no black employees. Farwest was worse. After several delaying tactics Mr. Fred Hosking, president of the company, refused to talk with CORE and stated that Farwest would not hire black drivers. Farwest was sure white passengers would refuse to get in a cab behind a black driver.[1]

CORE learned that there were contracts signed between Graytop and Farwest and the Port of Seattle. (Farwest also had an exclusive contract with the Seattle School District for transporting disabled children.) Reggie Alleyne, Tim Martin, and Walt Hundley called on the Port commissioners to insert a nondiscriminatory clause in all their contracts with private com-

TABLE 4.1 AFRICAN AMERICAN
DRIVERS EMPLOYED BY SEATTLE
TAXICAB COMPANIES IN 1964

Yellow Cab Company

All drivers	300
Negro drivers	35

Farwest Cab Company

All drivers	250
Negro drivers	0

Graytop Cab Company

All drivers	130
Negro drivers	0

TOTALS

All drivers	680
Negro drivers	35

Source: Data from an investigation by the
Washington State Board against Discrimination and confirmed by CORE investigations and negotiations (Valentine,
DEEDS: Background and Basis, 59, table 5).

panies and insist that these companies be equal opportunity employers. CORE was determined that the Port take some action. Finally, the commissioners, on February 25, 1964, announced they had passed Resolution 2158, specifically forbidding discrimination against any employee or applicant because of race, creed, color, or national origin.[2] But the March 1964 *Corelator* reported that this was "a very small step." Nothing had improved. Farwest and Graytop still did not hire African Americans. CORE continued to insist that this must change.

Under further pressure from CORE, the Port requested that the Washington State Board against Discrimination (WSBAD) conduct an investigation into charges made by our negotiators. CORE made a special effort to have a large and vocal presence at the WSBAD public hearing on July 16, 1964. Tim Martin, our chairman, testified, with the supportive presence of two CORE lawyers, Reggie Alleyne and Ed Singler. Many other active members, urged by the phone committee and an appeal in the June 1964 *Corelator*, helped to fill the hearing room. Representatives from all three cab companies attended this hearing. Also attending were staff from the City of Seattle comptroller's office, Seattle-Tacoma International Airport, and U.S. Veterans Administration Hospital and a concessionaire from King County Airport (Boeing Field).

In its report, the WSBAD found that although the Port announced Resolution 2158 to the press, television, and radio stations plus all the civil rights organizations in Seattle on February 25, 1964, a copy of the resolution had *not* been given to the cab companies. The WSBAD also reported that control over issuance of licenses for cab drivers was in the hands of the city comptroller, who required a recommendation by a taxicab company before issuing a license. This was another potential roadblock that could serve as an excuse for discrimination in hiring, since it was obvious that Graytop and Farwest would not recommend licensing a driver who was black. The WSBAD noted, "No authority in law exists for this [licensing] requirement." But WSBAD also found that "the Congress of Racial Equality presented no specific instances of racial discrimination

DON'T RIDE FARWEST-GRAYTOP CABS
CORE **THEY DISCRIMINATE!**

in the hiring practices of the taxicab companies, relying upon the all-white drivers in two taxicab companies as evidence of discrimination." CORE disagreed—pretty strong evidence we thought. In its final recommendation the WSBAD directed the Port to take affirmative action to make certain all contractors doing business with the Port knew of Resolution 2158. They directed the Port to determine whether there was racial discrimination in the hiring of taxicab drivers who served Port facilities and further recommended that if there was any racial discrimination, "the franchises of the offending companies be terminated."[3] *This did not happen.*

Given that no black drivers had been hired since CORE's first contact in October 1963, that these companies were in violation of Resolution 2158 set down by the Port, and that Farwest refused outright to negotiate with CORE, we had little hope that this WSBAD directive would cause any changes. CORE rarely found that hearings, commissions, or resolutions brought about changes without economic pressure. CORE called for a boycott of Farwest and Graytop on August 11, 1964. It was time to take the issue to the streets.

Chairman Tim Martin, in a press release, announced "Operation Pogo Stick." This direct action project, chaired by Don Matson, borrowed the phrase from Denver CORE. Roving pickets demonstrated at various places where high taxicab traffic would be found, such as hospitals, hotels, and restaurants. In addition to roving pickets, CORE members, church members, and friends attached bumper stickers to their cars with a message to all of Seattle: "DON'T RIDE FARWEST-GRAYTOP CABS / THEY DISCRIMINATE!" CORE asked supporters in this campaign to help "Drive Discrimination Away." Our flier reminded Seattleites, "Every time you ride in a Farwest or Graytop cab you support discrimination." We enlisted support from the porters at SeaTac Airport, who agreed that they would encourage their members not to load and unload luggage from Farwest and Graytop. A plan to start picketing at taxi stands was announced on Septem-

ARE YOU BEING TAKEN *for a* RIDE?

—NEITHER FARWEST NOR GRAY TOP CAB COMPANIES EMPLOY NEGRO DRIVERS.
—BOTH COMPANIES HAVE STATED THAT THEY "DO NOT PLAN TO HIRE NEGROES."
—QUALIFIED NEGRO DRIVERS HAVE APPLIED FOR JOBS AT FARWEST AND GRAY TOP CAB COMPANIES, BUT WERE NOT HIRED.

DON'T RIDE IN A FARWEST OR A GRAYTOP CAB

—DON'T SUPPORT DISCRIMINATION! . . . . . . .DON'T PATRONIZE JIM CROW TAXIS!—
—JOIN CORE IN ENDING THE DISCRIMINATORY HIRING PRACTICES OF FARWEST AND GRAY TOP CAB COMPANIES

DRIVE DISCRIMINATION **AWAY**

SEATTLE CONGRESS OF RACIAL EQUALITY   PHONE: EA 5-5496

ber 3. The *Corelator* urged readers to "Call MA 2–6500 for Integrated Taxi Service." (Yellow Cab still has this phone number, though the prefix "MA" or "Main" was changed to numerals long ago.) A leaflet listed our unsuccessful efforts with Graytop and Farwest over the past year that led to the boycott of these two companies.[4]

In September 1964, Fred Hosking claimed to a reporter that Farwest attorneys are "taking care of the entire thing . . . We are not unfriendly to anything they have to say."[5] Of course, CORE was not looking for "friendly" discourse; we were looking for an end to Farwest's discriminatory hiring. Ever hopeful, the October 1964 *Corelator* announced that Farwest had changed its hiring policy. Mr. Lancaster, president of the Taxi Union, told Don Matson that Farwest had agreed to hire Negro drivers.[6] However, there was no proof that anyone had been hired at Farwest or Graytop, and so the boycott continued.

The Seattle school administration had included a nondiscrimination clause in its exclusive contract with Farwest, but obviously, it was not being enforced. CORE negotiators met with members of the school administration and pointed out that Farwest was in violation of the school administration's employment guidelines, which forbade exclusion of workers based on race. Perhaps aware of the WSBAD's hearings at the Port in July and our ongoing boycott, the school administrators, albeit somewhat slowly, responded. Five months later, on December 18, 1964, Frank Brock, for Seattle Public Schools, reminded Farwest of its contract to transport handicapped children. The contract required that Farwest "not discriminate against any employee or applicant because of race, creed, or national origin."[7]

With pressure mounting from the Port, the school district, and the CORE boycott, on January 8, 1965, Farwest placed an ad in the black community newspaper *The Facts* for applicants. Both Farwest and Graytop requested the help of the Urban League and the NAACP to find black drivers. This was a real victory, as CORE remembered the adamant stance taken by Hosking against hiring black drivers. "Farwest Taxicabs Employ Negro Drivers" reported the March 1965 *Corelator*. Farwest had finally hired two African Americans. Again Seattle CORE's success was limited with respect to the actual numbers hired but was a victory in terms of changing overall hiring policies of the cab companies.

TRADE UNIONS

Farwest's recalcitrance was partly related to the fact that Farwest and Graytop were union shops, and union members were disinclined to open up job opportunities. Unions had also been a concern in achieving breakthroughs at the Bon Marché. Despite the fact that Seattle was known as a union town, CORE did not receive much cooperation from organized labor.

Somewhat isolated from the rest of the country, western Washington and particularly the Seattle area have a reputation for grassroots movements and citizen involvement. People formed cooperatives to share the responsibility and costs of everything from health care to preschools, food markets, and funerals. So too did citizens join together to form labor unions to change working conditions and achieve a better way of life. Joining together on February 6, 1919, 65,000 union and nonunion supporters shut down the city for five days in the Seattle General Strike for higher wages. Again, in 1934, a longshoremen's strike for improved working conditions and control over work assignments interrupted the unloading of cargo at West Coast docks, including Seattle, from May 5 to July 31.[8] The union movement continued to grow.

Therefore, it is not surprising that CORE members included men and women who were also active in the Aero Mechanics, American Federation of Teachers, Sleeping Car Porters, Longshoremen, Ship Scalers, Garment Workers, Office Workers, Warehousemen, Teamsters, and other unions. These CORE members felt a responsibility from the very beginning to approach union leadership in Seattle and request their support in the very first direct action project: the Safeway boycott. In mid-October 1961, Ed Singler was invited to explain the Selective Buying Campaign to the Executive Board of the United Garment Workers Local No. 17. Then on October 31 Ed Singler and Wallace Johnson spoke to the Committee on Political Education of the King County Labor Council to explain our campaign against supermarkets.[9] CORE members also made informal contacts with their individual unions, often handing out CORE leaflets at union meetings, for example. The Musicians Union granted Dizzy Gillespie a waiver to play at Dick Gregory's fundraiser for CORE. Otherwise, with the exception of the Ship Scalers Union and the Seattle Teachers Union, no official union support was ever given to CORE projects to end discrimination.

Even though unions refused to acknowledge racial discrimination in their ranks, CORE continued to hold to the union spirit. As part of our commitment to organized labor, it was an unwritten rule that all Seattle CORE's printed material had to be produced in a union shop and had to include the "union bug." Chet Kingsbury, a member of the University Unitarian Church who was very supportive of CORE, owned a union shop and produced most of our fliers. Other union printers were not so supportive. One union shop refused to print a banner announcing the forthcoming appearance of James Baldwin for a Seattle CORE fundraiser. To make certain the public understood our commitment to the labor movement, we always tried to mark "labor donated" on any material mimeographed by CORE volunteers for public distribution.

CORE felt there were many parallels between the labor movement and the civil rights movement: organizing tactics like boycotts and picketing, and union songs that were easily turned into "freedom songs." The civil rights movement, especially on the national level, included activists in organized labor who took on leadership roles in civil rights, like A. Philip Randolph, of the Brotherhood of Sleeping Car Porters; Herb Hill, who was labor secretary for the NAACP; and Marvin Rich, of CORE. Nationally, the participation of the United Automobile Workers, under the leadership of Walter Reuther, was very visible in the March on Washington in 1963; Reuther even urged Congress to enact a penalty on unions that discriminated.[10] The National Council of the AFL-CIO chose not to support the March on Washington, adopting a position of neutrality. The Teamsters Union was not regarded as a strong supporter of the civil rights movement in Seattle, though we appreciated that its members honored our picket line at Safeway. Under the leadership of Jimmy Hoffa in Detroit, representing the East Coast and Midwest, however, the Teamsters were strongly opposed to segregation of any kind.

Despite labor support for the civil rights movement on the national level, on the local level cooperation and support were lacking. This was particularly true of the building-trades unions—plumbers, electricians, sheet metal workers, carpenters, ironworkers, plasterers, and some Teamsters locals—which were not willing to address employment discrimination or to open up their ranks to minorities.

Seattle CORE's last significant attack on unfair employment addressed discrimination in the building-trades unions, the apprenticeship training programs, the companies that hired union labor, and federally funded government construction projects.

While many active members were working on DEEDS or trying to end segregation in the cab companies, CORE member Dick Cole drafted a proposal in May 1964 for soliciting the cooperation of unions. In his proposal, Dick pointed out to us that the approach CORE had used with the supermarkets and department stores would not succeed with unions. He reminded us, "Union resistance we encounter in our efforts will not stem only from racial prejudice, but from a policy of exclusion towards attempts by anyone to break into these unions."[11] Dick Cole, with the help of Don Matson and, later, Les McIntosh, continued to work on the union issue and made reports to CORE's membership but proposed no action plan at the time.

More than a year later, learning of a new federal office building to be constructed in Seattle, we pushed for local compliance with Title VII of the 1964 Civil Rights Act. In spite of all the exclusions written into the legislation, the

Equal Employment Opportunity Act gave us some basis to expect that blacks would be included in the workforce hired to construct this building. To be on record regarding those expectations, on September 2, 1965, Chairman Walt Hundley sent a letter to the General Services Administration in Washington, D.C., outlining past practices of the building trades and building contractors that could no longer be tolerated. His letter pointed out that

> the construction of a structure of this size [a skyscraper, filling an entire block from Second Avenue and Madison to First and Marion] will create a demand for a great many jobs in the building trades—an area that, for the most part, has been closed to Negroes in the past. There is no doubt that qualified Negroes are available in all job classifications that will be needed . . . They have the knowledge and the skills. We feel the Federal Government must use its influence to help bring a change in this shameful situation in Seattle. We will watch with great interest the progress of this contract. You must know how long CORE has tried to make meaningful changes in this area with little success . . . We see a tremendous opportunity for lasting change in this project and will not let it go by, but will do everything we can or must to see this hope fulfilled.[12]

We have found no response to this letter in CORE files, and we remember no improvement as a result of this letter.

APPRENTICESHIP PROGRAMS

Just a few months later a hopeful sign of possible changes by one union was reported in the December 1965 *Corelator*: "A training program announced some weeks ago and sponsored by Local 32 of the Plumbers and Pipefitters' Union has resulted in the employment of seven Negroes in local shipyards. James I. Kimbrough, Seattle Urban League president, noted that this is the first placement of its type handled through the League." The *Corelator* article concluded, "While encouraging, this is only a beginning, and most unions have done nothing to aid the fight against discrimination." Maybe our reservations as to whether this change was real had to do with other numbers. CORE's concern was confirmed: a WSBAD investigation in late 1965 and early 1966 reported no blacks in the Plumbers Union apprenticeship training program. (There were over four thousand members of the union in the state of Washington, but only one black member.)

In most building-trades unions, entering an apprenticeship program depended on "who you knew"; training slots normally were filled by relatives of members of that union. This nepotism certainly discriminated against all outsiders, but it functioned doubly as a racial barrier, since no black applicant would be accepted as "my cousin's brother's nephew's son" for whom an exception could be made. In February 1966 the WSBAD held hearings on the lack of minority enrollment in apprenticeship programs in businesses and unions. Testimony was taken from representatives of Boeing, Lockheed, the Washington State Employment Security Office, the Washington State Department of Labor, and other agencies that would be part of a program affecting apprenticeship and training programs. It was obvious from the testimony of the representatives of these agencies and companies that blacks would never be included in apprenticeship training programs, never be admitted to the unions, and never work for construction companies, or Boeing or Lockheed, at union wages. The WSBAD report revealed that the Boilermakers had 1 nonwhite apprentice out of 53, and the Carpenters had 1 nonwhite apprentice out of 240. The exception was the Cement Masons, with 5 nonwhite apprentices out of 11. All the other unions had *none* (see table 4.2).[13]

A decision as to CORE action on labor unions was set aside once more as we became involved in the urgent need to organize the community for what would become a citywide boycott of the Seattle Public Schools and the creation of an integrated learning experience for thousands of children in Freedom Schools.

CORE and WSBAD were not the only voices raised against discrimination in the building trades. The July 1966 *Corelator* announced Seattle CORE's full support for "Archbishop Thomas Connolly's 'Project Equality,' a campaign to bring about an end to racial discrimination in Seattle." The program was promoted by the Catholic Interracial Council under the leadership of Walter Hubbard. Project Equality not only focused on discrimination in the trade unions but urged groups and individuals to use their purchasing power to support integrated businesses in general.[14] CORE "reaffirmed its demand" that the Government Services Administration follow the principles of Project Equality for government contracts.

Union	Total Members	Total Nonwhite	Nonwhite Journeyman Applications	Nonwhite Journeyman Admissions	Current No. of Apprentices	Nonwhite Apprentice Applications	Nonwhite Apprentice Admissions	Geographic Jurisdiction
Boilermakers Local 104	5,200*	#	#	#	53	#	1	16 counties in Wash. and Alaska
Bricklayers Local 2	585*	13	0	0	32	0	0	King, Kitsap, Clallam, Jefferson
Carpenters Local 131	2,000*	#	#	#	260	#	#	North King Co.
Carpenters Local 1289	1,500*	15	#	#	240	#	1	South King Co.
Cement Masons Local 528	300*	65	#	#	11	#	5	All King Co. except southern tip, south half Snohomish Co.
Int. Bro. of Electrical Workers Local 46	3,000*	#	#	#	117	0	0	King, Kitsap, Clallam, Jefferson
IBEW Local 77	4,000*	20*	#	#	40 (King Co.)	0	0	State of Washington
Iron Workers Local 86	640	0	0	0	48	0	0	King, Skagit, Kittitas

Local	Membership							Jurisdiction
Lathers Local 104	110*	2	0	0	2	0	0	Snohomish Co. to Marysville; King Co. to Fed. Way
Oper. Engineers Local 302	6,800*	#	#	—	—	0	0	Alaska and 16 counties in Washington
Painters Local 300	1,400*	#	#	#	40	#	#	King and Snohomish
Plasterers Local 77	173*	9	0	0	4	0	0	
Plumbers and Pipefitters Local 54	2,300*	bldg trades 0 plumbers 3 pipefitters	bldg trades 0 plumbers # pipefitters	#	35* (1963–66)	2	0	King, Clallam, Jefferson, Chelan, Douglas
Roofers and Waterproofers Local 54	150*	8	1	1	0	0	0	Clallam, Mason-King, Snohomish, Kitsap
Sheetmetal workers Local 99	1,140*	bldg trades 0 shipyards #	bldg trades 0 shipyards #	#	45	0	0	King

Source: Washington State Board against Discrimination, "Building Trades Craft Unions: Conclusions," [October/November 1965].

* approximate figure

number unknown

— no apprenticeship program

On August 2, 1966, Governor Daniel Evans reissued the same executive order that Governor Albert Rosellini had signed on June 13, 1963, declaring that discrimination by state agencies or state employees would not be tolerated. It also applied to any company, contractor, or union doing business with the state of Washington. Those found in violation of the executive order would be subject to loss of their state licenses or positions. Governor Evans added article XII to that executive order, which called for a "review every year to determine that compliance with the provisions of this executive order is being maintained."[15] Again, lots of words on paper but no enforcement was evident—by anyone in the state.

Ken MacDonald, chairman of the WSBAD, issued a policy statement in September 1966 urging all those involved—labor unions, employers, educators—to adopt affirmative action and to include more Negroes as workers in the trade unions.[16] Of course, the WSBAD had no power to enforce the recommendations, and once again, nothing changed.

LATER EFFORTS

Finally, in November 1966, a little more than a year after Walt Hundley's letter to the federal government, Dick Cole and Don Matson made a presentation to the WSBAD. Using the WSBAD's own statistics on the lack of nonwhites in apprenticeship training programs, they made the case for addressing discrimination in the apprenticeship program as well as ways to open union membership to all. They stated that the whole process must begin with the public schools, cooperation and affirmative action by the unions, and finally the companies that hire union workers. They ended the presentation with a list of things that CORE could do to help:

1. Negotiate with firms to determine whether basic responsibility rests with union or management in order to best focus action.
2. Challenge any Federal contract where there is apparent discrimination, whatever the excuse by the firm involved.
3. Press for stronger state, county and city hiring and advancement procedures.
4. Organize Freedom Industrial Unions, if necessary.[17]

Within CORE, frustration with the unions was running high. The Union Labor Committee of CORE, as reported in the February 1967 *Corelator*, suggested printing leaflets for distribution "advocating the boycott of products carrying the union label." For liberal whites accustomed to always looking for union products, this was a startling—if necessary—proposal. CORE urged its members to hear an address on March 3 at the First AME Church by Herb Hill, national labor secretary for the NAACP, "Union Discrimination Why? What Can Be Done?"[18]

CORE considered possible picket lines and acts of civil disobedience, such as a "chain-in." Without adequate resources to carry out such action but inspired by Herb Hill, a group formed an umbrella organization called the Negro Labor Council. This group included CORE, the NAACP, the Baptist Ministers Alliance, the Catholic Interracial Council, and the Central Area Motivation Program, by now under the direction of Walt Hundley. A CORE member, Dan Young, acted as the spokesperson.[19] The purpose of the Negro Labor Council was to add weight to attempts to include blacks in the building trades, but it did not have much success.

A few men in CORE, particularly John Cornethan, Dan Young, Don Matson, and Les McIntosh, continued to work on trying to open up apprenticeship programs and jobs in the trade unions. For all intents and purposes CORE's power to bring about change in this area of employment ended in late 1967. But our work foreshadowed radical activity by others.

Later, the Central Contractors Association (CCA) was formed with the help of Walt Hundley, who had moved on to lead Seattle's Model Cities program. CCA's goal was to be included in the assignment of government contracts for new construction projects in Seattle that involved federal dollars. Starting in 1969, the CCA and the United Construction Workers under the leadership of Tyree Scott began to break the all-white hold on trade unions and the construction companies that hired them.[20] The prolonged legal and physical conflict that followed between black and white workers was confrontational and violent. Attempts to mediate black workers' grievances involved not only federal government officials but also the mayor, the county executive, and the governor. It took intense action to bring about any meaningful change. The history of that movement is detailed in a report by Trevor Griffey.[21]

Nationally, other apprenticeship programs slowly opened their enrollment to include blacks as well as women. Joan Singler remembers a conversation in the late 1960s with her brother, who taught in a union apprenticeship program for sheet metal workers in Detroit. He was resentful that his apprenticeship class, in just a few years, went from all white males (usually the sons or relatives of journeyman sheet metal workers) to include "colored and even women."

In Seattle some preferential hiring did occur in other jobs. By July 1, 1968, the Seattle Fire Department had increased the number of blacks from one to sixteen people.

Looking back, one can hardly deny that changes did occur—not only for blacks but for women too. With the exception of the trade unions, opening up jobs for minorities in all work categories turned out to be the most successful action taken by Seattle CORE. Did we hasten the day that barriers came down? We think we did. The work of CORE and community supporters between 1961 and 1968 certainly made Seattle a city with color a lot more visible.

Eager riders lining up on Twenty-Third Avenue for first run of new crosstown bus, with Reverend John Adams (back to camera) directing traffic. Others unknown except Ed O'Keefe (tall, dark-haired white man in dark suit), a key member of the Crosstown Bus Committee, and Joe White (man wearing white at front of bus). (CORE, Matson Collection)

THE CROSSTOWN BUS

Maid Adams

Why was I all alone on the Queen Anne bus in the middle of the night? Investigating. Here's why. Up through the mid-1960s the Central Area had no direct public transportation to the University District. Students wanting to attend the university and people who had jobs in that vicinity had to take a bus downtown and transfer from there to the University District, a time-consuming process. Late in the summer of 1966, Seattle CORE launched an action project to get the Seattle Transit System to run a bus along Twenty-Third Avenue, connecting the Central Area with the University District and points north and south. I was an active participant. When CORE negotiators discussed the need for this direct service, I remember the transit authority told us, "There is no need." "No one would ride," so it would "not be profitable."

CORE and other organizations formed the Crosstown Bus Committee. CORE members set about gathering facts about rider patterns on existing transit lines, as well as the numbers of people transferring downtown to the University District. We rode buses on existing lines and recorded the numbers of riders in the morning, afternoon, and evening and on the last runs of the night. Investigating the route from downtown to Queen Anne Hill, I rode the bus at 1:00 a.m. while my husband was home with our young son. I was the only passenger. My experience and that of other testers proved our point that many established routes had sparse ridership except at peak times. Armed with these facts, and after additional meetings with transit managers, CORE prevailed. Seattle Transit initiated a route using Twenty-Third Avenue directly to the University District. This was known for some time as the crosstown bus. It is now taken for granted as the number 48 bus, frequently full and clearly a success. This was a major victory for CORE—bringing a significant service to the Central Area's people.

PART III Housing

5 · SEGREGATED HOUSING IN SEATTLE

A proposed law against discrimination "WOULD COMPEL YOU TO RENT TO . . . non white persons who could be prostitutes, criminals and otherwise dangerous to you and your tenants and unless you could prove . . . these activities, you would also lose the privilege of evicting them," according to an inflammatory warning that the Apartment Operators Association sent to its members.[1] Blatant stereotypes like this helped perpetuate the fears of the white community. Similarly, the real estate industry endorsed the belief that black neighbors had a negative effect on property values, and that once a black family moved in on your block, all their friends and relatives would soon follow. When Reggie and Delores Alleyne were house hunting, he wrote, "We came across a number of persons who expressed a real desire to sell us a house—despite our color—but who were afraid . . . of pressure from neighbors. I also became personally aware of several instances in which neighbors used letter and telephone campaigns and other . . . harassment to prevent the sale of a neighbor's house to a non-white family."[2] Economist Robert Weaver wrote, "Among the basic consumer goods, only for housing are Negroes traditionally excluded from freely competing in the open market."[3]

For reasons like these, minority housing in Seattle resembled ghetto neighborhoods found in other northern cities around this country, though on a smaller scale. Dr. Quintard Taylor describes the Seattle ghetto in *The Forging of a Black Community*: "Seventy-five percent of the city's 26,901 black residents in 1960 lived in four Central District census tracts, and by 1965 eight out of ten black residents lived there—the highest percentage in the city's history."[4]

During World War II, Mayor William Devin was concerned about reactions from the black community to the race riots in Detroit, New York, and Chicago. Black soldiers were treated worse than Italian prisoners of war at Fort Lawton, Seattle. In 1944 Mayor Devin formed the Civic Unity Committee, a multiracial citizen task force charged with providing education to the public and business community on the need for an integrated city with fair and equal treatment for all citizens. Not giving a great deal of priority to housing, it took twelve years, until 1956, before the Civic Unity Committee created the Greater Seattle Housing Council to begin to address an open-housing policy. Open housing meant removing restrictions that prevented financially eligible buyers from purchasing a home anywhere they desired—because of their race, religion, or national origin. At the state level, the legislature passed the Omnibus Civil Rights Act in 1957, making housing discrimination illegal, although *only* when state and federal loans were involved, but the law was later challenged in court. In November 1959, Allen Potter, a member of Christian Friends for Racial Equality, was on the board of the Greater Seattle Housing Council. On behalf of Christian Friends, he asked the housing council to develop "a listing of homes available for open occupancy." The request was referred to the housing council's Program Committee, chaired by William Bannecker—who represented the Seattle Real Estate Board. After a year and a half, by May 1961, this committee agreed only "to *explore* the possibility of implementing a 'Clearing Service on Housing for Minority Families'" (emphasis added).[5] At the same time black buyers and renters with few exceptions were still refused housing outside the Central Area. Thus, from the forties to the sixties, while the issue of segregated housing was a topic for official *discussion* only, a housing ghetto became a reality. Most white Seattleites living outside the Central Area were happy to have no contact with Negroes.

HARMONY HOMES

While the mayor, the Seattle City Council, and the Greater Seattle Housing Council did nothing to change the fact that black people were restricted to living in the Central Area, others were working to overcome the restrictions. Some people, particularly in the Christian Friends for Racial Equality and in church social action groups, felt the need to reach out. For example, in the 1960s a group at Trinity Methodist Church in Seattle's Ballard neighborhood, home to many Scandinavians, formed the Committee to Welcome Non-whites to Ballard. An amusing incident illustrates the isolation of whites in Seattle. Harvey and Dorothy Jackins and their four children (including teenaged CORE activists Tim and Gordon Jackins) were members of this Ballard church. At one of the committee's first meetings, Harvey asked if anyone knew of people in their neighborhood who might be from a different race or background. One lady responded that she thought a Finn was living on her street.[6]

Early in 1960, Sidney Gerber and a few others formed Harmony Homes to build housing for minorities outside the Central Area. Gerber had previously chaired the Washington State Board against Discrimination but left, deciding he could do more as an individual citizen. Sid and a biracial group were contributing members.[7] These contributors raised $13,600 in operating funds for Harmony Homes, a nonprofit corporation that did not charge fees. James Kimbrough, treasurer for the corporation, was also the major buyer for the group. He recently noted that, being white, he became the contact person for purchases made on behalf of Harmony Homes, because Sid Gerber's name and reputation for selling to minorities were too well known in the real estate industry. Harmony Homes built houses or purchased lots that they then sold to black families wanting to live in other parts of Seattle and its suburbs. A good example of how Harmony Homes worked involved a real estate transaction for a black couple, Dr. Earl V. Miller, a urologist, and his wife, Rosalie, a dentist. Earl Miller, a member of CORE and the NAACP, served on the board of Harmony Homes. He had tried to buy a lot on Lake Washington Boulevard near Seward Park at the listed price of $12,000 to build a home for his family. The seller found out that Dr. Miller was African American and refused to sell him the land. Then Jim Kimbrough, on behalf of Harmony Homes, negotiated and purchased the lot for $10,000. Jim then resold the lot to Miller at the lower price, saving the Millers $2000. When the seller learned of this transaction he was furious. In answer to the seller's outrage, Jim pointed out that discrimination in this case had cost the seller $2,000.[8]

Early in 1960 Sid Gerber also brought together seven African American real estate firms to form the Central Brokers Association. The association set up a multiple-listing service, where each broker shared information with other black realtors on homes they had for sale. This service helped a few families to move outside the Central Area. The Central Brokers Association charged the normal fee for real estate transactions.[9]

Gerber also acted as a temporary loan agency, providing financing from his own funds at the going rate of interest until black buyers found a mortgage company that would pick up their loans. Denying funds for the purchase of real estate and homes was one aspect of "redlining," as discrimination in housing and insurance was called. If African Americans did find a home they wanted to buy, it was almost impossible to find a mortgage company that would lend them money. At the time of Gerber's death in May 1965, over $200,000 was outstanding in loans he had made to black purchasers. All the loans were eventually repaid to his estate.[10]

THE FAIR HOUSING LISTING SERVICE

University Unitarian Church members were well aware of racial discrimination in the sale of housing and the need to inform minority buyers of available houses. Allen Potter, a member of this church and of the Greater Seattle Housing Council, had not persuaded the council to establish a list of open housing. Potter knew that Unitarians Edna and Robert Jones had just been denied the purchase of a home in the north end based on the color of their skin. Despite the assistance of a white church member with the purchase, the seller, John O'Meara, returned the Jones family's deposit and refused to sell to a black couple. Jones filed a complaint against O'Meara, which was upheld by the Washington State Board against Discrimination. But on appeal, the Washington State Supreme Court heard the *Jones v. O'Meara* case and ruled in favor of O'Meara, stating that the relevant state statute was unconstitutional. Attorney Robert Winsor, also a Unitarian and later a Superior Court judge, represented the Jones family in this landmark case.[11]

Frustrated by the "do nothing" attitude of city officials and the ruling of the court and by the treatment received not only by Robert and Edna

Jones but also by interracial Unitarian couples, the Unitarians' Integration Committee decided to act. This small group, led by Don Matson and Doris Eason, placed a classified ad in the *Seattle Times* on June 10, 1962: "Church Committee desires listing of homes for sales. Open occupancy. If you have a home for sale and will sell to a minority, call . . . " As a result of the ad fifty people called to make inquiries, some with homes for sale. This was the beginning of the Fair Housing Listing Service (FHLS). When the committee tried to buy an ad again, the *Times* and the *Post-Intelligencer* refused, on the basis that the papers had a policy to not acknowledge the existence of discrimination in their advertisements. The papers said that someone had made a mistake in accepting the ad the previous week. The Unitarians then placed the ad instead in the *Argus*, *Seattle Observer*, and all community newspapers except the *West Seattle Herald*, which also refused to run it. Negative publicity, including an article in the *Argus*, led the *Seattle Times* to accept the ad a month later.[12]

Unitarians for Social Justice in Seattle invited their counterparts, members of the Public Affairs Committee of the suburban East Shore Unitarian Church, to get involved in this project. The Public Affairs Committee studied the issue, researching and contacting groups already involved in the cause of open housing. Under the leadership of Judy Esparza, along with Tom Foulds, Pat and Bob Davenport, and Shirley Buckingham, these eastside white activists launched a door-to-door solicitation in Bellevue and Kirkland. Using a direct approach they knocked on doors of homes with "For Sale" signs and asked if the owners were willing to sell to "any qualified buyer." Approximately one-third of those contacted said they would, and these homes were added to the inventory of the FHLS.[13]

News traveled fast, and Harmony Homes immediately became part of the FHLS, providing much of the funding for printing and mailings. CORE, the NAACP, the Urban League, Christian Friends for Racial Equality, the Anti-Defamation League, Bethel CME Church, and Mount Zion Baptist Church became partners in this effort. Eventually, the service expanded to more than twenty-four groups, including First AME, New Hope Baptist, United Church Women, St. Margaret's Episcopal, Madrona Community Presbyterian, Woodland Park Presbyterian, University Congregational Church, and Our Lady of Guadalupe Catholic Church. Other organizations and churches joined as the FHLS became more widely known.

CORE members became the foot soldiers for the FHLS. In July 1962 CORE members distributed seven thousand leaflets door-to-door in the Central Area, making people aware of homes for sale and soliciting interested buyers. Information about the FHLS was included in church bulletins in both white and black churches. Later, more than ten thousand fliers were distributed throughout the Seattle area. The flier, designed by Tim Martin, a commercial artist, graphic designer, and chairman of CORE, asked, "A New Home in Your Future? Outside the Central Area . . ." Tim's wife, Georgia Martin, was also a very active member of the FHLS.[14]

The Martins, a mixed-race couple with four children, had personally had a difficult time purchasing a house. It took them over eighteen months to buy a home outside the Central Area, with one rebuff after another. Often when the Martins were inquiring by phone, realtors asked if they were Negroes and said that they would not sell to Negro buyers. Other realtors, using a less direct approach, showed them only run-down properties. After a year and a half of futile searching, they finally purchased a home in Lake Hills, then an all-white suburb of Bellevue. As soon as the family agreed to sell their house to the Martins, Tim drove after dark to the seller's home with the down payment in cash. The same evening, according to Tim's later oral history, the seller phoned the Martins to say that neighbors who had learned of the sale called to "accuse him of 'scuttling' the neighborhood . . . bowing to NAACP intimidations [and even] threatened his life." Such atti-

Front of leaflet designed by Tim Martin to publicize the Fair Housing Listing Service. (CORE, Matson Collection)

tudes were widespread, but the Martins were not deterred. Tim later commented, "My wife and I got active in the Community Club . . . We joined the Samena Club so the kids could swim and play tennis. They went to Lake Hills Elementary and Odle Junior High. Some friends in Lake Hills said, 'Tim, you should keep a lower profile or you're going to get hurt.' I said, 'If I keep a low profile, I am *already* hurt.' I was determined to be a neighbor, not an oddity. We made ourselves visible . . . I wasn't testing anything, but I wasn't going to hide."[15]

The FHLS expanded, and so did its list of homes for sale. By 1963 the service listed over 140 homes for sale to any qualified buyer, ranging in price from $7,000 to $46,000. Homes for sale through the service could be found in all areas of Seattle, in the white suburbs of Lake Hills, Bellevue, Mercer Island, and Kirkland, and as far south as Federal Way. The service had sold twenty-two houses and assisted with two rentals. No commissions or fees were ever charged, unless the sale was made by a member of the Central Brokers Association. One lone white realtor, Elliot Couden, who had his office in West Seattle, defied the rest of the real estate industry and worked with the FHLS.[16]

Despite these scores of houses offered to buyers of all races, the vast majority of home sales were restricted by popular prejudice and the real estate industry policy of racial discrimination. CORE decided that to bring about an end to housing discrimination it was necessary to deal with the Seattle Real Estate Board.

CORE INVESTIGATES THE REAL ESTATE INDUSTRY

During its first two years CORE had focused on trying to break the color line in employment and raising funds for National CORE's projects in the South. Housing opportunities got only intermittent attention. Seattle CORE had grown to over a hundred active members by mid-1963, enough so we could add a full-scale project. The Housing Committee was established in May 1963 and chaired by Joan Singler, who was expecting her second child.

The first step in any CORE project required investigation and documentation, to prove that Afro-Americans were in fact being discriminated against. Expecting the possibility of boycotts, picketing, and even sit-ins, CORE knew we would need the support of both the black and the white communities. To us, discrimination in the rental, sale, and financing of housing was so obvious. Why take time to investigate? Seattle CORE, however, had to comply with National CORE's "Rules for Action." We must first investigate to establish the facts, then negotiate with decision makers, and finally demonstrate using nonviolent direct action. The Housing Committee decided that the best place to start would be with those realtors who already had discrimination complaints filed against them with the Washington State Board against Discrimination.

CORE's Housing Committee set out to prove by our own tests that discrimination existed. To ensure an accurate evaluation of each test, teams consisted of one white couple (the control) and one black couple (the tester). The tester and the control would agree ahead of time on similar personal information to be given to the realtor about their finances and family backgrounds. These couples would visit the same realtor, in most cases the same salesperson. Very often the black couple were bona fide buyers who wanted to purchase a home outside the Central Area. Both couples would inquire about the same house or houses. The black couple would see the realtor first and then inform the white couple of any service they did or did not receive, homes they looked at, the prices quoted, and so forth.

The first test took place on May 25, 1963, at Ewing and Clark Realty office at NE Fifty-Fifth Street and Thirty-Fifth Avenue NE, and the last test took place on October 20, 1963, at Loyal Realty in the Crown Hill area of Seattle. Close to half of the realty offices we tested had signed agreements with the State Board against Discrimination claiming they would not discriminate in the sale of housing. In every case the black buyers either were not shown the property they were interested in, or the price quoted was higher than the price offered to the white couple. Realtors often doubled the down payment for the black couple or sometimes just closed their offices when the black couple approached. If alerted by another realtor in the office, the salesperson simply did not show up for appointments and left the testers sitting in realtors' offices for hours. Many times the black couple would be told that a particular house they might be interested in had already been sold. The white couples invariably were shown the same house only a few hours later and were offered others in the same price range.

We also arranged tests at apartments. This was much more straightforward, often involving a single individual. Frequently owners or managers would tell the black tester that they did not rent to Negroes and Orientals. Other times, in a slightly subtler approach, the manager would say that the unit had just been rented. Once two black young women rang a doorbell and, looking in through the window, saw the landlady, clearly visible, crouching under a coffee table. She never answered the door. In each test, after a black renter had tried, a follow-up white "control" requesting the same apartment would be offered the unit. If the whites seemed uninterested in the first apartment, often they would be shown other units.[17]

CORE discovered another underhanded tactic to keep neighborhoods all white, initiated through the mail. When a "For Sale" sign went up, some realtors mailed the neighbors postcards that said, "You can decide who your new neighbor will be" or "You can choose your own neighbor." When CORE contacted several realtors asking why this was being done, we were told, "Some people are afraid that Negroes will move into the neighborhood," or "Since people gather for social functions it is desirable to have compatible neighbors."[18]

CORE documented all cases and forms of discrimination with dates, names of real estate firms, salespersons, addresses, phone numbers, and names of the white and black buyers or renters. We compiled the detailed results of our testing in "Report of Housing Discrimination by Real Estate Industry." We submitted our report to the Seattle City Council in October 1963 as it considered the proposed open-housing ordinance for Seattle. We sent copies to federal, state, and local governmental officials, including the mayor, the governor, and the Washington State Board against Discrimination, as well as to leaders of various church groups in Seattle and the media. We received no response from any government official or from reporters. One clergyman offered help: Reverend Lemuel Petersen.

OPERATION WINDOWSHOP:
THE REAL ESTATE INDUSTRY CLOSES DOWN

During this same summer of 1963 CORE used another technique, not only to test the degree of discrimination that existed, but also to encourage blacks in the market for a new home simply to *shop*. Millions of people across America "window-shop" all the time. What started out as a fairly straightforward CORE project—encouraging minorities to spend time on the weekend looking for a home and checking the prices—turned into a public exposure of the discriminatory and bigoted business practices of the area's real estate industry.

CORE set Sunday, July 28, 1963, for Operation Windowshop.[19] It was a day set aside to publicly encourage black buyers to look outside the Central Area at homes listed for sale in the newspapers or at open houses in new tract developments. To ensure that someone would actually "shop," Seattle CORE contacted black families who we knew were in the market for a new home. We asked these eight couples to participate in the project and report back to the Housing Committee on their experiences. CORE assumed that other minorities would also join in this day of looking/shopping.

We set in motion the approach CORE had used many times before. Several weeks prior to Operation Windowshop, we contacted Central Area residents in a massive door-to-door leafleting effort.[20] Black ministers announced the project from their church pulpits and encouraged those interested in buying a home to participate by going to look on July 28. We sent press releases to all the daily and weekly papers as well as the radio and television stations. CORE even hired a sound truck that traveled throughout the Central Area reminding people to spend the coming weekend window-shopping for homes. On July 26, KOMO TV arrived unannounced at the Singlers' home for interviews and to get more details on the project, which they then broadcast on the six o'clock and ten o'clock news.

On July 28, the first day of Operation Windowshop, the Seattle Real Estate Board countered with a quarter-page ad in the *Seattle Times* and *Seattle Post-Intelligencer* addressed to "Fellow Citizens." The ad claimed, "Operation Windowshop has been deliberately planned by a *nationally organized* group" (emphasis added). The actual planning group included a pregnant mother (the Housing Committee chair) with a two-year-old toddler and five other local members of Seattle CORE. The ad continued, "Persons who have no intention whatsoever of purchasing a home serve no purpose other than to disrupt and invade the homes of peaceful citizens." In another attempt to dismiss Operation Windowshop, the executive vice president of the Seattle Real Estate Board, Orville Robertson, told the *Seattle Times*, "There are all indications that a number of people have been shipped in to guide this demonstration." The *Times* quoted Robertson, "If these demonstrators are imported, they won't be too concerned with how outrageous they get."[21] This was a blatant attempt to frighten those with a home for sale and to discourage realtors from doing business with minority homebuyers! In fact, CORE knew black families who were actively interested in buying homes outside the Central Area. We had been able to confirm about eight couples who planned to participate that day as "shoppers." No one was imported from anywhere. The real estate board was blinded by its own prejudiced misconceptions. Realtors were unable to comprehend that many local whites and blacks cared deeply about injustice in housing.

The reaction of the real estate industry actually shocked us. On Saturday and Sunday, July 27 and 28, 1963, real estate offices closed and "open house" viewings were canceled. In the weekend edition of the two daily papers, more than 80 percent of the real estate advertising was canceled. To confirm what was happening, on Sunday CORE's Phone Tree Committee went into action and called individual real estate offices. That day 95 percent of the offices CORE tried to reach did not answer their phones. Orville Robertson, of the Seattle Real Estate Board, misinformed the *Seattle Times* on July 28 in saying he "thought most of the real estate offices would close, but that this was a voluntary gesture on the part of each individual realtor." However, one realtor in Bothell and one on Mercer Island called committee chair Joan Singler and told her they had been "instructed" by the Seattle Real Estate Board to close that weekend. There was nothing voluntary about it.[22]

This whole CORE project and the real estate industry response made the national AP wire news service. Chet Huntley, the national co-anchor with David Brinkley of NBC *Nightly News*, called Joan Singler. Huntley thought that closing down housing sales for a weekend in the entire Seattle area was unprecedented and wanted details of what was happening that weekend in Seattle.

At the CORE meeting the following Tuesday, we learned that approximately twenty-five people had participated in Operation Windowshop.

Fourteen of those at the meeting who tried to window-shop reported they were less than successful. Most offices and houses were closed. There were a few exceptions where individuals were shown a home and treated courteously and with respect. Sid Gerber had participated in Window-shop by taking a "Negro couple to look for houses in the $20,000/$25,000 range in Lake Hills" (a fairly expensive home in 1963). Marshall Wilson, a *Seattle P-I* reporter covering the July 30 CORE meeting, quoted Gerber as saying, "The real estate offices were all closed and there were no open house signs in the area that on the prior week had been covered with signs."[23] The following weekends we encouraged minorities to take advantage of open houses and to go and look. Our committee met on August 19 to explore other actions in the area of housing, including possibly negotiating with the Seattle Real Estate Board. We urged members to help organize Windowshop for the Parade of Homes scheduled for September 8 and 15, 1963.[24]

Operation Windowshop had several positive outcomes, despite the disappointment of those hoping to "shop" for homes outside the Central Area. First, the real estate industry by their actions—closing down for the weekend rather than showing homes to black buyers—made an undeniable admission of their blatant discriminatory practices. Second, many white people were outraged and called CORE wanting to list their homes for sale to any eligible buyer. CORE happily referred these calls to the FHLS.

CORE turned most of its attention to organizing strong participation in a march to the Seattle Federal Courthouse in support of the national March on Washington.[25] (Few Seattleites could afford the cross-country airfare to Washington, D.C.) We sold a button to show support and raise funds. A thousand people showed up, with monitors to keep us orderly and on the sidewalk. (We were exasperated that the government turned on the sprinklers. Of course we would stay off the courthouse grass! Who did they think we were?)

(Facing page) Rally in front of federal courthouse in Seattle in support of March on Washington, August 28, 1963. Note crowd staying off the grass and leaving space for people with business at the courthouse. (Seattle Post-Intelligencer collection, 1986.5.5929, Museum of History and Industry, Seattle)

March on Washington button (with "union bug") sold to raise funds. (CORE, Matson Collection)

NEGOTIATIONS

After our extensive investigation of realtors' discrimination, CORE policies called for negotiations. CORE's Housing Committee proposed to join with respected allies in talking with the Seattle Real Estate Board. On August 21, 1963, committee chair Joan Singler met with three members of the Seattle Conference on Race and Religion—Reverend Lemuel Petersen, Father John Lynch, and Rabbi Jacob Singer—and with Dr. Earl Miller, housing chair for the NAACP, and Reverend Samuel McKinney, of Mount Zion Baptist Church. Joan presented CORE's "Report of Housing Discrimination by Real Estate Industry," which detailed the tests carried out during the summer at local real estate offices, plus the outcome of Operation Windowshop. CORE's Housing Committee had documented beyond any doubt that the real estate industry was a major barrier to integrated housing. Joan explained that copies of the incriminating report had been sent to government leaders and agencies at all levels.

This group agreed that they should meet with representatives of the Seattle Real Estate Board. Reverend Petersen, acting as spokesperson for the group, tried to contact Harold Cooper, president of the board. Reverend Petersen attempted to arrange a meeting, first by letter and, when there was no response to his letter, with a follow-up phone call. After several weeks Cooper finally sent a reply. Despite CORE's proof of obvious discrimination in one test case after another, the real estate board responded that since there was no problem and no discrimination by realtors, there would be no point in meeting.[26]

Around the same time, September 11–14, 1963, a Six State Real Estate Conference was held at the Seattle Center. CORE sent a mailing to religious leaders summarizing our documentation of discriminatory practices of the real estate industry and asking them to join our demonstration. Many responded. Clergy of all faiths participated with CORE and the NAACP in a three and a half day picket of this event. On the first day of the protest, an anonymous source sent in a false report that demonstrators had locked arms and prevented delegates from entering the Opera House. The Seattle Police Department sent three squad cars to deal with the (nonexistent) situation. (We wondered how many times the police sent three squad cars out to respond to an anonymous tip.) What the police did observe was the overwhelming support of the religious community. Among the demonstrators were nineteen ministers and rabbis, both black and white, from various neighborhoods in Seattle and the white suburbs of Bellevue, Clyde Hill, and Mercer Island, who joined our picket line with dozens of their parishioners.[27] We were overjoyed at this powerful support from so many religious leaders. The long list of participating clergy was reported in the September 1963 *Corelator*. Verbal support was even offered by some realtors attending the conference. Grace Walker, a real estate agent from Oregon, told us she sold to any client in Portland and had no problems finding buyers or sellers. She actually joined our picket line on Friday and Saturday.

Governor Albert Rosellini was one of the keynote speakers at the conference. CORE and other organizations urged him not to address the realtors. More than a year earlier, on July 23, 1962, at the Benjamin Franklin Hotel in Seattle, the governor had given a speech to the National Conference of Commissions against Discrimination. He had told them, "We look forward to next year to the passage of a law designed to prohibit anyone in the business of selling, leasing or renting real property from discriminating against any person on the basis of race, color, creed, or national origin. I plan to have such a bill introduced in the next session of the Legislature." We had sent the governor CORE's report proving blatant discrimination by realtors. We were hopeful that the governor would be sympathetic to the plight of the black citizens of his state. He ignored our request, however, and crossed the picket line to speak to the conference.[28]

Because of the large size and the duration of our demonstration, we expected more news coverage. Seattle media, however, paid little attention to this public opposition to the real estate industry's barriers to open housing, reporting only CORE's objection to Rosellini's speech.[29] Similarly, the media ignored the CORE Housing Committee's detailed report of realtors' deliberate discrimination against African American buyers.

The next day, September 15, 1963, two thousand miles away in Birmingham, Alabama, a dynamite bomb exploded in the Sixteenth Street Baptist Church, injuring twenty-one children and killing four girls preparing for Sunday school. Racism in Seattle might take a less violent form, but our culture was badly infected by the same virus.

HUMAN RIGHTS COMMISSION—INSTEAD OF AN ORDINANCE

Like the governor and the media, local officials persistently ignored segregated housing. On December 11, 1961, the NAACP had proposed that the city council pass an ordinance prohibiting discrimination in the sale and rental of housing in Seattle. Despite detailed testimony with personal stories from black citizens at a public hearing, the city council declined to take any action. In July 1962 Mayor Gordon Clinton appointed a Citizens' Advisory Committee for Minority Housing. This committee was chaired by Alfred Westberg, a reasonable-minded white former state senator, and included one member of the black community, along with representatives of the Seattle Real Estate Board and the Apartment Operators Association. The Citizens' Advisory Committee called an all-day public hearing on October 19, 1962. People representing CORE, the NAACP, church groups, faculty from the University of Washington, and other organizations gave testimony on the degree of segregation and discrimination in housing in Seattle. Within two months this advisory committee returned a formal recommendation that Seattle adopt an antidiscrimination housing ordinance, with penalties for noncompliance. The committee also recommended the creation of a Seattle Human Rights Commission to administer and enforce the ordinance.[30] Finally someone had understood the depth of the problem and made recommendations to correct this longstanding injustice.

Mayor Clinton, however, stated he would not sign any city council ordinance that included enforcement provisions. He agreed to the creation of a Human Rights Commission, but the commission would work by conciliation and persuasion only. The black community was outraged. This approach was just more of the same—segregated housing would be a "topic of discussion," only this time the "discussion" would be led by the Human Rights Commission. On December 28, 1962, Reggie Alleyne, CORE's new chairman, sent the mayor an angry letter expressing frustration at the mayor's inaction. In their "Statement on the Need for a Seattle Anti-discrimination Housing Law" a few months later, the leaders of CORE, the NAACP, Reverend Mance Jackson, Reverend Samuel McKinney, Reverend C. E. Williams, and State Representative Sam Smith urged the

Tim Martin, after eighteen months of obstacles in trying to buy a house, testifying before a crowd that includes many realtors at one of the numerous hearings on open housing. (Seattle Post-Intelligencer collection, 1986.5.5938.2, Museum of History and Industry, Seattle)

black community to boycott a "powerless Human Rights Commission."[31] On June 18, 1963, CORE and other civil rights and church groups participated in a march and mass protest rally outside city hall, proclaiming, "No more talk. We want action NOW!"

On July 1, the city council held another hearing on a housing ordinance. At the hearing Alleyne gave detailed evidence of the many forms of blatant discrimination used by the real estate industry to prevent blacks from purchasing homes outside the Central Area. All these had been documented by CORE's housing investigations that began in May of that year. Army Major John Cannon, a member of CORE, testified at this hearing on his inability to find a place to live outside the Central Area. In dramatic testimony he told the committee he had a teenage son, an age when a young man needs a father's guidance, but "I have just received orders to go to Korea. I don't want to go. I was there during the war. I am going to Korea to maintain democracy, but I would rather stay in Seattle and try to achieve democracy. But I will go to Korea. It is my duty. Your duty is obvious. Do your duty." Equally powerful was the challenge put forth by Reverend John Adams, who charged the council, "The problem before you is a clear-cut moral

Reverend Mance Jackson, with bullhorn, addressing rally at Seattle city hall on June 18, 1963, in protest of Mayor Clinton's appointment of a commission instead of taking immediate action on open housing. (Seattle Post-Intelligencer collection, 1986.5.5923.14, Museum of History and Industry, Seattle)

issue, namely whether all citizens in this community have equal rights. For good Americans to need to debate whether to provide legal redress to fellow citizens when they are denied the right to live where they want to, and can afford, is in reality to betray the Constitution. It turns the American dream into a horrible nightmare."[32]

Instead of passing an open-housing ordinance, the city council established a Human Rights Commission and directed it to draft an ordinance. Angry and frustrated at the city council's stalling, more than twenty young people staged a twenty-four-hour sit-in at the city council chambers. This was not a CORE-sponsored action, but CORE members Infanta Spence, Patti Rabbitt, and Ray Cooper joined with the Central District Youth Club, which organized the sit-in. These young people hoped their presence would focus public attention on the decision makers who ignored the urgency of open housing. Negroes were tired of having others tell them where they could and could not live.[33]

Support from the Catholic Church for a housing ordinance was immediate. In the July 5, 1963, issue of *Catholic Northwest Progress*, the Most Reverend Thomas A. Connolly made an impassioned plea to citizens of all denominations. He urged "all citizens to pay special attention to the housing issue which seems to be the key to dissolution of segregation as it appears in our community. There must be no delay in the passage of a fitting, responsible ordinance with proper sanctions that will eliminate the abuses to which our fellow-citizens are being subjected." Archbishop Connolly's words fell on deaf ears.

A little more than two weeks later the Human Rights Commission was appointed, with Phil Hayasaka, an Asian American, as the director and only two African Americans among the twelve commissioners. Many in the Central Area viewed these appointments as an outrage. How could the mayor not involve more of the black community on such a crucial issue? Frustration and outrage surfaced immediately after the commission appointments were made. "Negro Leaders Plan Demonstration Here" was the lead story of the July 19 *Seattle Times*. Two days later a protest for greater black representation on the commission became a reality. On July 21, 1963, twenty-three black and white young people began a sit-in to convey this message. The sit-in lasted until four days later, when they were arrested for refusing to leave city council chambers.

Phil Burton and Charles Johnson, representing the NAACP, and others declared that having only two Negroes on the commission was unacceptable. Reverend Mance Jackson, speaking for the Central Area Committee on Civil Rights, made the same objections and supported the stand taken by the young people who were arrested: "The incidents [the sit-in and arrests] were unfortunate but I really believe what the young people did was heard louder than all the speeches we have made in presenting the Negro's cause for equality and representation." Expressing deep frustration with the lack of progress, Jackson declared, "A paternalistic concept of human relations in the country is all over . . . We don't need to be taken care of. We want to be equal participants in our problem-solving process." Mayor Clinton "grieve[d] that arrests were necessary to end city hall demonstrations" and called on Seattle citizens to support open-housing legislation.[34]

A HOUSING ORDINANCE REFERENDUM

Within four months the Human Rights Commission drafted an open-housing ordinance with penalties for discrimination and submitted it to the city council.[35] But instead of making the ordinance effective immediately, the council allowed it to be referred to the voters on the general election ballot of March 1964. Although most of CORE's energy and people-power in late 1963 were being directed at A&P, with picket lines at their stores three days a week, we began an all-out effort to support the ordinance.

Feeling that picketing realtors might have a negative influence on the vote, Seattle CORE decided to suspend demonstrations on housing until after the election. We made an exception when the Seattle Real Estate Board held its annual "Man of the Year" awards at the Olympic Hotel. Almost a hundred of us demonstrated outside the hotel entrance, handing out our message, "Racial Discrimination Hurts Seattle," to passersby and those attending the event. We reminded people, "There Are No Innocent Bystanders, Vote for Open Housing on March 10."[36] As the campaign for the ordinance continued, CORE handed out leaflets wherever possible to educate the public and counter the scare tactics of the real estate industry.

Seattle's religious community tried other avenues. Churches United for Racial Equality (CURE) was an umbrella organization representing Baptist, Episcopal, Lutheran, Methodist, United Church of Christ, Presbyterian, and other congregations in the Seattle area. Quoting a challenge from Reverend John Adams, CURE undertook to "alert the community to its moral responsibility to support full rights." On February 19, 1964, wearing "I Believe It's Right" buttons, CURE activists hosted nearly one thousand coffee hours in homes and churches to encourage their friends and neighbors to vote in favor of the open-housing ordinance. CURE cited Reverend Adams on the need "to call attention to the vicious fact of segregation in Seattle; [and] that Negroes and other minority groups want and need guarantees of full civil rights under the law."[37]

Archbishop Connolly presided over a solemn High Mass at St. James

Cathedral for civil rights, sponsored by the Catholic Interracial Council, on Tuesday evening, March 2—one week prior to the election. About seven hundred priests, nuns, and laity attended. The archbishop spoke to the moral issue: "We believe that the entire question of racial justice, with particular reference to the matter of open housing at the moment, confronts the conscience of every citizen of this community . . . Remember that the most crucial test of the love of God is the love of neighbor." Adding weight to this message Father Lynch preached to "all men who have any concept of justice and charity that the present state of racial discrimination in our country and in the City of Seattle is a violation of our Christian conscience."[38]

The *Catholic Northwest Progress* reported that twenty-four hours after the Mass, the King County commissioners unanimously adopted an open-

John Cornethan and others picketing in front of Olympic Hotel in Seattle. The woman with a headscarf in the foreground is Judy Esparza. (Seattle Post-Intelligencer collection, 1986.5.5952.1, Museum of History and Industry, Seattle)

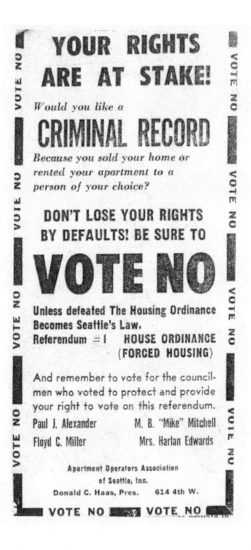

YOUR RIGHTS ARE AT STAKE!

Would you like a

CRIMINAL RECORD

Because you sold your home or rented your apartment to a person of your choice?

DON'T LOSE YOUR RIGHTS BY DEFAULTS! BE SURE TO

VOTE NO

Unless defeated The Housing Ordinance Becomes Seattle's Law.
Referendum ≠1   HOUSE ORDINANCE (FORCED HOUSING)

And remember to vote for the councilmen who voted to protect and provide your right to vote on this referendum.

Paul J. Alexander   M. B. "Mike" Mitchell
Floyd C. Miller   Mrs. Harlan Edwards

Apartment Operators Association
of Seattle, Inc.
Donald C. Haas, Pres.   614 4th W.

VOTE NO   VOTE NO

Apartment Operators Association inflammatory advertisement against open-housing referendum (Seattle Times, March 9, 1964, reproduced courtesy of The Seattle Public Library, Campaign Literature, Spring 1964, R324.79 C152)

housing ordinance for the unincorporated parts of the county. The commissioners had heard seven hours of testimony for and against the ordinance, then deliberated for about ten minutes before passing this law. Unfortunately, passage of the county law did not convince city voters.[39]

The Seattle Real Estate Board ran an attack campaign with newspaper ads and leaflets that claimed a YES vote would mean "Forced Housing, and the loss of your rights." Realtors continued to play on fears that having black neighbors would lower property values. The Apartment Operators Association ad even threatened a "Criminal Record" for any landlord who rented "to a person of your choice" or, for renters, a $500 fine and jail if "accused of moving because your landlord accepts a tenant whose color is . . . different than yours."[40]

Three days prior to the vote, on Saturday, March 7, 1964, the Central Area Committee on Civil Rights led a "March to the Housing Rally." The Central Area Committee on Civil Rights by this time included all the civil rights organizations and many of the area churches. Our friends and supporters had grown beyond the Central Area and included the Catholic hierarchy and the many, mainly white, churches in CURE. This time the demonstration marchers could choose among four gathering places: First AME Church, St. James Cathedral, the Federal Courthouse, or the Seattle Center. Approximately 1,500 people, both black and white, walked from these four starting points, merged, and marched together to a rally at Westlake Mall, the triangle of paved street adjacent to Fourth Avenue that widened as it stretched from Pike north to Olive Street. (The monorail terminal was south of Pine Street then.) The afternoon before

the vote, we picked up leaflets at Plymouth Congregational Church and fanned out across downtown to hand them to people leaving work.

But on election day, March 10, 1964, Seattle voters defeated the referendum decisively—by a margin of two to one—despite our earnest efforts. Those whites who wanted to be convinced that the ordinance could infringe on their rights had a rationale for their negative vote. Dorm Braman, running for mayor on the same ballot, opposed the ordinance, as did several candidates for the Seattle City Council who were all voted into office. Council candidate Jim Kimbrough, who was active with the FHLS and supported the ordinance, was defeated. The attack campaign, which equated open housing with "forced housing and the loss of your rights," had succeeded. Obviously, many whites in Seattle were still not willing to live in an integrated world.

"The defeat of the Open Housing Ordinance is keenly disappointing," a white civic leader wrote. "We can understand that the Negro community

From left, Reverend Samuel McKinney, Reverend Paree Porter behind Reverend John Adams, and Father John Lynch leading demonstrators from Seattle Center to join marchers starting from the federal courthouse, St. James Cathedral, and First AME Church for open-housing rally at Westlake Mall, March 7, 1964. (CORE, Matson Collection)

White and black demonstrators marching for open housing on the Saturday (March 7, 1964) before the vote on the open-housing referendum. (Richard Heyza/Seattle Times photograph 19640307)

After marching from four different locations, open-housing supporters at rally under the monorail at Westlake Mall, March 7, 1964. (Seattle Post-Intelligencer collection, 1986.5.9654, Museum of History and Industry, Seattle)

Volunteers to hand out downtown Monday afternoon pick up flyers at 4:15 Monday at Plymouth Congregational Church, 1217 6th Ave (6th & University St., 1 block east of Olympic Hotel).

THESE CHILDREN ARE EQUAL NOW

- *Will they have an equal opportunity for good housing?*

- *Will they have an equal opportunity for good education?*

- *Will they have an equal opportunity for social development?*

They will if you vote

YES FOR OPEN HOUSING

SEATTLE CITIZENS' COMMITTEE FOR EQUAL OPPORTUNITY
James N. O'Connor, *Chairman* • 127-39th Avenue East, Seattle

Open-housing leaflet produced by a coalition of supporters, this copy with typed instructions for volunteer distributors. (Special Collections Division, UW 28822z, University of Washington Libraries; leaflet photo by permission of Carla Anette Chotzen)

interprets the 2 to 1 defeat as conclusive evidence that Seattle is not yet aware of the plight of its minority citizens and that only dramatic events will bring about recognition and determination to correct it."[41]

Four months later, on July 2, President Johnson would sign the Civil Rights Act of 1964, outlawing discrimination in public places and in schools—but offering no help for segregated housing, a major problem all over America, particularly the North.

6 · DIRECT ACTION TO END SEGREGATED HOUSING

I s it ever just for the public to vote on withholding rights from a portion of the citizenry? Is it ever ethical to deny rights based on a popular vote? CORE did not confront this underlying moral aspect of the referendum—neither when the city council sent the open-housing ordinance to the voters nor during the campaign. Religious leaders urged support for open housing on moral grounds, as did CORE, but we did not directly address the basic ethical question, a question that our democracy still faces. Instead, CORE attempted to win the hearts and minds of the public by sharing facts we had researched and through exhortations from pulpits and at rallies.

Before the election CORE avoided any confrontational demonstrations on housing, but we could hold off no longer. It was time for direct action to publicize injustice. Determined to end segregation in housing, we had prepared for the next step. Acting on new reports of denied service at the real estate offices of Picture Floor Plans, Inc. (PFP), CORE had opened an investigation into discriminatory practices there.

Three bona fide black buyers, who had been contacted by CORE, and a white CORE tester documented their experiences with the sales staff of PFP at both the main office on 183rd Street and Aurora Avenue and a branch office in Bothell. On February 29, 1964, at the Aurora office, Mrs. Norwood Brooks requested to see homes in the $18,000–$25,000 range in the north end of Seattle. She and her husband were eminently respectable;

Norwood Brooks, a Republican, later was comptroller of Seattle and then King County assessor, among the first blacks elected to office in Greater Seattle. The real estate industry had now reverted to "token showings," a subtle form of discrimination, as a way of discouraging blacks from purchasing homes outside the Central Area. Unimpressed by her respectability, a realtor showed Mrs. Brooks two houses in very undesirable areas and not acceptable to Mrs. Brooks. She was told that that was the extent of homes in her price bracket and she left. Shortly after Mrs. Brooks departed, CORE sent in a white shopper asking for homes in the same price range. The white shopper was given an office file that contained listings of any number of homes that the realtor was willing to show. The salesman urged the shopper to return that afternoon with the shopper's wife so that the salesman could show them these houses. The next day, March 1, a PFP realtor at the Bothell office showed a black couple, Mr. and Mrs. Leroy Gordon, several dilapidated houses. In some cases the realtor would point out a house but did not stop to allow them to get out of the car to look. He also drove them past properties that the Gordons were interested in and claimed he did not have keys to show those houses. The realtor said he might have something later in the week and would give them a call—he did not.

Judy Esparza, new chair of the CORE Housing Committee, submitted a report to the membership covering the investigation of this one real estate company. Based on past history of the real estate industry and these two cases, CORE voted to take action directly against PFP and all its branch offices. Our purpose for demonstrating was to draw attention to racist sales practices. At the same time CORE tried to establish a dialogue with the owner or managers and to negotiate an agreement for fair treatment of minority customers. Our objective was to have realtors sign a nondiscriminatory agreement, which CORE would follow up to ensure the realtor lived up to the agreement. Attempts at negotiations failed.[1]

On March 22, Judy Esparza sent out a press release announcing the beginning of a sit-in and "A Statement of Principles by Seattle Congress of Racial Equality" summarizing why this was taking place. "In proceeding with our sit-in, we ascribe [sic] to the words of Dr. King: 'Actually, we who engage in nonviolent direct action are not the creators of tension. We merely bring to the surface the hidden tension that is already alive.'"

She also alerted Seattle citizens, "Members [of CORE] have moved into a realtor's office where they will sit and wait until it is realized that non-discriminatory service must be given to all, regardless of race, creed or color. These persons will continue to demonstrate until not only the realtor but the silent community finds the courage to face the principles and reality of justice."[2] To us it was obvious there was no other course of action left. Simultaneously with the press release, we held the first sit-ins on Sunday, March 22, at the Aurora Avenue and Bothell offices of PFP. CORE members entered the outer offices, occupied seats provided for prospective customers, and maintained a silent vigil for the entire afternoon. Picketing and leafleting went on outside each office.[3]

As the sit-in began at the Aurora office, a black couple who were bona fide buyers waited for a salesman, Mr. Barnett, to show up for their 2:00 p.m. appointment. After an hour and a half, another realtor told them that Mr. Barnett was late, and there were no other salespeople who could take care of them. The couple left that office and went to the Bothell branch of PFP hoping someone there could serve them. At that office they were shown several cards with listings of homes for sale but were told there would be no time to show them houses because the office was closing. We observed these obvious acts of discrimination at the very same time that white customers were ushered into realtors' back offices and then taken out to look at houses.

Tim Martin, CORE chairman, explained why the demonstrators were there. He asked the realtor to look at a "Suggested Provisions for a Written Agreement between Seattle CORE and Any Realtor Practicing Racial Discrimination."[4] (Looking back, how could we have expected any realtor to read this draft when the title required him to admit to practicing racial discrimination? How naïve! How sure we were that right would prevail!) Mr. Paul Appling, manager of the Aurora office, refused to talk about any agreement and claimed that his office would show houses to any qualified buyer. How could he have missed the black couple who had just been refused service for an hour and a half?

Demonstrators sitting-in or picketing were committed to stay for the entire afternoon. Many of us wondered whether we would be arrested. CORE's rules for expected behavior of demonstrators included a commitment to nonviolence and instructions that participants leave the premises

only if ordered by the police. If anyone in the realty office attempted to remove a CORE member, that demonstrator would "go limp" in passive resistance. Our past experience with the police had been verbal exchanges that involved warnings but no arrests. Many Seattle CORE activists had not experienced the uncertainty and tension of sitting-in. Yes, we had participated in shop-ins, but these small offices were a whole new environment. The first day of demonstrating was very stressful.

Church members played a role in the demonstration. At CORE's request, churches in the Central Area listed PFP office phone numbers in their Sunday bulletins. As soon as church services ended, PFP phones started ringing with callers asked PFP to sign the CORE agreement and end their discriminatory practices. The disruption to their business, with phones ringing constantly and demonstrators inside and outside the offices, prompted

Picketers at Picture Floor Plans include, from left, Oscar Hearde, Tommie Lamb, unidentified sign carrier, Judy Esparza, and Esther Hearde, in one of many demonstrations at PFP. (Seattle Municipal Archives photo, 63932)

the realtors to call the police. Three police cars were sent to the Bothell office and one to Aurora. The police conferred with the management at each office, did not talk with any representative of CORE, photographed all cars, but made no arrests and left. Demonstrators at both locations stayed until the offices were officially closed. The following weekend, because it was Easter, the demonstrations were suspended, though callers continued phoning offices.

When the sit-ins resumed on April 4 and 5, 1964, a third branch office of PFP, located in the Greenlake area, became a target. Reverend Paree Porter, pastor of Ebenezer AME Zion Church, led this demonstration; he was a leader or active participant in many CORE projects and picket lines. From late March until May 10, Seattle CORE demonstrated at PFP offices every Saturday and Sunday. CORE officers Tim Martin, Walt Hundley, Bettylou Valentine, and John Cornethan picketed or sat-in each weekend. Other active members, such as Judy and Gilbert Esparza, Dick Morrill, Oscar and Esther Hearde, and Cara and Harold Newman also became dedicated regulars, as did students Elizabeth Fusco and Aaron and Iris Bodin. Two young black students, Ernestine (Ernie) Rogers and Barbara Davis, made an exceptional commitment since there was no direct bus service to the north end. Ernie and Barbara, carrying their picket signs, would board a bus from the Central Area to downtown Seattle. Downtown they transferred to whatever route would take them many miles to a PFP office on Aurora Avenue or in Greenlake or Bothell. They spent the day picketing and returned home by the same long bus route.[5]

We also demonstrated at Maywood Hills, a housing development operated by PFP in Bothell. Here demonstrators sat-in at the open houses and also picketed in front of the houses. They were joined by Reverend Floyd E. Cronkite, of Bothell Presbyterian Church, and Mrs. Fumi Yasutake. Mrs. Yasutake, of Japanese descent, had been denied access to the new homes. The minister and CORE representatives carried on a long discussion with Mr. Stan Parker Sr. (a relative of the PFP owner) about his signing an agreement that the firm would not discriminate. Parker said that the Seattle Real Estate Board controlled everything and PFP could not enter into such an agreement by itself. This "passing the buck" between PFP and the real estate board went on for the duration of CORE's housing activities.[6]

The possibility of arrests was a constant concern among CORE mem-

Walt Hundley and Gilbert Esparza sitting quietly at the front door of a Picture Floor Plans office. The Seattle police officer (left foreground) wrote down the names of the demonstrators but took no other action. (Seattle Municipal Archives photo, 63897)

bers. At the Maywood Hills development, Elizabeth Fusco brought her guitar to a demonstration and picketers joined in singing freedom songs. As a result of the music and singing, the Bothell police were called to answer a neighbor's complaint that the group was too noisy. When the police arrived, picket captain Joan Singler asked, "Will we be arrested if the singing continues?" The police captain said no but that a citation might be issued. CORE member Oscar Hearde (a member of the Longshoremen's Union) told the police officer, "If the group stopped singing, the next thing the police would ask would be to stop demonstrating." The officer said the group "had a right to demonstrate," and the picketers continued to sing. On that particular day, April 12, 1964, in addition to the group at the Maywood Hills development, CORE demonstrated at PFP branch offices in Bothell and Greenlake. Then in the last week in April, CORE started a new procedure against PFP. Instead of smaller groups picketing or sitting-in at several branches, all the demonstrators moved en masse from office to office.[7]

As a result of the sit-ins and picketing, PFP changed the way it did business. Some branches eliminated the public waiting areas in their offices so there would be no room for demonstrators to sit-in. Others did not close down the waiting areas but posted "Private" or "Employees only" on the

From left, Val Valentine, Liz Fusco with guitar, in front of unidentified picketer, Barbara Davis's back, and Judy Esparza (partially obscured by sign), on May 4, 1964. (Seattle Municipal Archives photo, 63911)

desks and chairs. On April 19 at the Aurora office, Jean Adams, a white CORE member, was forcibly removed from a chair in the waiting area by two realtors. They claimed that the chair was designated for "employees." When she was carried out of the office, she was replaced by ten other CORE members who occupied the area. The police were not called, but the office was closed immediately after that, and the demonstrators left. Another tactic involved locking the doors. Salesmen and their customers entered the office through a back door opened by another realtor. If locked out, some of the CORE demonstrators tried to enter the office when customers were being shown in. This resulted in several pushing-and-shoving matches. At one point, petite Elizabeth Fusco was pinned between the wall and a door and was able to get free only with the help of two other CORE members.[8]

As tensions increased, Chairman Tim Martin appealed to Mayor Braman to use his office to end the need for demonstrations against PFP and, we hoped, end discrimination in housing. On April 23, 1964, the mayor held a meeting at his office. Attending for CORE were Tim Martin, chairman, Judy Esparza, chair of the Housing Committee, and Reverend Paree Porter, chair of CORE's Direct Action Committee. All three CORE members had participated in almost all demonstrations against PFP. Harold Cooper and Orville Robertson attended for the Seattle Real Estate Board but no one represented PFP. Cooper and Robertson made a point of telling the mayor that they could not negotiate for PFP—another way of avoiding any meaningful resolution. The real estate board suggested that one way to resolve the housing problem would be for CORE "to concentrate on discussions and seminars for the public." CORE asked if the board would cosponsor such an activity but they declined. The mayor did say that he felt that the public considered the board to be opponents of open housing, and they needed to correct that image. He also hoped that an agreement between CORE and the real estate industry could be reached. CORE agreed that this was one of the goals. The board, however, made no commitments to change anything. The meeting ended with the mayor saying that he hoped this meeting would not be the last—but it was.[9]

CITY LEADERS' SECRET PLANS

CORE was not aware that arrests were being contemplated by the mayor, the city attorney, and the police, with the involvement of the real estate industry. An "Intra-department Communication of the Seattle Police Department" summarized meetings held on April 13 and 14, 1964—ten days prior to the mayor's meeting with CORE and the Seattle Real Estate Board. Attending the first meeting with the mayor were Police Chief Frank Ramon, Assistant Chief C. A. Rouse, and King County Prosecuting Attorney Charles O. Carroll. Having planned their strategy, city officials were joined the following day by Paul Appling, manager of PFP; Ken Paulsen, representing the North End Brokers Association; David Smith, attorney for the North End Brokers Association; and two members of the Seattle Real Estate Board. City officials presented an outline of the circumstances that might allow the police to arrest CORE demonstrators. After several exchanges, the real estate leaders indicated that "the course of conduct planned by [the city] was a sound one; that it would be better to initiate criminal action as a result of demonstrations at a bank, rather than at a real estate office." Internal police memos alluded to a CORE action project aimed at First National Bank. (CORE was not planning action against any bank.) The mayor seemed to think bank demonstrations would be the point where CORE members could be arrested: "It probably will be in the picketing of banks that the first arrests will take place."[10]

These city officials and representatives of the real estate industry agreed that PFP would wait two weeks, and hopefully there would be "criminal prosecutions" of CORE demonstrators. At this meeting it was further agreed that during this two-week waiting period, the city "will generate publicity favorable to Mayor Braman's program of jobs for Negroes." If no grounds for a legal arrest had occurred during this time, PFP would seek an injunction and file a civil damage suit against CORE. In May Mayor Braman was quoted as saying, "Sooner or later arrests will be made to stop CORE and other active civil rights groups from interfering with the business function of the City."[11]

The police department worked with the realtors and asked brokers to try to get the names of demonstrators if possible. Protesters involved in the demonstrations were constantly photographed by the police and realtors working for PFP. The police recorded license plate numbers and checked for names and home addresses of the owners. The police also filmed us on a regular basis. CORE chairman Tim Martin wrote to Police Chief Ramon in protest over this type of intimidation. Chief Ramon responded that this practice was "within the law." Why was there a need for the photos? He answered, "That's police business."[12]

CONFRONTATION

Superior Court Judge Eugene Wright had ruled on April 13, 1964, that real estate offices were places of public accommodation subject to the Washington State Law against Discrimination, RCW 49.60. This ruling was under appeal to the State Supreme Court, but it became the rationale for more aggressive action by some CORE demonstrators, including Judy

Esparza, chair of the Housing Committee. Relying on the lower court's decision, Esparza pointed out that CORE sat in a real estate office "representing a clientele wishing to negotiate a settlement providing equal service for all the public." This was conducting serious business in a place of public accommodation.[13] Earlier, in March, Judy had written, "OUR CAUSE is just: the Negro in the free land of America has suffered, like no other American, from the cruel institution of slavery. That institution, through its consequences reaching down to today, makes many white Americans bigots and many black Americans their victims. If, eventually, CORE members break a law to break through to the human heart, we must."[14] With this viewpoint, the militancy of each confrontation with the realtors at PFP became more pronounced and more frequent.

The first weekend in May 1964, in a dispute over which areas were public and which were private, Captain Fred Pingrey and six other officers of the King County Sheriff's Office responded to a call to intercede at the PFP office at 183rd and Aurora. CORE members sitting-in that day included CORE officers Walt Hundley, Bettylou Valentine, and Judy Esparza. Also present was Philip Burton, legal counsel for the NAACP, who pointed out to Captain Pingrey that in the absence of a formal complaint from the realtors, if he made arrests he would be assuming judicial responsibility on which areas in the office were public and which were private. The captain took two copies of our proposed "Written Agreement between Seattle CORE and Any Realtor Practicing Racial Discrimination" and left without arresting anyone.

On May 9 a confrontation became much more physical. At the Greenlake branch, when David Paul tried to enter a realtor's private office, three salesmen picked him up and dropped him on the floor outside the office. At the Aurora office those sitting-in refused to leave when PFP stated the office was closing. A frequent PFP tactic was to lock the doors and close the office for a brief period, then to reopen and admit only customers escorted by salesmen. CORE explained this tactic to sheriff's lieutenant Patrick F. Burke, whom the realtors had called. Burke assured the demonstrators that today the salesmen would leave and no customers would be allowed through the doors. The demonstrators left. Doors were locked and the office closed. Within the hour, however, the Aurora office was ablaze with lights, the open sign was out, and business continued.

Sunday, May 10, turned out to be the last day of demonstrating against PFP. Picketing began at the Bellevue office. The office was locked, so no sit-in took place. Demonstrators moved to the Greenlake office and managed to enter, but immediately it too was locked. The group moved on to the office at 183rd and Aurora. Demonstrator Elizabeth Fusco managed to enter the locked office by following customers as they were admitted. Four realtors immediately dragged Liz across the floor as she went limp and threw her out the back door. When Lieutenant Burke arrived, Liz Fusco and witnesses submitted a complaint against the realtors. Later when two new customers were being admitted through the front door, there was a great deal of pushing and shoving among several demonstrators, the realtor, and the customers. When the second customer tried to enter, Gilbert Esparza was in the office doorway. At this point the realtor struck Gil Esparza in the face, knocking him and his wife, Judy, off the steps. He fell backward. Bleeding profusely, Gil returned to try to talk to the realtor, who continued to try to push him out of the office. The realtors called the police again, and we called NAACP attorney Phil Burton, who advised Gil that he could file a civil action against the realtor. Gil then went to University Hospital to have five stitches in his upper lip. Other demonstrators noted that the entire incident was photographed by the person who had driven the two customers to the PFP office.[15]

END OF DIRECT ACTION PROJECT

Two days later, at the May 12, 1964, CORE meeting, Chairman Tim Martin, Vice Chairman Walt Hundley, and Secretary Bettylou Valentine recommended that the direct action project against PFP be suspended for sixty days for further evaluation. Before voting, members spent some time discussing the value and disadvantages of pursuing a project to the point of being arrested. Seattle CORE was then also working on projects in employment, education, and fundraising for National CORE and programs in the South. A majority at the meeting reasoned that being arrested and going to jail would consume the group's money and energy. By a vote of twenty-one to nineteen, we agreed to suspend demonstrations at PFP.[16]

Three days after we voted to suspend our demonstrations, Picture Floor Plans, Inc. and the Seattle Real Estate Board obtained a restraining order from Superior Court. On May 15, 1964, nine members of Seattle CORE were served with the restraining order and a demand for payment of $1,000 in damages for PFP's loss of business.[17] CORE member Bob Winsor was our attorney and, fortunately, represented us pro bono. (Winsor had also represented Robert Jones in the *Jones v. O'Meara* case on housing discrimination that had been appealed to the Washington State Supreme Court.) Winsor's first act on CORE's behalf was to request postponement of the court date. The second was to have the case transferred from Judge Lloyd Shorett's court. Judge Shorett had ruled in favor of the Seattle Real Estate Board in *Jones v. O'Meara*, and Bob was concerned about possible bias.

Attorney Winsor made the case to Judge Theodore Turner, Shorett's replacement, that the disruption of PFP's business and any loss in sales could equally be due to the behavior of the realty company. He used the doctrine of "clean hands" in CORE's defense—Picture Floor Plans was not blameless. First, PFP deliberately engaged in unfair practices in places of public accommodation, offering service to white customers that they routinely denied to black customers. Second, they conducted business on Sundays, which was specifically prohibited by state law. The realtors claimed that they operated by ethics based on the Golden Rule, but this was refuted in depositions by several leaders of the religious community in Seattle. Tim Martin, who spent more than eighteen months trying to buy a house outside the Central Area, testified that the plaintiffs "do unto Negroes vastly differently from the way they do unto Caucasians."[18]

Judge Turner denied the plaintiffs' claim for financial damages. The court ruled, however, that any further demonstration at PFP must be scaled down drastically. No demonstrators would be allowed inside the sales offices, and no phone calls could be placed to a PFP office except for official business. CORE would be allowed no more than one picket at each real estate office, though that person would be allowed to hand out leaflets.

Phil Burton, who also represented CORE during the PFP demonstrations, had a completely different view on the court case. In an interview with the *Seattle Observer*, Burton stated, "The State Board Against Discrimination should intervene in the PFP/Real Estate Board's suit [and] ask that the injunction be immediately dissolved, and in addition make the Real Estate Board a defendant in a restraint of trade counter-claim."[19] But the State Board against Discrimination took no action.

While the restraining order was in effect against Seattle CORE, an independent Ad Hoc Committee against Discrimination (not to be confused with "the faction" Ad Hoc Committee that split from Seattle CORE; see chapter 9) continued the picket line at several PFP offices in June and July 1964. These were mostly University of Washington students, including Esther Hall, John Whittenbaugh, and Colin Heath, plus some members of the church community. Police files show that the Seattle police kept this group under surveillance. Police in unmarked cars closely monitored the apartment house where demonstrators would meet and disperse to picket PFP.[20]

CORE did not undertake any more testing and picketing at real estate offices. We turned our attention to school segregation, which was, of course, caused by segregated neighborhoods.

ONGOING EFFORTS FOR OPEN HOUSING

The Fair Housing Listing Service (FHLS) did continue its work. Its March 1965 newsletter listed total housing sales at one and a half million dollars. No fees were charged in those sales. The newsletter also reported that a number of small brokers, seeing that neighborhoods were being opened to black buyers, had contacted the FHLS to ask about prospective buyers. The editor of that March newsletter noted, "We [FHLS] expect to lick the whole problem in the next year, by showing the large realtors that they cannot keep areas all white."[21] The editor was Sidney Gerber, one of the driving forces of the FHLS. Sadly, he was killed in a plane crash on May 15, 1965, only two months after this newsletter was distributed.

It was not until after the assassination of Martin Luther King Jr. on April 4, 1968, that Seattle finally passed an open-housing ordinance prohibiting discrimination in the sale and rental of housing based on race—and it included an emergency clause making the ordinance effective *immediately*. It took only fifteen days from the death of Martin Luther King for the city council to act. The Open Housing Ordinance of 1968 was further amended in 1975 to cover sex, marital status, sexual orientation, and political ideology. A 1979 amendment added age and parental status; in 1986, creed and disability were included; and in 1999, gender identity. With the housing situation in Seattle rapidly changing from single-family dwellings to condo living, housing bias was addressed once more. State gay rights legislation in 2006 encouraged "homeowners' associations to remove all remnants of discrimination from their governing documents." This law found "these discriminatory covenants, conditions or restrictions . . . contrary to public policy and repugnant to many property owners."[22]

Legislation, however, did not change neighborhoods very quickly. The 1980, 1990, and 2000 censuses show African American families moving south into less expensive areas in Rainier Valley, Beacon Hill, and Renton. There were some black families living in all-white areas that had not previously been integrated but not in great numbers. By the year 2000 the Central District, now considered an area of "in-city living," had become a desirable place to buy a home. African American families were rapidly replaced by young white families who remodeled older houses. The sale and rental of housing now are determined by financial considerations more than by race.

PART IV Education

7 · SEATTLE'S SEGREGATED SCHOOLS

I n the South, laws had required separate schools for black students. In the North, segregated housing produced the same result. Unable to purchase homes elsewhere, minority families were concentrated in one small geographic area of Seattle. School assignments were based on neighborhoods, so elementary schools in the Central Area were overwhelmingly black. Despite the Supreme Court's 1954 *Brown v. Board of Education* decision that separate schools were inherently unequal, Seattle schools in 1961 were still, in fact, segregated. The civil rights community was convinced that integrating the school system was essential to improve educational levels. Furthermore, integrated schools would provide important experiences in the multicolored world that our children would be entering.

Because well-paid jobs for African Americans were so scarce, the Central Area also tended to have a high incidence of poverty, with its attendant problems for its families and their children. The Seattle School Board, like school boards in most northern cities, had done little to correct the imbalance.

As early as 1961 the NAACP had filed a suit against the Seattle School Board on behalf of black children, demanding a change in Seattle's segregated schools. The Seattle School Board responded to the NAACP lawsuit two years later, in 1963, by creating the Voluntary Racial Transfer (VRT) Program. This program allowed black children to transfer to schools where the majority of students were white and allowed white students to transfer to schools with a majority of minority students. The cost of transportation, however, was left to the parents. The first year, 1963–64, at least 235 black children transferred out of Central Area schools and 8 white students transferred in. In the 1964–65 school year, 369 black students transferred out and 17 white students transferred in. But these numbers were not significant in a total Seattle public school population of over 90,000 students. Voluntary Racial Transfer barely affected the racial percentages in Seattle schools.[1]

Seattle CORE felt compelled to address the school situation. With more than 140 members by 1964, we thought we could take on education as a major project, even though CORE was simultaneously involved in many other activities—direct action against Tradewell, negotiations with taxicab and other companies, research and negotiations with the Chamber of Commerce on downtown employment, regular orientation sessions to train new CORE members, efforts on housing discrimination, and a rent strike against Central Area slum landlords. We also were responding to appeals for food and clothing for Mississippi Negroes whose public assistance had been cut off by their state. The Klan in central Mississippi was vicious, burning homes and churches, shooting people, and sowing fear. From June 26 through 29, 1964, Seattle CORE held a round-the-clock vigil at the federal courthouse, ending with five hundred marching to the Westlake Mall, in honor of three voter registration volunteers missing in Neshoba County, Mississippi. Their fate had been unknown for two weeks, but we were sure they had been murdered.[2] We only recently had learned their names: James Chaney, Michael Schwerner, and Andrew Goodman. It would be five more endless weeks before their bodies were unearthed.

We were busy, but segregated schools affected the future of all Seattle children; addressing the problem became a priority. We established an Education Committee in the spring of 1964, first chaired by Delores Alleyne. Our official investigation was led by CORE member and University of Washington anthropologist Dr. Charles (Val) Valentine, aided by University of Washington geographer Dr. Richard Morrill and others. Val produced a twenty-three-page analysis covering the details and statistics of de facto segregation in the Seattle schools, reporting the number of students enrolled and the percentage of minorities in each school, from first grade through high school. These statistics showed that eight Central Area schools were more than 85 percent nonwhite; 90 percent of all black elementary school children were enrolled in just ten schools out of a total of eighty-six Seattle elementary schools; in seventy-five Seattle schools the enrollment averaged between 90 and 100 percent white. Garfield High School, located in the Central Area, had its black student population increase from 33 percent in 1957 to over 50 percent in just five years.[3]

CORE'S FIRST ROUND OF NEGOTIATIONS

Representatives from CORE's Education Committee requested a meeting with the Seattle School Board and began negotiations in late summer of 1964. Based on the statistics and recommendations in Dr. Valentine's analysis, CORE requested:

- compulsory human relations classes for all teachers;
- changes in the attendance zones of senior and junior high schools that would limit black attendance to no more than 30 percent;
- combining pairs of neighboring schools near edges of the ghetto, such as predominantly black Harrison Elementary and predominantly white McGilvra Elementary, to integrate students of three grades in one building and three in the other, a pattern called the Princeton Plan;
- transferring students out of Central Area schools where changing attendance boundaries would not improve racial balance;
- reopening the enrollment period of the VRT Program started in 1963; and
- public financing of the transportation costs of busing students in this program.[4]

The school board agreed to only two of these. They agreed to hold three compulsory closed-circuit TV programs in human relations for all teachers and to extend the VRT Program enrollment period to mid-September. The school board pointed out that they had instituted some compensatory education programs in Central Area schools and recruited approximately two hundred voluntary tutors to help carry out this program. A compulsory program to move children out of neighborhood schools, they said, would not work.[5] "Neighborhood schools" became a rallying cry for people who opposed transferring children in order to integrate Seattle schools.

"Neighborhoods" were in fact a large part of the problem. Black families were not able to buy or rent housing outside the Central Area. This, of course, created an ever-larger concentration of black children in Central Area schools. CORE was simultaneously trying to address segregated housing but was not accomplishing broad-scale change.

By January of 1965, the biracial team of Carla Chotzen and Beatrice Hudson (who replaced Delores Alleyne as cochair of CORE's Education Committee) was still trying to raise money for "Operation Transfer." This was a program to provide bus fare for black students interested in transferring to white schools in Seattle. Their goal was to raise $347, which would provide transportation for twelve students for one school year.[6]

The spring of 1965 and on into 1966 saw the big push to try to end segregated schools through negotiations and, failing that, by direct action. CORE had already gone through the steps of investigation and negotiation with the school board. The VRT Program was far too small to have any chance of integrating the school system since there still was no public money to cover the transportation costs incurred by participation in the program. Furthermore, the "receiving" schools had done nothing to make Central Area children welcome—no teacher awareness or student education, no program to show respect to newcomers who might feel uncomfortable in an unfamiliar situation.

OTHER PROPOSALS FOR INTEGRATING THE SCHOOLS

The NAACP also proposed a version of the Princeton Plan realignment of school zones, particularly the boundaries of Harrison and McGilvra elementary schools. (Harrison was later renamed Martin Luther King Jr. Elementary School and then closed in 2006.) Baby boomers' children were still swelling school populations, and in June 1963 the NAACP asked the

Seattle School Board to locate new schools in areas that would maximize integrated classes. The board responded that nothing was planned beyond the limited transfer program. Again in July 1964, Dr. Earl Miller, NAACP education chair, repeated the requests of 1963 and added more details: urging the board to look at "educational clusters," close Horace Mann School, and pay transportation for voluntary-transfer students. The school board responded by reaffirming their commitment to neighborhood schools. The NAACP also submitted to the Washington State legislature a bill that would eliminate racial imbalance in public schools. The state legislature did nothing. In 1965 the NAACP began preparing a second lawsuit requiring the Seattle School District to submit a plan that would bring an end to racially segregated schools. The case was actually filed in March 1966 and coincided with the school boycott.[7]

In April 1965 the Urban League submitted the Triad Plan to the Seattle School Board. While CORE picketed the school board meeting on May 12, 1965, James Kimbrough, board president of the Urban League, made the official presentation of the Triad Plan to the school board. This plan was written by Ivan King, who was on the staff of the Urban League (and was also a member of CORE). The Triad Plan proposed ending segregated elementary schools by combining clusters of schools in a geographic area. In this plan, elementary school students from three neighborhoods would attend two grades in each of three schools. Students would attend one school together for first and second grades, then third and fourth together at a second school, and fifth and sixth grades in a third school. Some students would be bused out of their neighborhood some years, but they would be with the same classmates throughout.[8]

Before the school board meeting to decide on the Urban League plan, CORE and the NAACP sent a letter to the board, calling for adoption of any effective plan for school integration. The civil rights groups reemphasized that compensatory education was not a substitute for integration. The letter cited the school system's own *Intergroup Guide:* "Traditional education has not proved to be an effective answer to prejudice." They condemned the Seattle School Board's inaction to date and concluded by quoting the *Intergroup Guide:* "As the problem grows, the necessity for action grows too."[9]

INTEGRATED EDUCATION

=

QUALITY EDUCATION

Poster reflecting the
idea that integrated
education equaled quality
education, a tenet of faith
in the 1960s following
the 1954 Supreme
Court decision on school
integration. (CORE,
Matson Collection)

THE SCHOOL BOARD RESPONSE

The school board flatly turned down the Triad Plan, as it had turned down the CORE and NAACP proposals. Superintendent Ernest Campbell told the Urban League, "The public schools do not exist for the purpose of imposing broad social reforms upon the people."[10] Even the school board's own Citizens Advisory Committee had urged that some action be taken to end segregated schools in Seattle, but was ignored.

We were outraged. CORE and the NAACP immediately issued a press release, signed by John Cornethan and E. June Smith: "The School Board . . . continued to perpetuate the illusion that all is well in Seattle." They went on to point out that civil rights advocates "have worked in good faith," but that "never again will we allow ourselves to be duped into thinking . . . the School Board intends to do anything about ending segregation in the schools voluntarily."[11] They pledged to undertake direct action or any effort necessary to integrate Seattle schools.

In August 1965 Phillip Swain, chair of the Seattle School Board, announced that Summit School would be closed and school boundaries would be changed. In September, the school board also approved a plan to transfer approximately five hundred students from Horace Mann and Leschi elementary schools to north end schools, but the cost for transportation would be the responsibility of the parents of these students. This would be in addition to approximately five hundred VRT students who were paying for their own transportation. Horace Mann and Leschi were chosen because, the school board claimed, they were overcrowded. In letters to University of Washington professors Thomas Barth, sociologist, and Richard Morrill, geographer, Carla Chotzen, cochair of CORE's Education Committee, stated her belief that there was no overcrowding at these two schools.[12] She felt that these closures were announced to placate activists in the black community. CORE, the NAACP, and the Urban League all acknowledged that the transfer of five hundred children was a step in the right direction but still insisted there needed to be a plan for total integration of all Seattle schools.

Meanwhile, CORE's Executive Board started planning for some sort of public demonstration to persuade the school board to integrate the schools. To educate the community and gain support for direct action, they proposed door-to-door leafleting, house meetings, and continuing the picket line at school board meetings. This would lay the groundwork for another yet undetermined action project, this time directed at the Seattle School Board and the new superintendent of schools, Forbes Bottomly.

The pace of CORE's involvement with the school desegregation plan was heightened when Sue Gottfried agreed to cochair the Education Committee with Carla Chotzen. In the spring of 1965, Sue wanted to participate in the Mississippi Freedom School project and asked Walt Hundley, then chairman of CORE, to write a letter of recommendation. Instead, Walt persuaded her to take on the issue of integrating the schools in Seattle.[13] Because CORE had already conducted an investigation and had tried negotiations and had a specific plan for integrating the schools, it was time to prepare for a direct action campaign.

Education was now Seattle CORE's highest priority, while we also continued working on many other concerns. At the same time we were inspired and horrified by news from the South—and not only Mississippi. For months we had seen brutality visited on Negroes attempting to register to vote in central Alabama. Then the murder of Jimmie Lee Jackson in February 1965 brought hundreds of silent marchers to the bridge in Selma, Alabama, where they were viciously bludgeoned and teargassed by state troopers in what became known as Bloody Sunday (March 7, 1965). John Lewis, now a member of Congress, suffered a fractured skull. Supporters from across America came to Selma to repeat the march; one of them, Reverend James Reeb, was clubbed on the head and died.

Seattle could not ignore these horrors. Bettylou Valentine, Joan Singler, and Elizabeth Patton started phoning. By 6:00 p.m. the next evening, Friday, March 12, 1965, hundreds of us were picketing or standing in mourning at the federal courthouse, in a silent vigil that lasted around the clock through Sunday and concluded with a prayer service. More than two thousand people signed in, including a large contingent from Garfield High School, many

Silent vigil for Jimmie Lee Jackson and Reverend James Reeb killed and many injured in Selma, Alabama, held on the steps of the federal courthouse in Seattle in March 1965. From left, Tommie Lamb, John Cornethan, Reverend John Adams partly obscured behind Willie Crawford, unidentified couple, Joan Singler, and Bettylou Valentine. (Bettylou Valentine personal collection)

whites driving by who just stopped and joined the vigil, and "one career Marine officer who. . .stayed throughout the night . . . bought coffee for us all, and remarked that his whole pattern of values had changed."[14] We sent the two thousand names to President Johnson to urge passage of a voting rights bill, part of a nationwide upwelling of demonstrations for the cause. The next evening, March 15, 1965, President Johnson spoke to a joint session of Congress and called for protection of the right to vote and "the full blessings of American life" for Negroes, famously proclaiming, "We shall overcome." Seattle CORE then resumed our campaign for integrated schools.

EDUCATING OUR SUPPORTERS

Even though civil rights groups had tried every possible approach to persuade the school system to end segregated schools, CORE felt it was imperative that the broader black community be involved. Widespread community support for a direct action campaign was crucial. CORE's Education Committee focused on setting up meetings with clubs and churches and in people's homes. Carl and Frenchie Klee chaired the Church Committee; Felisa Hundley chaired the committee responsible for arranging meetings in homes; and Beatrice Hudson took responsibility for contacting clubs. David Lamb replaced Felisa Hundley as chair of the Home Committee later in the summer. In this campaign CORE and the NAACP shared responsibility; cochairing the same committees for the NAACP were Randolph Carter, Yvonne Beatty, and James Washington Jr., respectively.[15]

On Saturday, June 19, 1965, a group of volunteers from CORE and the NAACP leafleted 10,000 homes in the Central Area. "All Seattle children need quality integrated education" was the message. The leaflet also explained the attempts to move the school board into action on the proposals submitted by CORE, the NAACP, the Urban League, and the board's own Citizens Advisory Committee. Included in the leaflet was a direct appeal for the community's support and participation in this project. The newly opened CORE office at Twenty-Second and Union became the main distribution point and coordination site for this leafleting effort. Each team, normally two people, was given a map marked with the area they would cover. They were to leave a leaflet at each house or apartment within their map boundaries. In addition to the door-to-door leafleting, the NAACP mailed the leaflet to over 1,500 people on its membership list.[16]

Later our outreach tactic changed to knocking on doors and talking with anyone who would take time to discuss schools. It was important to point out to the parents of school-age children how segregated—and inadequate—the schools were and what other options might be available. We asked parents and residents of the Central Area to sign a pledge card to support an integrated-school campaign and become part of the information network. Teams made up of members of CORE and the NAACP gathered in people's homes to talk with their friends and neighbors about the need for integrated schools. All CORE members were urged to work through their church and neighborhood groups to build awareness of the need to integrate our schools. Churches played a major role in lining up support. Ministers and their congregations took time to talk about the segregated schools and the role people needed to play to change them. As an example, one Sunday in July, ten members of First AME Church signed up

NAACP   CORE

ALL Seattle Children Need . . .

QUALITY INTEGRATED EDUCATION

- More Equal Educational Opportunity
- Better Preparation for Good Citizenship
- Better Preparation for Getting a Job
- Better Background for Going to College
- More Effective Teaching for All Groups
- More Efficient Use of the Schools
- More Rich and Varied Experience

Front panel of leaflet distributed to 10,000 Central Area homes urging public support for school reform. (CORE, Matson Collection)

to host meetings in their homes.[17] For the rest of the summer and well into the fall of 1965 the Education Committee worked to build support for some sort of action to draw citywide attention to segregated schools. CORE and the NAACP collected pledge cards from parents willing to transfer their children or join in other direct action against segregated schools.

While the exact plan for a massive demonstration was still being discussed, NAACP attorneys Philip Burton and Charles V. Johnson and a legal team from the New York office of the NAACP were planning action through the courts. Their suit, brought on behalf of thirty black students, was actually filed in Federal District Court against the Seattle School Board and Superintendent Forbes Bottomly nine months later—on March 18, 1966. The NAACP asked the court to order a district plan for the elimination of racially segregated schools and stated that the VRT Program was not working. The basic tenet of the lawsuit was that "segregated education of any kind deprives children of the equal protection guaranteed in the 14th Amendment to the Constitution." The NAACP requested further that the most segregated schools in the Central Area be closed. This list included Horace Mann, Leschi, T. T. Minor, Harrison, and Colman elementary schools plus Washington Junior High. Finally, they demanded that no new schools open on sites that would further entrench segregation and that teaching assignments for black teachers not be based on race. Furthermore, they requested the court to address the failure of the school administration to promote minority teachers to positions as principals.[18] Courts proceed slowly.

David Wagoner, a school board member, responded that the board had

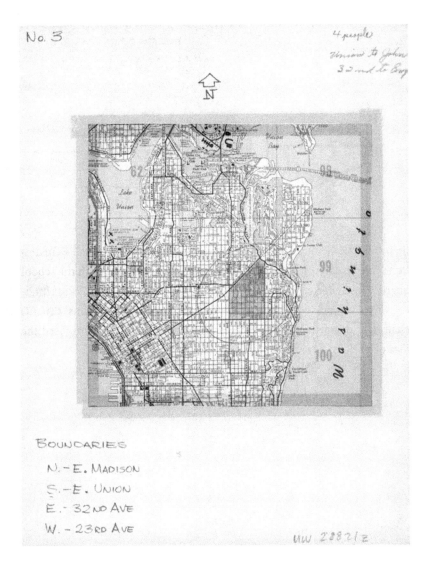

No. 3

4 people
Union to John
32nd to Eng

BOUNDARIES

N. – E. MADISON

S. – E. UNION

E. – 32ND AVE

W. – 23RD AVE

UW 28821z

a program of compensatory education in place and that each child must be treated by staff without prejudice. The school board reaffirmed "its philosophy . . . that integrated education provides better racial understanding among all children," and that it would "work to bring this about by whatever just, reasonable and educationally sound means are available to us."[19] We thought the school board was in denial regarding the basic problem. The Central Area Civil Rights Committee (CACRC—the combined body of representatives from CORE, the NAACP, black churches, the Catho-

CORE

Integrated Education

Quality Education

NAACP

SEGREGATED SCHOOLS CANNOT BE EQUAL!

1. I would transfer my child (children) if special school busses were provided. (Number of children____)

2. I join with others in demanding that the School Board promptly produce plans to end the pattern of segregated schools.

3. If the School Board failes to work out adequate plans, I pledge to join in a course of direct action.

NAME_____

ADDRESS_____

TELEPHONE_____

Front and back of pledge card for parents to promise support for integrating the public schools. (CORE, Matson Collection)

lic Interracial Council, and other church leaders) shared CORE's frustration. This leadership group no longer believed that talking with the school board would end segregated education in Seattle. At this point Walt Hundley, CORE's representative to CACRC, and Reverend John Adams, CACRC chairman, decided it was time for a bold action plan. They proposed the idea of a school boycott.[20]

A MULTITUDE OF ACTIVITIES SIMULTANEOUSLY

CORE's newsletter, the **Corelator**, provides a month-by-month description of almost all of CORE's activities from 1962 to 1968. The following brief summary of just one issue gives a taste of how very many activities the group carried out simultaneously. It also gives some examples of projects that we were not able to include in this book. Summaries of all **Corelators** can be found at www.civilrights.washington.edu. Look for CORE, Timeline.

September 1965, Summary

Agenda includes reports on School Integration Campaign; Negotiations with the Restaurants; Discrimination in the Unions; and the petition campaign related to the Freedom Patrol. A Rally is set for Sat. Sept. 18th at Mt. Zion Church addressing police brutality. Send telegrams (85 cents) to our Congressional delegation to support Mississippi Freedom Democratic Party's challenge to be the representative from that state. Dance raises money to pay some of the office bills but more contributions needed. Nominations for officers to be taken at October meeting. Support Leon Bridges for School Board. The second Jobs Fair being held in October, and sponsored by the Chamber of Commerce. Estimates are that 50 Negroes have been hired since DEEDS project, and many with college degrees and many more with some college education and hundreds who were high school graduates. Appeals for clothing for children ages 5–11 years old to be sent to Lexington, Mississippi.

8 · BOYCOTT AND FREEDOM SCHOOLS

School attendance was an almost-sacred obligation. Awards were given for attendance as well as for grades. A proposal to take students out of school to press for integration flew in the face of basic public values. Yet, at a special meeting on February 17, 1966, CORE's Executive Board recommended that we help lead a boycott of Seattle schools. The membership voted yes—with not one dissenting vote. CORE would take on this project. The boycott would not be just a couple of days to skip school but would provide a quality integrated education, to be called Freedom Schools. The very next evening, interested participants started meeting to plan the boycott, to be held on March 31 and April 1. Carla Chotzen, from CORE, volunteered to be overall coordinator. Freedom School staff and curriculum were under the direction of CORE member Frenchie Adam. Later, CORE's integrated team of Nancy Norton and Frances White assumed the major responsibilities and daunting tasks of creating the curriculum and class schedules. Reverend John Adams, from First AME Church, took on the job of obtaining sites for the schools. Sue Gottfried, an author and cochair of CORE's Education Committee, would write, produce, and distribute mailings and leaflets to encourage the widest possible support and participation. Sue was also responsible for producing signs for this campaign.[1]

CORE understood the immensity of the task. We were calling for a boycott of the public schools and providing a two-day substitute educational program for children from kindergarten to high school seniors, all to be planned in only forty-two days. Could we do it? Yes, but we would need lots of help. CORE membership was not a prerequisite for involvement in the boycott and Freedom Schools—if you were interested, you were welcome to join us.

One week later a letter from John Cornethan, E. June Smith, and Reverend John Adams gave notice of the boycott to the school board and the superintendent of schools. The letter explained, "the loss of a few days of school by children who participate in the demonstration constitutes a serious loss, but one that will be less serious than growing up to adulthood conditioned to life by an all-black or all-white education."[2]

To begin the process, Adams found space for classes at all the major churches in the Central Area, including Mount Zion Baptist, Tabernacle Baptist, First AME, Madrona Presbyterian, Goodwill Baptist, and Cherry Hill Baptist. He also received commitments from the East Madison YMCA, East Cherry YWCA, Prince Hall Masonic Temple, Woodland Park Presbyterian Church, St. Peter Claver Center, and, later, the Atlantic Street Center. The University Friends office became a transportation site for north end and north Capitol Hill students. Woodland Park Presbyterian Church was later changed from a classroom site to a transportation site.[3]

The safety of all the children was uppermost in our minds as we planned. We needed to provide a good experience of learning in integrated classrooms. Endless meetings took place to set the curriculum and to find staff for all these sites. Each Freedom School would require two volunteers, one black and one white, trained by CORE to serve as coprincipals. These coprincipals shared overall responsibilities for each site set for elementary, junior high, or high school classes. They would greet the children, get classes started, keep the momentum going, deal with emergencies, and assist the teachers. These individuals, de facto principals, felt apprehensive at the uncertainties ahead. With their help, a hundred volunteer Freedom School teachers went through a training program and were instructed to bring ideas and activities for their assigned age group. Training volunteer teachers required the concentrated effort of both the trainers and those assuming this new role. Every person who participated in this project was a volunteer.

Volunteers had to put together a transportation plan with chartered buses to move children to the schools. Supplies for the Freedom Schools, such as paper, pencils, glue, movie projectors, milk, crackers, and juice, had to be ordered and paid for. The task of raising the funds and paying the bills was ably handled by Boeing mathematician Ed O'Keefe. While soliciting these funds, he also had to secure money to keep the CORE office open. Major contributors to the Freedom Schools project were Anne Gerber, Dean Harvey McIntyre, Phyllis Nagel, and Jean Adams. The Catholic Interracial Council raised $200 for the purchase of milk for the children. In all, we raised $800 to cover the costs of the Freedom Schools. Even in 1966 dollars, this was an unbelievably small budget for educating, first, three thousand, and then, almost four thousand students for two days.

Ten thousand fliers mailed to selected zip codes on March 16 read, "Do You Want Action on School Integration? Join the Boycott of Seattle Schools, Send your children to Freedom Schools." The following week an additional six thousand copies of this flier were mailed to an expanded zip code list. Printing and mailing added another $200 to the costs of this campaign. Hundreds of parents signed and returned the response coupon on the flier, agreeing, "I will send my children to Freedom School, March 31–April 1," giving us some idea of how many children to expect. But we hoped many more might attend. Some parents and high school students were hesitant because of exams set for the days of the boycott. Some students were deterred when told their participation in the boycott would be listed as an "unexcused absence," and makeup exams would not be allowed under these circumstances. As the boycott date drew near, Sue Gottfried reported "a strong shift in favor of the boycott" from Garfield students.[4]

On March 25, six days before the boycott, representatives from CORE, NAACP, Central Area Civil Rights Committee (CACRC), and several churches gathered to report on final arrangements. The meeting was intense and the process messy. We had no reliable prediction of how many youngsters would come. Would Negro parents send their children? We had to prepare for all eventualities. Representatives reported on many details that were already arranged. Day care for preschool children of volunteers would be at the First AME Church, staffed by other volunteers. NAACP president E. June Smith had lined up people to register students as they arrived for school. Nancy Norton reported that of the hundred teachers needed, eighty-five had been recruited. Frenchie Adam was still concerned that there was not enough staff for the secondary level. Les McIntosh thought he could recruit a few more men to teach high school students. Carla Chotzen announced that high school students would not be allowed to leave the Freedom School once they had checked in for classes. (Exceptions would be made for a few students who had exams scheduled at Franklin High School.) Frenchie reminded the teachers to emphasize creating *dialogue* rather than *talking* to kids. Eighteen pastors had committed to talk about the

NAACP **CORE** CENTRAL AREA COMMITTEE ON CIVIL RIGHTS

Do You Want ACTION on School Integration?
Join the BOYCOTT of Seattle Schools
Send Your Children to FREEDOM SCHOOLS
March 31 and April 1

WHAT IS THE PROBLEM?

In 1954, the United States Supreme Court handed down the doctrine that separate schools cannot be equal. The Court ordered schools across the country to integrate.

Twelve years later, Seattle schools have become steadily more segregated. Seattle has 13 predominately "black" schools and over 100 "white" schools. Our Negro students are so few that they would not make up one busload to each segregated "white" school.

Segregated schooling perpetuates segregation in employment, in housing, in every area of our daily lives.

WHAT HAS BEEN DONE?

Appeals for action on this problem are already a decade old. Steady negotiations with the School Board have been going on for three years. These pressures helped to produce the voluntary transfer program and led to a school-administered transfer of 400 children this fall. But no further action is contemplated by the School Board. Neither token school transfer, nor voluntary transfers, nor segregated compensatory education will stop the ever-enlarging pattern of school segregation.

WHAT DO WE ASK?

We ask that the Seattle School Board *immediately* adopt a comprehensive plan to integrate Seattle schools. *The public announcement that a master plan has been adopted would cancel the boycott.* There is no lack of available plans. CORE, NAACP, the Urban League and others have offered workable plans for school integration. The School Board has not adopted any of these, *nor has it ever put forward any desegregation plan of its own.*

boycott at their March 27 Sunday services. Phil Burton was working with some other lawyers to prepare a statement on the legality of the boycott, that it might not be a violation of school law. Dr. Earl Miller would ask some doctors to be on standby for any emergencies during Freedom School hours. The session concluded with a reminder of a staff meeting for elementary school volunteers on Tuesday, March 29, at the CORE office, and for secondary school volunteers on Wednesday, March 30, at the Prince Hall Masons.[5]

Top of flier mailed to 16,000 homes urging parents to send their children to Freedom Schools, with coupon for response on their intention to participate. (CORE, Matson Collection)

A final rally to generate support for the school boycott was held on Saturday, March 26, at Tabernacle Baptist Church, at Jackson and Twenty-Eighth. Dr. Miller summarized the community's efforts over the years with the school board, so no one could doubt the need for action. Enthusiasm overflowed, as at every rally. We took up a collection for the Freedom Schools and raised more much-needed funds.

PUBLIC REACTION IN ADVANCE OF THE BOYCOTT

In building awareness, though not necessarily support, we were aided by two television programs and by daily coverage in Seattle newspapers, starting on March 15, 1966, and continuing after the boycott. Articles in the papers covered interviews, reactions, and divisions within the Seattle church and civic community regarding the boycott. One issue dividing the church community was the stand taken by the board of directors of the Greater Seattle Council of Churches. The church council board supported the boycott and the Freedom Schools, writing, "It is pretty well conceded that there is little, if any, social progress in the world without protest of some form."[6] Similarly, the Seattle Presbytery supported the boycott and "gave its blessings to clergymen and church members who volunteer" in Freedom Schools.[7] But the following day fifteen leading ministers from downtown churches, including three Presbyterian pastors, met for two and a half hours with Superintendent Forbes Bottomly. They released strongly worded resolutions opposing the boycott and disassociating themselves from the stand taken by the Council of Churches. They claimed to "support the goals . . . toward an integrated society," but "the boycott calls for illegal action, . . . is a deliberate attempt and 'treacherous use of undiscerning young people as the tools . . . of adults' and . . . condones insubordination thinly veiled by the program for civil rights."[8] They objected to the boycott "as exploiting children and disrupting their education" and said it would "foster disrespect for the law." Reverend John Adams's response was pointed: "I remind these custodians of the status quo that these segregated schools against which we boycott have been illegal for 12 years and they [the ministers] never have said a mumbling word."[9]

The legality of the boycott was argued many times before and after the event. Michael Rosen, executive secretary of the American Civil Liberties Union (ACLU) of Washington, had recently been in the South with the legal team supporting the Mississippi Summer project. He stated it was the school board that was breaking the law, by allowing de facto segregated schools to continue in the face of the Supreme Court ruling twelve years earlier.[10]

The *Seattle Times* dedicated more coverage on March 25 and 29. It cited comments from Reverend Peter Raible, who supported the boycott and was a volunteer Freedom School teacher leading student discussions on civil rights. Raible also engaged his congregation at University Unitarian Church. A meeting on March 28 had the specific purpose of hearing the congregation's views on what official position the church should take. The congregation adopted a resolution requesting "the Seattle School Board to take steps as may be necessary to end racial imbalance at the earliest possible date." The resolution passed with 141 in favor and 19 opposed. Although this was not an official endorsement of the boycott and the Freedom Schools, many Unitarians sent their children to be part of the demonstration. Raible pointed out, "I know no other church in our community which dares risk a congregational meeting to decide policy on this issue."[11]

Support for the boycott from the black churches was robust, as expected. What was not expected was the strong public stand in support of the boycott by Archbishop Thomas Connolly and Father John Lynch of the Catholic Interracial Council. In a Catholic newsletter Archbishop Connolly urged Catholics to become involved in ending de facto segregation. Father Lynch, reported Herb Robinson, stated that support for boycotting school was "based on a principle of 'double effect,' [and] explained that the term means condoning breaking a law to 'achieve a greater good.'"[12]

On the other hand, some white clergy protested that the children were being used as "pawns" and stated that the boycott would "implant the idea of lawlessness in children's minds." A number of white clergy, including the Very Reverend John C. Leffler, of St. Mark's Episcopal Cathedral, were "whole heartedly in support of integration in schools" but opposed truancy as a means of protest. Lutheran pastor Dr. Donald A. Clinton, however, overcame his initial negative reaction and became "convinced such a protest is necessary and right." In answer to charges that children were being manipulated for adult ends, Reverend Raible wrote, "I conclude that all children, white, Negro and Oriental, are significantly deprived by current patterns of segregated education. A fundamental obligation upon me as a parent is to prepare my children to live in a world where the vast majority of the people belong to the colored races . . . I think I reverence rather than use my children when I involve them in any effort for an integrated society."[13]

Rabbi Raphael Levine, of Temple de Hirsch, made the front page of the *Seattle Times* when he called for a "conference . . . to discuss racially-imbalanced school enrollments." He said that because of neighborhood patterns, "The schools are helpless to implement their publicly stated belief that 'an integrated education provides better racial understanding among all children in our pluralistic American society.'"[14] Other leaders disagreed and pointed out that three intense years of "conferencing" had produced no change. There were many letters to the editor in the two daily newspapers, both positive and negative.

The *Seattle Times* editorial writer Herb Robinson commented on March 20, "Even if only a handful of children are absent from class those two days, the boycott sponsors have accomplished their purpose by stirring up the most vigorous public debate in Seattle to date on racial imbalance in the schools." He further noted an "interesting development . . . that Seattle school officials are recruiting specifically for black administrators, a marked change in previous policy."[15]

On March 29, 1966, the two daily papers carried a total of five featured stories on why Seattleites should or should not support the boycott. On March 30, the day preceding the boycott, the *Seattle Post-Intelligencer* editorialized that the boycott would be wrong and quoted from a report the Seattle school administration had sent home with every student that same day. The school system's efforts to integrate the schools were listed in "Education for Understanding: A Report on Intergroup Education in the Seattle Public Schools." The *P-I* editorial praised the school district for

- institutes for teachers assigned to the Central Area to eliminate racial prejudice,
- textbooks that credit Negro contributions to democracy, to help eliminate the prejudices of white students,
- compensatory education or enrichment programs to close the achievement gap,
- the voluntary transfer program, which enabled Negro pupils to transfer to white schools.

To further bolster the school board against giving in to an "involuntary crash program," the *P-I* editorialized that in a forced-transfer program "the Negro pupil will be the loser. If it is true that there is an achievement gap at present due to various environmental conditions, thrusting Negro youngsters en masse into more advanced classroom situations would, it seems, create more problems for them than it would solve."

The school administration's report cited by the *P-I* reflected Superintendent Bottomly's search for solutions to educational inequities. In internal records Dr. Bottomly indicated that integrated education could provide a better environment for students. Nevertheless, he was pursuing plans only for compensatory education, for faculty "Prejudice Seminars," for curriculum improvement on Negro experience, and for improving the voluntary-transfer programs.[16] He was not working for timely, complete integration.

THE FREEDOM SCHOOLS OPEN

Throughout the weeks of preparations, volunteers felt anxious and expressed reservations—would we get enough participants to impress the school board? Hundreds of parents had signed their children up, but the committee was concerned whether a substantial number of black families would send their children, and whether total attendance would be large enough to impact school policy. On Thursday, March 31, 1966, to the happy amazement of the volunteer staff, the Freedom Schools were filled to overflowing. More than three thousand smiling, eager children arrived, two-thirds of them black and one-third white. Most brought their sack lunches; for those who forgot, 525 McDonald's hamburgers had to be quickly purchased. To accommodate the overflow crowd, additional space had to be found on a moment's notice, but a few phone calls quickly secured more classrooms at Temple de Hirsch, Herzl Conservative Synagogue, and St. Clement's Episcopal Church.[17]

Jean Adams, coprincipal at First AME Church, remembers that excited kids started bounding up the church stairs an hour early, in joyful anticipation—far more than we had planned for. Even after some children were moved from First AME to new sites opened at Herzl or St. Clement's, 175 children needed to squeeze in where we had thought we could accommodate seventy-five or, at most, a hundred. "Every nook and cranny was bulging."[18] Children were well behaved amid the confusion, as adults improvised solutions. In spite of the crowded conditions, "there was a joyous atmosphere and a spirit of working together, sharing a real glow of happiness and unusual satisfaction. Under these circumstances the children and adults did remarkably well not only to maintain themselves but to do so with pleasure and composure and a sense of purpose."[19] Ministers from black churches as well as white clergy on the CACRC board were there to help out and in some cases actually taught a class. "The children seemed to enjoy each activity [even though] most of the time there wasn't room enough to turn around in. [They had] worthwhile learning experiences, stimulating new social contacts, and a remarkable personal involvement in one of the ways changes can be brought about in our society."[20] The curriculum, developed by Nancy Norton and Frances White, emphasized Negro history. Age-appropriate classes in music, reading, science, art, crafts, and creative games were offered to elementary and middle school children. Older students were also offered career counseling and movies about civil rights.[21]

Well-known academicians, artists, and musicians participated. At First AME Freedom School, Rabbi Norman Hirsh fascinated a large group of fifth- and sixth-graders with stories about the parallels between the prejudice suffered by Jews and Negroes in the United States. Civic activist Kay Bullitt spontaneously offered to take third- and fourth-grade children on a neighborhood walk.

Henry Siegl, concertmaster of Seattle Symphony, playing "Flight of the Bumblebee" and "Farmer in the Dell" on his violin for attentive elementary school pupils at First AME Freedom School, March 31, 1966. (Ron DeRosa/Seattle Times original photo has been lost; clipping from CORE, Matson Collection)

Nationally recognized artist James Washington Jr., Seattle Symphony concertmaster Henry Siegl, actor Keve Bray, sculptor Rich Beyer, ACLU lawyer Michael Rosen, university professors Alex Gottfried and Richard Morrill, Presbyterian pastor William H. Creevey, jazz musicians Floyd Standifer and Overton Berry, all taught classes at Freedom Schools.[22] On April 1, the second day of classes, the number of students increased to 3,918. With this larger crowd the volunteers breathed a sigh of relief—support for integration was overwhelming—and they geared up to teach Freedom School all over again. The modest contribution of each participant had added up to an impressive, meaningful total. The Freedom Schools had been a stupendous, overwhelming success.

We were rewarded by comments from parents. A mother delivering her

Reverend Ralph Mero, East Shore Unitarian Church, in discussion with middle school students at Mount Zion Freedom School, March 31, 1966. (John Valentine/Post-Intelligencer collection, 1986-5.11603.1, Museum of History and Industry, Seattle)

child to school was heard to say, "I'm so proud to be a Negro!" One mother sounded thrilled, saying how overjoyed she was when her children came home "with a new sense of pride in being Negro and a new knowledge of the part that Negroes have played in America."[23] One man appeared unexpectedly after school and, for six to eight hours both days, helped clean up before his full night shift at work, in proud appreciation of "how much his daughter had learned at the high school Freedom School." Children wanted to "come to Freedom School again!"[24] This was a life-changing experience for participants.

Three Seattle schoolteachers violated their contracts with the school administration to serve in the Freedom Schools. School librarian and TV

Mike Rosen, ACLU attorney, leading Freedom School high school class at Prince Hall Masonic Temple. (AP images 660331010)

moderator Roberta Byrd served as coprincipal at the YMCA. Felisa Hundley, middle school teacher and wife of Walt Hundley, and Dick Warner, a history teacher at Ballard High School, were volunteer faculty. Warner explained his participation: "One cannot be an active and responsible citizen without taking action—that is what I teach my pupils in school. I strongly believe in integrated schools. It is my duty to participate."[25] An opposing view was taken by Dee Raible, wife of Reverend Peter Raible and head of the art department at Meany Junior High School. She stated, "I feel very strongly about compensatory education. As the community at large faces its problems, the kids will be ready to fit in."[26] Ms. Raible spent the two days of the school boycott teaching her regular classes at Meany Junior High, while their children attended the Freedom Schools with their father. Obviously, the Raible household was split on this issue.

It should be noted that the absences of children who attended the Free-

Roberta Byrd, coprincipal of the East Madison YMCA Freedom School, teaching Negro history to some of the more than three hundred students at that site. (Richard S. Heyza/Seattle Times original photo has been lost; clipping from CORE, Matson Collection)

dom Schools were listed as "unexcused" by the school district. Absenteeism in some Central Area schools was over 50 percent.[27] About 30 percent of the Freedom School attendees were white. In addition to parents and students, whose enthusiastic response made the boycott a milestone, we received support and endorsements from the Seattle Presbytery, Catholic Interracial Council, Archbishop Thomas Connolly, American Federation of Teachers Local 200, the University of Washington chapter of Friends of the Student Nonviolent Coordinating Committee, Students for a Democratic Society, Northwest Conference of Women's Auxiliaries of the International Longshoremen and Warehousemen's Union, and the leadership of the University Unitarian Church and of the Greater Seattle Council of Churches.[28]

EVALUATION OF THE FREEDOM SCHOOLS

The first evaluations of the Freedom School experience came from the students themselves. After the boycott a full page of the *Seattle Times* printed interviews with ten teenagers who attended Freedom School. Gordy Sanstad, a white Roosevelt High student proclaimed, "The boycott has been a total success." He further observed, "There's something wrong with Seattle's racial situation—I don't think any student can get a complete education from an all-white or all-Negro school." Two black Garfield students had other comments. Leasa Farrar admitted she was not fully aware of the extent of segregation in the schools. "I started to listen to people and found out how little I knew before. I'm for the Freedom Schools and the boycott because, if nothing is done, the central area schools will be 100 percent Negro in a few years . . . The School Board doesn't have any choice—they have to do something." Donald Zackery thought, "When the School Board members see what the Freedom Schools and the boycott are trying to accomplish, they'll have to do something about this segregation problem." According to Linda Navarro, also from Garfield, "The transfer programs aren't doing a thing . . . it takes a lot more than that to achieve integration. I don't know what they [the School Board] can do, but they have to try. The Freedom Schools have been great—we've learned a lot about Negro history and what the boycott is all about."[29]

Empty seats reflecting the high absenteeism rate in Central Area public schools due to school boycott.
([Ken Harris]/ Seattle Post-Intelligencer collection, 1986.5.11483, Museum of History and Industry, Seattle)

Organizers of the boycott felt we had accomplished what we set out to do. We had been able to involve more than three thousand students for two days in a peaceful and creative protest. At the same time, children came away from this experience having learned something about Negro history and the civil rights movement in a multiracial setting. The level of involvement and the attendance said a great deal about the mood of many citizens and their children. The human resources required to put together an all-volunteer force to make the project happen had not been seen before in Seattle. The civil rights community had demonstrated to the Seattle School Board and Superintendent Forbes Bottomly that this was a responsible and serious undertaking with significant community support. De facto segregation in the schools would no longer be tolerated.

On Friday evening, April 1, after the close of the Freedom Schools, most of the volunteers met at 8:00 p.m. at Carla Chotzen's home to evaluate the two days of classes. Leaders and teachers reported on what had happened, on what worked and what did not work. The overwhelming consensus was that the boycott had been a huge success and that a clear message had been sent to the Seattle School Board. Some enthusiastically called for another boycott immediately. Others, including Roberta Byrd, insisted that the school board was about to act and we should wait and see what they did. After the official evaluation meeting, a celebration by some of the very tired volunteers lasted late into the night.

A few weeks later, Cal Harris and Les McIntosh, who served on CORE's Education Committee, proposed to the membership the following actions: picketing the Seattle School Board; sending CORE representatives to school board meetings; a major citywide boycott of the schools the first week of September; and organizing white students to transfer to Central Area schools. To do this CORE would engage in leafleting, organizing neighborhood meetings, canvassing door-to-door, and contacting the parents of the children who had attended the Freedom Schools. Cal and Les also recommended a mass march to the school board meeting on May 21.[30] Given that the campaign against segregated schools had taken over a year, and the boycott and Freedom Schools had taken six weeks to execute at a cost of nearly $1,000, it is not surprising that the membership took no official action.

Then on May 31, 1966, two months after the boycott, civil rights leaders called a town hall meeting at the First AME Church. CORE, the NAACP, and CACRC wanted the community's input on what should be done next.[31] A second boycott was suggested but never took place. By this time the school board and Superintendent Bottomly had let community leaders know that the Voluntary Racial Transfer Program would now provide free transportation, by chartered buses with chaperones on each bus. The school administration also promised that a program would be set in place at the "receiving" schools to prepare principals and teachers to create a receptive atmosphere and provide fair treatment to all children.[32]

By July 6 leaders of the black community were urging parents with children attending segregated schools to participate in the voluntary-transfer program. The Central Area Motivation Program (CAMP—a War on Poverty program) sent a letter to parents stating, "Some . . . have worked extremely hard to bring about a paid transportation program for our youth and now it is up to our community to support the program by volunteering to transfer our children." The letter was signed by Reverend John Adams, chair of CACRC; John Cornethan, chairman of Seattle CORE; Walter Hundley, executive director of CAMP; Charles V. Johnson, Northwest area president of the NAACP; Reverend Samuel McKinney, chair of the Seattle Opportunities Industrialization Center; Edwin Pratt, executive director of the Urban League; and E. June Smith, president of the Seattle NAACP. The initial transfer program was to include eight hundred children.[33]

Obviously, the boycott had an impact on several fronts. Newspaper, television, and radio coverage put the public spotlight on an issue that most white Seattleites were not willing to face. It forced church leadership and church congregations to debate what they should do personally to bring about an end to de facto segregation in the schools. By this action the Seattle School Board and school superintendent were put on public notice that drastic changes were expected.

Some benefits from the pressure created by the boycott, although not the solution CORE, NAACP, and CACRC were looking for, included paying transportation costs for students in the voluntary-transfer program. Sensitivity training for teachers and staff at receiving schools was set in motion. (Val Valentine taught one of these human relations classes and was shocked when one teacher accused him of racism because he had referred to "a chink in the armor of segregation.") The curriculum continued to be updated, a change that had started with the lawsuit brought by the NAACP in 1961. Finally, administrative positions within the school system were being filled by African Americans: Robert Bass was appointed assistant vice principal at T. T. Minor Elementary, Warren Burton became vice principal at Sharples Junior High School, Dorothy Hollingsworth was hired as the director of Head Start, Mildred German became assistant supervisor of the district's guidance office, and Roberta Byrd Barr was appointed the community liaison coordinator for Title I programs.[34]

Our attention, however, could not be limited exclusively to Seattle's serious problems. News coverage in June 1966 showed James Meredith shot and injured in Mississippi near the beginning of his "March against Fear," his walk alone down the highway toward Jackson. The hundreds who took up his cause, walking through dangerous rural parts of the state to the capital, included Martin Luther King, Stokely Carmichael, Floyd McKissick, and Seattle's Val and Bettylou Valentine. Bettylou remembers seeing Marlon Brando and James Brown at the closing ceremony when marchers arrived in Jackson.

OTHER EFFORTS ON EDUCATION

Just three months after the Seattle school boycott, segregated schools drew the attention of the federal government: the Department of Education funded a Desegregation Training Institute run by the political science department at the University of Oregon. This six-week intensive course trained forty-five community people in tactics that hopefully would help to integrate schools in their respective communities. National experts in the fields of race relations, education, political science, sociology, and community organizing staffed the institute, teaching techniques for breaking down de facto segregated schools and how to deal with problems caused by segregation.

Four members of Seattle CORE—Ernestine Rogers, Cal Harris, Carl Klee, and Margaret Crocker—were selected to attend, along with two Seattle school principals and other leaders. In a recent interview Ernie Rogers shared her enthusiasm and the positive impressions of what she learned in those six weeks. If such an institute had been established in Seattle at that time, she felt, it might have made a big difference in dealing with Seattle's segregated schools. Unfortunately, this did not happen.[35]

In 1967 Frances White, a CORE activist who had created some of the Freedom Schools curriculum, started a program to teach Negro history to children in the Central Area. She was encouraged by a visit from Lou Smith, West Coast field secretary for CORE and an advocate of the Black Power movement. Her classes attracted mostly black children, who met each Saturday in private homes. Teachers and guest lecturers traced the historical course from ancient African civilizations to the present, outlining the contributions of black people. Out of this experience and led by Frances, CORE went on to publish the story of the first Negro pioneer in Washington State, George Washington Bush, written by Sherry Hopperstad and illustrated by Tim Martin. Copies of this booklet, *Washington's Negro pioneer . . . George Washington Bush* (based on "The Saga of George W. Bush," by Ruby El Hult), were sold to libraries and Seattle schools. The Seattle Public Library acquired ten copies. The Catholic Archdiocese spent $300 for five hundred copies to distribute throughout its school system. Frances White, determined to spread this story, was often seen standing in front of supermarkets selling the $1.00 booklet she believed would educate both children and their parents about their Negro heritage.[36]

After our boycott, some CORE members continued their involvement in the school issue by working with CAMP under the direction of Walt Hundley. Ernie Rogers and Barbara Davis recall being community liaison workers. Knocking on doors and talking with black parents about their children's education, they were able to enroll many families in the voluntary-transfer program.[37]

The school district requested that CACRC and CAMP work on enrolling students in the Voluntary Racial Transfer Program in the summer of 1967, as they had in 1966. But CAMP would not cooperate in a "year by year reaction to the problem of racial imbalance." Speaking for the civil rights leaders, Reverend Adams explained, "We are not going to commit ourselves until it is shown to us that these efforts are part of a larger, viable plan to end school de facto segregation." The black community was looking for a long-range plan that went beyond the Voluntary Racial Transfer Program. Andrew Young (a local NAACP leader, not to be confused with Martin Luther King's lieutenant from Georgia) added, "These problems [segregated schools] must be met by the Seattle Public Schools with a comprehensive plan, which we hope will be the proposed continuous progress centers."[38]

Other CORE members took a contrary approach. Questions were raised by members who no longer supported CORE's goal of integrating schools. Many black parents were beginning to question the value of the voluntary-transfer program. Did attendance at white schools necessarily mean that their children received a better education? Why should the black community carry the burden of busing their children to white schools to bring about integration while the majority of white students continued to attend their neighborhood schools? After the announcement that Horace Mann School would be closed, Ron Carson wrote, in the March 1968 *Corelator*, "It is imperative that the citizens of the Central Area be that deciding factor of the closing of schools. The citizens should realize that John Adams, Walt Hundley, and the school board can no longer decide our destiny."

The groundwork, however, had been laid for change. The school board and superintendent of schools continued to introduce programs to begin to racially balance Seattle schools. Two later studies provide detail on the challenges and turmoil that the administration and students faced in these and ensuing years. These are "Desegregating the Public Schools, Seattle,

Washington, 1954–1968," a PhD dissertation by Doris Hinson Pieroth, and "Tradition to Transformation: How Seattle Is Reinventing Its Public Schools," a report in 2002 by former *Seattle Times* editor Mindy Cameron for the Alliance for Education.

If we measure the results of our efforts to integrate the schools against what CORE achieved in the fields of employment and housing, the changes are disappointing. Would the patterns of de facto segregated schools have improved without the school boycott or the constant push by CORE, the NAACP, CACRC, and the Urban League? In those early years of the 1960s and 1970s some changes were instituted that have carried through to today. The school curriculum now includes the history and experience of black citizens. School faculties, including administrators, are no longer all white. Parents of Central Area schoolchildren became activists and now demand some input as to how their children are educated. An increase in federal dollars became available for Head Start and compensatory educational programs in the Central Area schools. Sensitivity workshops became mandatory for teachers, staff, and administrators. More white students started voluntarily transferring in at the elementary, junior high, and high school level. Mandatory busing was tried from 1978 until declared unconstitutional in 1982. An Afro-American, John Stanford, became superintendent of the Seattle schools in 1995 and another, Dr. Maria Goodloe-Johnson, in 2007. Certainly the school district, once it committed to integrating the schools, tried many different approaches. Sadly, the statistics for the school year 2007–8 indicate, particularly at the elementary level, a resegregation of Seattle schools. As of 2010, the situation does not seem to have changed substantially.

Even in the twenty-first century, in Seattle and across this nation, north and south, Americans have not been able to resolve the issue of segregated schools. Many white parents still fear that their children would get a lower-quality education at predominantly black schools. Many black parents and teachers fear that their children would not be respected or taught appropriately at predominantly white schools. As our cities and our nation become more diverse, there is an ever-greater need for children to attend schools with a mix of cultures and race. Regretfully, many Seattle citizens, including parents of school-age children, still do not view this as a priority.

PART V **Internal Matters**

9 · MAINTAINING THE ORGANIZATION

S eattle CORE's first activity, in 1961, was to support a jail-bound Freedom Rider. Jail, per se, was not his choice, but jail was Southern segregationists' response to lunch counter sit-ins, to attempts to integrate buses, and to voter registration and other civil rights activity. Dr. Martin Luther King Jr.'s "Letter from the Birmingham Jail" became one of the most famous statements of the movement. So spending time in jail for the cause of civil rights became a badge of honor to some activists. One Baptist minister on the picket line was heard to say that he "hoped that he would get arrested," apparently wanting to follow in Martin Luther King Jr.'s footsteps.[1] For some activists, jail became a measure of one's commitment to the movement. By mid-1964 the place of jail in the local civil rights movement became a divisive issue in Seattle CORE.

By then CORE demonstrations against Picture Floor Plans had gone on for months. Direct action against A&P and Tradewell had escalated to shop-ins. At times some of our demonstrators became confrontational. At the April 23, 1964, membership meeting, Elizabeth Fusco moved that "CORE members be willing to be arrested." Reggie Alleyne followed with a motion that "CORE members who are ready and willing to go to jail this weekend do so, and that specific acts leading to arrests be planned by the Executive Board." Those opposed worried that money, time, and energy would then be directed at raising bail and enlisting lawyers for legal proceedings instead of finding jobs and houses for minorities. (Similar disputes embroiled civil rights workers during the Mississippi Freedom Summer over whether to go to jail or register voters.) After a long heated debate, Reggie's motion failed, twenty-one to nineteen.[2]

This vote brought to the surface divisions in the chapter that had been brewing for months, especially around direct action involving grocery chains and the real estate industry. Going to jail "this weekend" was only one of the issues raised by a group of people within CORE who were unhappy with the leadership and wanted to take a more militant stand. Their influence was frequently a challenge to CORE rules and procedures.

As our numbers had grown, it took effort to maintain CORE's discipline of investigation and negotiation before we undertook action. Dramatic portrayals of racial injustice on the nightly news attracted many new volunteers. One member later voiced concern that Seattle CORE was "growing faster than we can assimilate the numerous capable new people and ideas," and others remembered, "It became increasingly difficult to function democratically."[3] Some newcomers were impatient with our insistence on orientation and our rules for nonviolent demonstration. Since the support of the greater Seattle community, both black and white, was essential for our projects to succeed, CORE constantly tried to overcome public perceptions that we were agitators or troublemakers. Thus, if CORE demonstrators actually were disruptive, we feared our effectiveness would be compromised. Longtime members believed our command of facts and principled negotiations were necessary tools to achieve equality in hiring, housing, and education. As time went on and many projects were under way simultaneously, our preliminary investigation and negotiation were sometimes abridged. As happened in other CORE chapters around the country, "there was a tendency to shortcut some Rules for Action—to reduce the period of negotiation to a minimum and turn to demonstrations quickly."[4] But even if negotiations were abbreviated, we did not abandon those requirements, and we always nurtured our image of respectability and reasonableness.

On many occasions at Picture Floor Plans demonstrations and at the Tradewell shop-in, a group of CORE members (whom we called "the faction") violated the CORE Rules for Action. Longtime CORE members listed numerous complaints: faction members saw no need to check in with the picket captain, let alone follow directions. They tried to provoke adverse reactions by engaging in verbal confrontation with passersby or business personnel. Members of the faction seemed to need to prove their commitment by lengthy picketing, sometimes lasting all day, in contrast to the more usual two- or three-hour shifts—commendable dedication but with the potential for escalating tensions. Val and Bettylou Valentine and Jean Adams identified numerous disruptive episodes during demonstrations, including the following:

- At Picture Floor Plans, "faction members . . . refused to follow instructions . . . For example, A. Bodin and C. Howlett returned again and again to handing out leaflets in the midst of Aurora traffic after W. Hundley and B. L. Valentine had repeatedly instructed them to cease this dangerous practice."

- "During the Tradewell shop-in . . . A. Bodin and I. Bodin both disobeyed . . . instructions against taking perishable and breakable items. This behavior was repeated after the authorized project leader, W. Hundley, called the group together and went over the instructions again."

- "Last Saturday afternoon . . . new people joined the line [who] shared the philosophy of this questionable group . . . With their addition the composition of the line changed dramatically from an orderly peaceful line to a raucous, sauntering, casual looking line . . . They in effect 'took over' and the entire tone of the demonstration was changed. Several people expressed their concern to me over the underlying tone of violence in the chants and shouts."

- "Malicious and vulgar slogans, such as 'let them see my backside' were repeatedly sung or chanted during the picketing of Picture Floor Plans offices. This practice continued after it was pointed out that such behavior is a violation of the Rules for Action . . . engaging in this behavior were E. Fusco, M. Howard, I. Bodin, J. Howlett, D. Paul, K. Cooper, and R. Sherman."[5]

- "They also share an attitude of provocation. They seem to hope something will happen. They are excited by the sight of police cars or policemen and react in a challenging or chip on the shoulder manner. It is a thrill-seeking attitude, as though they hoped to become heroes or martyrs in the movement."

- "With one or two exceptions these persons are all white. I continue to question the appropriateness of such persons shouting phrases of 'I want my freedom.'. . . etc. The vigor and relish with which they shout these phrases is also unsettling . . . as they contain elements which *cannot* be described as non-violent. These same people . . . ask more quietly 'why aren't there more Negroes out here?' . . . This question expresses an attitude of condescension."[6]

Objectionable behavior at demonstrations was not the only issue separating the faction from other members, and the division grew bitter. The faction worked to undermine CORE leadership. Esther Hall cited numerous charges she heard from members of the faction, among which were the following:

- The leadership was "too responsible"; many of them "had jobs" and therefore were not willing to go to jail.
- Correspondence from National CORE was withheld from the membership.
- Judy Esparza was forced to resign her chairmanship of the Housing Committee and her position as assistant secretary.
- The Executive Board held secret meetings and exercised illegal powers to start, stop, or frustrate direct action projects.[7]

Several members of the Executive Board did hold jobs, but all other charges against the leadership were false.

The faction operated within Seattle CORE and identified themselves as members of Seattle CORE, but at the same time they organized themselves as a separate Ad Hoc Committee. They held meetings that other CORE members were not invited to attend. At one point Ed Singler learned of such a session and showed up, only to have the group break up. One member of this group, David Paul, wrote articles for the *Seattle Observer* allegedly as a representative of CORE although not approved to do so. Chuck Howlett attended an NAACP meeting claiming to be representing CORE. He then presented himself at CORE meetings as a representative from the NAACP. Neither position was authorized by either CORE or the NAACP.

At the May 11, 1964, Executive Board meeting, Walt Hundley advised Seattle CORE against joining in Liz Fusco and Gilbert Esparza's civil lawsuit against Picture Floor Plans salesmen. Liz Fusco had been forcibly removed from the office and Gil Esparza had been hit by one of the salesmen who was trying to remove him from the office. Members were distressed at the realtor's mistreatment of Liz and Gil, but a basic tenet of nonviolence was to accept violence without retaliation (which would include a lawsuit). The majority agreed with Walt that CORE should stay out of the lawsuit.[8]

During this period of dissension, CORE members were working on a multitude of projects. Jointly with the NAACP we were negotiating to persuade Seattle schools to discontinue their contract for student transportation with Farwest cabs. Negotiations with Nordstrom and picketing at Tradewell went on through July 30, 1964. We were planning a dance to raise funds for the chapter and National CORE. The groundwork was being laid for the Drive for Equal Employment in Downtown Seattle (DEEDS), one of CORE's biggest action projects. Internal strife impeded our progress.

The faction's refusal to adhere to CORE basic principles and unwillingness to cooperate with established CORE leadership finally led to an intense confrontation. Seattle CORE set a special meeting for August 24, 1964, to address the faction's charges in an open session of the entire membership. Giving notice of this meeting, the officers (all four black) wrote to all active members: "When CORE's effectiveness in Seattle is increasing, when the power structure and other civil rights groups respect our civil rights leadership, we are being torn apart internally by bickering, vying for power . . . There can be no objection to open criticism of the leadership or program . . . or to suggestions on policy and activities openly brought before the membership . . . Our objection is against systematic private propagandizing." The letter spelled out the allegations that the faction had been circulating and named six members of the faction: David Paul, Judy Esparza, Aaron Bodin, Mona Howard, Charles Howlett, and Richard Cole. The letter made it clear how detrimental this factionalism was to CORE's ability to carry on projects.[9]

The August 24 meeting was extremely emotional. It was an open confrontation with people who not only had been working to divide the chapter but were recruiting members with lies. After heated debate, a motion was made to publicly identify and censure those who were guilty. That is exactly what a majority of the membership voted to do. Most of the dissident group finally left Seattle CORE. Some members of the faction remained in the chapter but were willing to adhere to CORE rules and procedures on projects. One white faction member left for civil rights work in Mississippi. No members of the faction remained in CORE by 1968, when the transition to Black Power occurred.

THE FBI WATCHES US

A former CORE member recently noted that the FBI used to infiltrate groups to foment discord, hoping to dilute an organization's effectiveness, cause its demise, or both. We do not know whether the FBI was involved with the faction in Seattle CORE, but it would fit FBI practices. The FBI was definitely watching us. In the mid-1950s Don Matson, an active socialist, had refused to sign a loyalty oath and was fired from his job as a chef at Frederick and Nelson's Tea Room. Don's wife, Donna, who was raising their four small children, was visited by the FBI after Don refused to sign the oath. Donna recounted that the FBI visited on a damp day when the house was filled with freshly washed diapers hanging from every laundry line she could rig in their small house. Outraged that tax dollars were being spent to investigate her family, she told the FBI agents to leave and go investigate some real criminals.[10]

Norm Johnson, a founder of Seattle CORE, had a security clearance for his job at Boeing, but in the fall of 1961 his pastor told him that the FBI had been checking on Norm's recent activities.[11] Under the Freedom of Information Act, Joan Singler recently was able to obtain her husband Ed's and her own personal FBI files, the files of two deceased CORE friends, and the four-inch-thick file on Seattle CORE. This file on our organization, COMINFIL SEATTLE CORE 100–25362, dates from October 12, 1961. Names of informants and most details are deleted, but the files indicate that over time the FBI had fifteen confidential informers reporting on our members and activities. Individuals are identified by FBI file numbers. Dates, other details, and personal relationships make it clear that from the early months of CORE two people, a husband and wife, were assigned to attend all CORE activities and report to an FBI agent.[12] These people, we thought, were our trusted friends. Collaboration between the Seattle police and the FBI is also well documented. A police department memo of April 6, 1964, mentions a request for "more and better information the FBI might have concerning CORE's intention" in demonstrating against First National Bank (a project CORE had only discussed but never planned). Two weeks later special police investigators W. Larkin and S. Dimek reported learning from "informants" about demonstrations at Picture Floor Plans.[13] An FBI summary on November 29, 1966, stated that a Seattle police officer "regularly attended CORE meetings for several months (between Nov. 1965 and Nov. 1966) and found no reason to feel that the Communist Party or other subversive element has infiltrated or is influencing the Seattle Chapter of CORE."[14]

We were not completely naïve. Even without specific proof, we assumed someone was reporting our plans. Several times we withheld details on where and when we were going to picket until the actual day of the demonstration so informers would not have advance notice. In one example, our plans for the Nordstrom's shoe-in must have been passed on to company executives. On the day before the planned demonstration, Mr. Nordstrom contacted CORE with a plan to integrate his sales force.

What we do not know is whether the informers in Seattle CORE were only reporting on us, or whether any of them were provocateurs. We cannot prove that the FBI instigated the faction in Seattle CORE, but the pattern fits. Abundant proof exists of J. Edgar Hoover's disdain for civil rights groups and of FBI infiltration tactics. FBI informers penetrated many groups—CORE, Southern Christian Leadership Conference, Black Panthers, and even the Ku Klux Klan—for the sole purpose of monitoring and eventually destroying them. Undoubtedly some members of the faction were simply carried away by their passion for racial justice. But the tactics the faction used—challenging the strong leaders, trying to discredit them on false charges, holding secret meetings, and breaking the rules of discipline at CORE demonstrations—have all the standard earmarks of an FBI operation.[15]

SOCIALIST/COMMUNIST ATTEMPT AT CONTROL

Before the faction, a previous division had occurred early in the development of the CORE chapter. A proposal to put much of the power to run the organization in the hands of an *organizing secretary* was defeated when some leaders learned that a few people active in either the Socialist Workers Party or the Communist Party were behind this plan. The struggle over who would control the chapter continued well into December 1961, especially after the successful boycott of Safeway. Writing the constitution and voting in officers became a contest between this socialist/communist group and those who were concerned that political affiliation not be part of our agenda. When the executive offices were established for our new constitution, CORE secretary Joan Singler had just delivered her first daughter, and some people assumed that she would no longer be able to carry out her duties as secretary. Those seeking to gain control had circulated this notion because they had a candidate they were planning to run for secretary, a step toward control of the chapter. Other CORE officers were alerted to this plan. At their request Joan wrote to the membership that she was capable of handling the duties of both secretary and motherhood. The FBI file records our effort, including many phone calls, to ensure that a large turnout of responsible people would attend the November meeting. Joan's letter was read, and attempts to replace her ended. Those who planned this tactic eventually left the chapter. Some other Socialists and Communists stayed on and were active in CORE. Political affiliation was never an issue as long as members agreed to CORE's Rules for Action and made a commitment to being nonviolent.

There were times when our demonstrations were perceived as too radical for some other organizations, but we were usually able to work closely with the NAACP and frequently with churches. The DEEDS project reflected a major difference of opinion between CORE and the NAACP and Urban League as to tactics but not as to goals. There were no "turf wars" such as other chapters experienced, especially in the South.

WOMEN HOLD UP HALF THE SKY

The slogan "women hold up half the sky," which comes from the 1950s Mao revolution in China, had not become well known in the United States in the early 1960s, but it describes the workload realities of Seattle

CORE. Shop-ins, real estate testing, picketing, police patrol oversight, school boycott, Freedom Schools, fundraising to support the civil rights efforts in the South—all required a great deal of work. Securing meeting space, producing meeting notices and the newsletter, typing, mimeographing, preparing envelopes, distributing thousands of materials door-to-door, recruiting and training volunteers, preparing picket signs, providing food and drinks, and staffing the CORE office every day were only some of the activities necessary to enable CORE to work on issues of employment, housing, and school discrimination. Much of this was done by women.

Seattle CORE was an all-volunteer organization. We had no paid staff. Some of the work was done in the evenings by people who had spent the day working, going to school, or searching for employment, but much was done during the day. Volunteering for CORE was like being on call seven days a week for twenty-four hours a day. Several names stand out for their continued willingness to always be available and undertake any task given them. White housewives and mothers included Mary Provo (north end mother of five), Nancy Norton, Donna Matson (mother of four), and Cara Newman. Black students were Ernie Rogers, Barbara Davis, Esther Hall, and Bettylou Valentine. Senior women of both races gave countless hours, notably Ethel Lightfoot, Sarah Lynch, and Charlotte Bosserman.

A postcard from Jean Durning gives a flavor. After describing her babies' cute new accomplishments, she wrote, "Saturday, CORE put on an all day conference on CORE methods and projects. In addition to leading discussion groups both morning & afternoon (and a breakfast meeting beforehand for final planning) I had 2 people (+ a child) from Eugene, Ore. who attended the conference staying with us overnight . . . Last Tues. and Wed. nights I had CORE committees."[16]

Most of the support work was done by people who were "free" during the day. Because of the social structure of the early 1960s, the people who were "free" during the day were women—wives, mothers, women in the home and not in the paid workforce, and students with somewhat flexible schedules. Many of these women were white. Even in the 1960s many black women were unavailable because they were employed in low-paying jobs such as domestic help and cleaning women—not because of women's liberation but because black women filled service jobs when their fathers, husbands, and brothers were excluded from jobs that would support a family.

Whatever their skin color, women in Seattle CORE may have held up more than half the sky. Over the course of a few years CORE women were at times pregnant, giving birth, or caring for newborns, infants, and toddlers at the same time that they were doing full-time volunteer work on an ongoing basis.

In some cases where both members of a couple were not equally committed to the cause, there were CORE "widows" or "widowers." The intensity and continual activity of the group led to serious wear and tear on marriages, especially when only one partner was so actively involved. For instance, Maid Adams remembers a parallel group made up of two members who called themselves "Rotten Core" and took comfort in talking to each other about the endless involvement of their spouses in CORE. Tasia Young and David Adams were these two (spouses of Dick Young, attorney and active member, and Jean Adams, committee chair). Had Rotten Core made any effort to make their group more visible, surely other spouses would have joined.

Joan Singler remembers that being active in Seattle CORE and having children just seemed to go together: "My first daughter, Carrie, was born on October 30, 1961, two days after my first picket line at the 23rd & Union Safeway store. Then in February 1962, when she was only three months old, Carrie and I flew to Chicago. There I met my mother who had flown in from Detroit. I gave Carrie and a supply of formula and diapers to my mother. She took Carrie to Detroit to visit with my Michigan relatives, while I flew on to Cincinnati for my first National CORE Convention, just across the river in Covington, Kentucky. Our daughter Sandra was born on August 18, 1965, four days after Daisy Boyetta and I completed a door-to-door canvas of black families in the Horace Mann school district, knocking on doors and trying to convince people that something had to be done about the segregated schools."

Maid Adams's son Mark was around five when he occasionally became involved with CORE activities. He has recollections of "stamping things" at CORE mailing parties, where often two or three kids were present. He also remembers going on a march downtown and being aware of picket lines.

Jean Durning recalls arriving at the A&P picket line with her preschool daughter but having picket captain Ed Singler send her home. The picket line would not look dignified with a toddler among us. Two years later the rules must have relaxed. Cara Newman pushed a stroller in the Picture Floor Plans picket line, with her baby in a hat emblazoned "Freedom."[17]

In terms of child care for CORE activities, it was usually possible to find someone to take kids since it was normal for mothers to be at home during the day. There was frequent exchange of babysitting, especially in the Madrona neighborhood,

Volunteers at CORE office, March 26, 1966: from left, Barbara Davis, Betsy Putnam with her twins, and Nancy Norton. (Seattle Post-Intelligencer original photo has been lost; clipping from Special Collections Division, UW 28887z, University of Washington Libraries)

which had an active babysitting co-op. Informal exchanges also seemed to occur naturally.

Although Seattle CORE was in the forefront of civil rights activity in the early 1960s, it was in other ways a reflection of its time. For example, although women were nearly always elected to the position of CORE secretary, no woman was ever chairman or vice chairman of the organization. This was true despite the desire of some CORE women to stand for election and lead the organization. When Bettylou Valentine wanted to run for chairman, two male CORE officers informed her that CORE had to be represented by a man. No woman led negotiating teams. Negotiations were always male-to-male, despite the fact that CORE women may have organized and led the investigations, compiled the statistics, written the reports, and voted for the action. Some women participated in negotiating teams, but usually as note-takers and never as the designated leaders. CORE's male leaders assumed—probably correctly—that they would be speaking to white male businessmen who would not take women seriously.

CORE's battle was for a more just racial society; gender had not yet become a recognized issue.

RAISING FUNDS

CORE volunteers used their personal typewriters to cut mimeograph masters for fliers printed on the Unitarians' machine in Don Matson's basement, and they met in space donated by the YMCA or the YWCA. Even with in-kind contributions, there were many costs: materials for picket signs, postage for mass mailings, hot coffee for winter picketers, and funds for Seattle's Freedom Riders. Of high importance, National CORE constantly needed financial support for its work in the South.

Raising money was a regular challenge, while we simultaneously continued direct action campaigns for equal employment, housing, and schools. Active CORE members paid dues of $2.00 a year (equal to about $15 today) and were frequently urged to donate more. Ed O'Keefe, as mentioned, contributed $10–$25 each month; sometimes he gave $80, $100, or even $150. Many individuals and groups contributed, especially churches—for example, at one point Blaine Memorial Methodist Church, Nisei division, contributed $82, and for several years Unitarians for Social Justice gave close to $100.[18] Dollar amounts would be seven and a half times larger in 2010 dollars.[19] In addition to dues and contributions, CORE put on fundraisers.

A few memorable events provided publicity in the wider community as well as bringing in money. As described in chapter 1, early in 1962 Seattle CORE received a copy of the 30-minute film *Freedom Ride*, which depicted the integrated groups who rode a Greyhound or Trailways bus across the South to challenge state segregation laws. The violent southern reaction to these rides focused the national spotlight on the segregation in interstate travel—which despite being outlawed by the Supreme Court was still widespread. *Freedom Ride* was screened at churches and other locales in Seattle and around the state, where contributions were collected. Proceeds were dedicated to support Ray Cooper and Jon Schaefer and sent to National CORE for other Freedom Riders.

BIG NAMES COME TO TOWN

In May 1962, Seattle CORE was informed that comedian Dick Gregory, who had a regular gig in San Francisco, had volunteered to fly up on a Sunday and perform a fundraiser for the benefit of both National and Seattle CORE. The date was set for Sunday, June 24. Within a few short weeks the Seattle chapter arranged to rent the Moore Theatre and hired Earl Kelly, drama coach at Ballard High School, to organize the event. With lots of publicity and many hours of work, CORE sold enough tickets to nearly fill the Moore. Three local bands volunteered to perform at this fundraiser— the Gentrys, the John Lewis Trio, and the Billy Tolles Combo. But after their names were printed on our posters, the Musicians Union barred them; by union rules they could not play more than six days in a row.

Shortly before the June 24 performance, four CORE members (Norm Johnson, Joan Miracle, Ed and Joan Singler) visited Dizzy Gillespie, who was playing at Jazz Alley in Seattle, to ask him to step in and play at the fundraiser featuring his friend Dick Gregory. Gillespie agreed to do it if the Musicians Union agreed, which it did; the six-day restriction did not bind an out-of-state performer. But CORE could not advertise his participation due to his contract with Parnells (a jazz club) and Musicians Union rules.

The morning of the fundraiser Ed Singler and Norm Johnson met Dick Gregory's plane and checked him into a motel. Norm and the Singlers then took him to visit the World's Fair, where he noticed black employees in many positions—as Century 21 management had twice promised us.[20] At lunch in the restaurant atop the Space Needle, Joan Singler recalls that Gregory ordered a Scotch and water. The waitress apologetically explained that Washington State did not allow the sale of liquor on Sunday. "Well, all right," said Gregory. "Bring me an ice tea, but make it look as much like a Scotch as you can."

Poster advertising Dick Gregory's show, printed before Musicians Union rules required the bands to drop out, which resulted in their replacement by Dizzy Gillespie's band. (Singler, personal collection)

C.O.R.E.
presents

dick Gregory

MOORE
THEATER
SUNDAY
JUNE 24
8:30 P.M.

Illustration on program for Dick Gregory performance. (CORE, Matson Collection)

That evening, backstage at the Moore Theatre, with the audience already assembled, Dizzy Gillespie declared he was not going to go on. CORE organizers were frantic. But his pianist knew Dizzy's moods. He told the other musicians, "We'll just start, he'll come on—you'll see." They did, he did, and the crowd cheered as Dizzy Gillespie and his band opened the show.[21]

Dick Gregory's opening line was that he checked in to the Olympic Hotel and they offered him a room on the top floor. "No way," he said. "Put me on the second. If there's a fire, I'm not going to jump with nobody looking like me to hold the net."[22] It was a line he could adapt to any city he was in; all firefighters everywhere were white. Gregory turned psychic pain into a hall full of laughter. The show was hailed as "a tremendous success." The *Corelator* reported, "Gregory and Gillespie put on a terrific show" and thanked Tim Martin, Don Matson, Norm Johnson, Erv Smith, and Joan Singler for their "overwhelming contributions and self-sacrifices."[23] Costs included taking Dizzy Gillespie and his band to dinner at the "Spanish Village" at the World's Fair. Net proceeds provided $1,500 for National CORE, plus enough for Seattle to buy a much needed mimeograph machine of our own.[24]

Early the next year, in February 1963, National CORE notified its West Coast affiliates that famous author James Baldwin would do a six-city speaking tour to raise money for CORE. Since his usual speaking fee was $500, the tour meant he was donating $3,000 to the cause.[25] Baldwin had already published *Go Tell It on the Mountain, Notes of a Native Son, Giovanni's Room, Nobody Knows My Name,* and *Another Country;* in 1963 his "Letter from a Region in My Mind," originally appearing in the *New Yorker*, was published as *The Fire Next Time*.

Tim Martin chaired the local committee for Baldwin's Seattle lecture, to be held May 6, 1963. The committee began with trepidation, unsure how it could possibly pull together a quality event for a national figure. We had no money to hire a professional event organizer. It was up to us. How would we generate adequate publicity? A local sign maker refused to print a banner publicizing a Negro, whether famous or not. After getting each store manager's permission, Norm Johnson put up posters in store windows along Broadway on Capitol Hill, an upscale shopping destination. As soon as Norm was out of sight, some managers pulled down the posters.[26] Tim and his volunteers were able to rent the Masonic Temple (now The Egyptian movie theater), print and distribute advertising posters, and arrange for selling tickets (adults $2, students $1) at six different book or music stores in Seattle, Bellevue, and Burien. CORE members Joan and Hugh Miracle hosted a dinner reception at their home for patrons—people who contributed $10.00 or more—to meet Mr. Baldwin before his lecture.[27]

More than 1,400 people packed the main floor and the balconies of the Masonic Temple. Backstage at the theater, CORE member Jean Adams remembers seeing Baldwin, a small man, peering at the waiting crowd. She politely asked, "How are you?" to which Baldwin responded, "Scared to death." Shocked at his reply, to her lasting regret she could think of nothing reassuring to say to alleviate his stage fright.

James Baldwin began his talk by forbidding any taping of his remarks, which were copyrighted as material for an upcoming book. He said living in New York slums was expensive. Richer people would look down on him for wearing a $100 suit, but it cost him the same as a $300 suit since his possessions were stolen so often that he had to replace a suit three times. To escape the tenements, he used a ruse to rent a better New York City apartment. He would identify himself as the butler making arrangements for "a rich man who would move in when he got back from Europe." He then would live in the apartment for months as the butler until the landlord discovered no white employer would be coming. Then Baldwin would repeat the subterfuge to find a new apartment. Tiring of such tricks, he found refuge by moving to Paris. But now, he explained,

"JAMES BALDWIN IS ONE OF THE
BRASHEST, BRIGHTEST, MOST PROMISING
YOUNG WRITERS IN AMERICA."
—TIME

Seattle CORE presents

JAMES BALDWIN

MASONIC TEMPLE
MONDAY, MAY 6-8 P.M.

Tickets : $2.00 students $1.00 (UNRESERVED)

HARTMANS, UNIV. DIST.
LITTLE RECORD MART
AVAILABLE AT   BELL BOOK AND CANDLE
MAISON BLANC
LEA'S BOOK SHOP, UNIV. VILLAGE
FARMER MUSIC, BURIEN

Poster advertising James Baldwin's lecture; many copies were torn down by proprietors who had given us permission to post them in their store windows. (Singler, personal collection)

he felt compelled to leave the comfort of France to participate in the epic struggle for civil rights that his people were waging in the United States.[28]

A sixteen-year-old CORE member, Carole Dianne Smith, did not hear his talk. Standing at the back of the auditorium just before he was introduced, she was available for a task that arose suddenly: Baldwin needed his suitcase packed so he could leave immediately for his next city. Carole drove her beat-up old car to his hotel and packed his belongings—she still remembers his navy blue silk pajamas and that his Swedish toothpaste, called Vademecum, struck her as very cosmopolitan. Looking back from the present security-conscious age, she is amazed that she was allowed into his hotel room without much question.[29]

Baldwin's speech helped increase CORE's visibility among the audience and the wider Seattle population. A recent critic comments on "Baldwin's seething insights and directives, so disturbing to the white liberals and black moderates of his day."[30] His Seattle speech had a similar reaction. The *Corelator* reported, "Responses of the audience ranged from anger at Mr. Baldwin's approach to the problem to slight disappointment in this same approach. Which probably goes to show why Mr. Baldwin is such a controversial yet highly regarded commentator on the struggle of the Negro in this country."[31] Financially, his lecture was a success. Ticket sales and patron contributions brought in over $2,000 for civil rights efforts, most of which was sent to National CORE.

Not to raise money but for publicity, James Farmer, founder and national director of CORE, came to Seattle in October 1962 and gave a public address at the New Hope Baptist Church. The November 1962 *Corelator* reported that Farmer "gave us a dynamic . . . glimpse into the civil rights struggle in other parts of the country . . . 97 restaurants have been desegregated in North Carolina. [He] introduced many citizens of Seattle to the meaning and purposes of CORE."

Three years later, in December 1965, when both CORE and Mr. Farmer's name were well known, he returned to Seattle for a fundraiser held at Mount Zion Church. It would benefit both CORE and the American Civil Liberties Union (ACLU). Dinner tickets were sold at $15 a couple, $10 single, or, for a sponsor, $25. According to the advance publicity, "Only 400 people will be able to attend." Although some 350 people bought reservations in advance, and tables were set for 380, "about 460 eager patrons showed up. There was a lot of confusion in setting up tables and serving but no one seemed to mind too much." Hardworking CORE volunteers included Frances White, in charge of tickets, and Herb Harris and Don Matson, the chefs. Don and Herb managed the Herculean task of planning and cooking the whole meal, including a scramble to feed eighty last-minute unexpected guests. This "Bill of Rights Day" dinner brought in $4,300, of which $2,000 went to National CORE, $1,000 to the ACLU, and the remainder to Seattle CORE.[32]

Seattle CORE also publicized visiting dignitaries who raised money or publicity for other civil rights groups. Reverend Ralph Abernathy addressed a civil rights rally on October 15, 1963, at the Opera House, sponsored by the American Friends Service Committee. Roy Wilkins spoke on September 27, 1964, for the NAACP. In September 1966 Sammy Davis Jr. performed for the NAACP, and James Meredith appeared for the ACLU. Herb Hill came for the NAACP on March 3, 1967.

OTHER VENTURES

Some of our fundraising was dedicated specifically for National CORE's work in the South. For example, for several years we sold CORE Christmas cards. In the spring of 1962 we sold tote bags made in Haywood, Tennessee, to support displaced farmers. One year, folk-style dolls made in Sunflower, Mississippi, were sold for Christmas gifts. Hal Newman and Barbara Davis chaired CORE's solicitation drive to "adopt a civil rights worker." Churches, clubs, unions, and individuals in Seattle gave a total of $1,300—enough to support a civil rights worker in Mississippi for the whole year of 1965.[33]

CORE sponsored a number of dances as fundraisers. Musicians Al Larkins and Floyd Standifer offered to play for CORE events several times. In what the *Corelator* called CORE's "first public social event of the year," we put on a cabaret-style dance on August 9, 1964, downtown at the Chamber of Commerce auditorium. Flo Martin and her committee enlisted "a real fine group of musicians . . . and top notch entertainment," all donated for the cause. All CORE members were urged to sell tickets, at $2.00 per person, and to volunteer as waiters, bartenders, and so on. Ads urged, "Let's all do the Freedom Twist!" Six months later, on February 21, 1965, CORE held another cabaret dance for $2.00, advertised "with Live Music" at the Norselander (the building at 300 Third Avenue West that later became the Mountaineers Clubhouse and is now gone). This event, the night before the George Washington's Birthday holiday, was successful: "We had a ball. Over three hundred people attended and we cleared $500." A repeat of the event, a cabaret dance on Saturday, August 28, 1965, "was really terrific [and] enabled us to pay a few bills." On Sunday, May 29, 1966, the evening before Memorial Day, CORE again held a cabaret dance at the Norselander, again charging $2.00 for tickets, with music by the Floyd Standifer Group. On June 3, 1967, there was a fourth cabaret dance at the Norselander with live music; this time tickets cost $5.00 a couple or $3.00 for singles.[34]

A different sort of fundraiser was Frances White's lawn party in August 1966, with music and refreshments. It lasted from midafternoon into the evening. The *Corelator* reported, "Attempts to raise money through CORE parties have been very successful . . . Anyone with additional moneymaking schemes or gimmicks, please call the CORE office."[35]

The most persistent theme, repeated in nearly every *Corelator*, was simply a request for funds: "Have you paid your dues? $2.00 please." "Part of your obligation is financial support of this chapter." "You can become a 'Friend of CORE' by contributing $2.00 (or more if you can afford it)." "There have been many appeals in this newsletter for money. Although I wish we did not have to spend time soliciting for all manner of funds, it takes money to help keep the drive for integration a meaningful drive. THANK YOU." "Pay Your Dues, D_m It!" "We need more money, so dig a little deeper." "CON-

TRIBUTIONS NEEDED. Sound like a familiar subject? Well it is an ever present one." On August 8, 1967, a financial statement showed outstanding bills of $282.61 and funds in the bank of $42.41—"one of the most helpful things you can do at this point is to send money."[36]

10 · BLACK POWER AND SEATTLE CORE

Black Power! Two words that, until the mid-1960s, were seldom spoken in the same sentence. A revolutionary idea that took the racial lexicon to a new level in terms of self-identity—from colored to Negro to Black. The idea that African Americans had power, were powerful, could exert power, was a call to action that challenged the nonviolence of the 1960s civil rights movement.

The first mention of Black Power in Seattle CORE appeared in the July 24, 1966, *Corelator*, reporting on an all-day retreat on July 23 at Seattle University. Participants reaffirmed CORE's mandate of nonviolent direct action and a "vital role for Caucasians to play" and deplored the media's distortion of the Black Power slogan. We endorsed James Farmer's definition as meaning that CORE must be "building equality and trying to organize the Negro community politically and economically." We also approved the statement of Floyd McKissick, who became the leader of National CORE in 1966, that it should mean "not black supremacy, but a unified black voice reflecting black pride."[1]

The July retreat foreshadowed a lengthy period in the mid- to late 1960s of ongoing confusion, contradictions, and mixed feelings about the term "Black Power" and its meaning. This was true at the national, as well as the local, level and was not confined to CORE. Many civil rights and other groups were grappling with this confusion. To put this complexity into perspective, it must be remembered that this was a time of multiple simultaneous revolutions—the movements for civil rights, Black Power, black nationalism, peace, women, the United Farmworkers, and against the Vietnam War. Powerful voices from youth, both black and white, were saying they "weren't going to take it anymore."

It was an unprecedented time of upheaval in the status quo at every level. Civil rights work in the South had involved ever-present danger with massive marches, police brutality, and arrests. In Mississippi in one year alone, four civil rights workers had been killed and four critically wounded, eighty Freedom Summer workers beaten, one thousand arrested, thirty-seven churches bombed, and thirty black homes burned or bombed. Thousands rioted in Watts in 1965 and in Detroit in 1967. In a different vein, there was the Motown Sound and, in 1968, James Brown's influential "I'm Black and I'm Proud." Dress codes changed dramatically, with many blacks wearing dashikis and intricate head wraps. Giant Afros appeared seemingly overnight. Learning Swahili was favored, African names were taken, and slave names were replaced with an "X." On the West Coast a contrasting revolution was taking place in San Francisco, with huge demonstrations against the war in Vietnam, the 1967 "Summer of Love," and counterculture events of rock festivals, light shows, the Grateful Dead. Street and university protests led to police brutality and arrests. Hippies grew shoulder-length hair. Tie-dyed shirts and blue jeans were everywhere. Across the nation, people of all ages were affected by these changes, but especially youth from all backgrounds. A recent review noted, "the world seems to have 'spun faster' in 1968 than in neighboring years. Authority everywhere was under furious attack. The civil rights movement was fracturing between nonviolent and violent strategies."[2]

Seattle experienced all these changes, including a Black Panther office that opened at Thirty-Fourth and Union in the Madrona neighborhood. At that time Madrona was an economically and racially mixed community, predominantly black. The local Madrona school functioned well, encompassing everyone—black, Asian American, and white—and was led by a powerful multiracial PTA (including Aki Kurose, Jeri Ware, Diana Bower, Frances Carr, Sheila Bodemer, Carol Richman, and Roger Sale).

University of Washington students were agitating politically—with a Black Student Union, efforts to initiate a black studies program, and a chapter of Students for a Democratic Society (SDS). There was pressure for a women's studies program and for more women instructors. The University of Washington experimental college sprang into being, at that time considered a radical alternative educational direction. Numerous coffeehouses were filled with intense political discussions. Various alternative newspapers arose, such as the Helix.

It was the time of Stokely Carmichael, H. Rap Brown, Malcolm X, Elijah Muhammad, and Huey Newton, all espousing ideologies that drastically departed from long-standing integrationist beliefs and policies. In comparison, the NAACP, the Urban League, and CORE all seemed pretty tame. The Student Nonviolent Coordinating Committee (SNCC) was in transition to becoming a Black Power organization.

CORE, locally and nationally, was under pressure from these militant forces, leading to serious questioning of our commitment to nonviolence, the negotiation process, and interracial cooperation as a way to bring about change. In Seattle CORE, members could look to a long list of accomplishments in bringing about significant improvements in employment, housing, and education. But we also realized that an enormous amount of work still urgently needed to be done. These factors contributed to turmoil in beliefs and scrutiny of tactics within our chapter, with many CORE members questioning what it would take to bring about equality—nonviolence or "by any means necessary"? Perspectives differed. To many whites, working in integrated teams was important to demonstrate their strongly held beliefs in equality and as evidence that the American democratic ideal was achievable. Some whites also saw integrated efforts as reassurance that they individually were free of dreaded racism. For some blacks, interaction with whites was mainly useful to the extent that it helped in gaining improvements for black people. Interacting with whites was not a novelty; black people had been doing so all their lives. If black people were hopeful, they were also skeptical as to whether whites could be trusted. These concerns were rarely voiced to white members but were evidenced in subtle behavior. As Floyd McKissick said during a Seattle visit, "Dealing with white people is like holding a bag of snakes. Only one of them might be poisonous, but if you reach your hand in the bag, you don't know what you're gonna get."[3]

Also affecting CORE was President Johnson's War on Poverty. Beginning late in 1965 War on Poverty programs addressed issues that had been primary concerns of CORE: jobs for blacks, housing, education, voter registration, transportation, and youth services. These poverty projects had the advantage of paid staffs and local offices. It was a mixed blessing that many active Seattle CORE members were hired full-time by these programs, resulting in excellent leadership for the new agencies but a serious drain in workers and experience for CORE. A prime example was the appointment of CORE's chairman, Walt Hundley, to design and organize the Central Area Motivation Program (CAMP)—one of the most successful poverty programs anywhere in the United States. A similar example was Ed Singler's appointment to the Western regional office of the War on Poverty program in late 1965, for which he and Joan moved to San Francisco. In this rapidly changing landscape, more questions arose on the role that CORE could play. In August 1966 Seattle CORE formed a committee to "keep abreast of local poverty programs and how they might affect civil rights in Seattle." Skepticism, apprehension, and distrust were present in our concerns. We had been pressing for such federal programs, and the nationwide civil rights movement was partly responsible for their existence. But none of us knew what to expect from them.

There followed a sustained period of uncertainty, confusion, and frustration. CORE now was left with less vital leadership. It is apparent, in looking back, that the organization began a slow death around 1966. We lacked clear direction and goals, which led to fewer projects, which in turn led to fewer participants, which led to fewer donations. In part, we were surviving on momentum from previous successes. Some attrition is normal in any enterprise. For instance, after Bettylou Valentine was awarded her master's degree from the University of Washington, she and Val moved to St. Louis. Jean Durning, with her husband increasingly involved in politics, had no time to volunteer after their third baby began to crawl. Other members drifted off. They took jobs, moved out of the area, and became involved in other groups, leaving an organization that was depleted but did not realize it. Unable to afford the recently doubled rent, in February 1967 we gave up our rundown office at Twenty-Second and Union and temporarily rented space in a member's home at Sixteenth and Union. Even that small rent was not sustainable, and the CORE files were moved to storage in Frances White's basement (until later donated to the University of Washington Libraries and identified as accession number 1563).

It was the beginning of the end of an era focused on civil rights and integration and the dawn of an era of insistence on black identity and self-determination. National CORE, while trying not to offend whites personally or jeopardize their significant financial support, directed local chapters to become more involved in the black community and to work with black groups, suggesting more militancy. The role of whites was not spelled out on either the national or the local level.

TURNING POINT

The CORE national conference held in July 1967 in Oakland, California, marked a crucial turning point for the organization. Four Seattle CORE members attended, two black and two white. The white members, Mary Provo and Jean Adams, gave their votes to Frances White, one of the black members, the other black member being John Cornethan. Three Seattle votes supported amending the National CORE constitution. The amendment passed: the definition of CORE as a "multiracial" organization was replaced by "CORE is a mass membership organization to implement the concept of Black Power for black people."[4] Self-determination as expressed by Black Power became the overriding direction. Integration was no longer a goal of CORE.

The Seattle CORE meeting held on July 27, after the July national conference, focused on this change of direction. Chairman John Cornethan, an integrationist, did not support the changes and felt the local chapter could continue with long-established policies. In support of this position, the July 1967 *Corelator* republished Seattle CORE's 1966 resolutions that had reaffirmed nonviolence and the vital role of white members. John expressed support for the aspect of Black Power dealing with economic improvement but objected to changes he believed were antiwhite.[5] Emotions at our July 27 meeting were intense. Twenty-two blacks and sixteen whites were in attendance, along with the West Coast regional director, Lou Smith. Smith made it clear that Seattle CORE could not reject national policy and retain the CORE name. A few members spoke against Black Power, but after Smith's persuasive presentation, the voice vote to go along with national policy passed without objection.[6]

At the next Seattle CORE meeting, in August 1967, members called for Cornethan's resignation because of his refusal to implement national policy. After heated discussion, Cornethan left the meeting, which was taken over by the treasurer, Ed Russell. Members voted to hold a special meeting September 7 to impeach the chairman. An interim all-black governing committee of Ed Russell, Ira Oakes, Barbara Davis Robertson, and Bob Redwine met to outline Black Power goals to be presented to the membership. They held that "whites who accept the black-power philosophy have the primary role of working to remove prejudice . . . in the white community."[7]

This was the first time this sentiment had been expressed. Most whites were stunned and disbelieving that such a change applied to them. It was inconceivable to people who had given so much and believed so fervently in this interracial cause that they were no longer needed or wanted. Whites found this transition startling, despite a series of conflicting messages over the previous two years regarding whites' participation. Whites wondered if they could be involved at any level, even fundraising.

In September 1967 CORE voted John Cornethan out as head of the Seattle chapter and selected Ed Russell as the new chair. Despite the emotional intensity, members did not disparage John. The next *Corelator* explained, "replacing the Chairman should *not* be construed as criticism of Mr. Cornethan as a person, but rather . . . desire [to] reflect National CORE policy."[8]

Through this uncertain period and acting on momentum, a group of half a dozen blacks and whites with long-standing personal relationships continued to work on projects that had previously been planned or were in process. As difficult as it may be to understand, this cooperation seemed very natural to those involved. In November and December 1967 these few CORE members worked diligently together on a booth at a community bazaar, selling products from a southern cooperative and holiday cards from the National CORE office. They were proud that the CORE booth was located immediately next to the display by Black Muslim artist Gregory X. Participating in the bazaar was an attempt to meet national expectations of cooperating with more black community organizations. The same handful

John Cornethan, CORE president in the challenging year of 1967, who tried to accommodate both black and white membership. (From 1966 group photo of civil rights leaders with Congressman Adams, Brock Adams Photograph Collection, Special Collections Division, UW 28888z, University of Washington Libraries)

All-black interim
committee officers,
September 13, 1967:
Ira Oakes, Barbara
Davis Robertson, Bob
Redwine, and Ed Russell.
(Vic Condiotty/Seattle
Times photograph)

of blacks and whites raised money for black students to attend a Black Power conference in California. The small group also sponsored "an evening with George Washington Bush" to publicize and promote our recent booklet on the first Negro pioneer in the state of Washington. Such was the dedication of these members that it seemed normal, even though CORE's policy was changing, to work together on projects that furthered the group's goals.[9]

It was a strange time of transition not fully comprehended by anyone in Seattle CORE. It was an intense time of heightened awareness of black identity with a lot of questions in the black community. Was someone black enough? What did it mean if a woman did not wear an Afro? Any black man involved with a white woman faced serious criticism. Commitment to getting an education began to be suspect as maybe "too white." Exclusively black groups like the Black Panthers and Black Muslims had power and energy and presented persuasive examples of the advantage of all-black organizations. These groups influenced a belief that only blacks could effectively produce results for the black community and affected the direction of Seattle CORE. Almost inevitably, CORE too went in this direction, and whites drifted away.

The March 1968 *Corelator* carried the headline "CORE ALL BLACK," with a short paragraph stating that the previous meeting had decided, "In order for CORE to function in the community it must be an all black organization. It was agreed by most of the people there, that this was the best thing." As the tone of this quotation indicates, the separation was not done with anger or hostility but as a practical matter.

Without a doubt some African Americans breathed a sigh of relief to have an all-black CORE and relished the banishment of whites as long overdue, while some had mixed feelings and serious reservations. White CORE members had varying reactions to the decision that CORE needed to be black—that only blacks could work successfully in the black community toward black self-determination. Some did not see the necessity of this change in policy and left feeling hurt. Some were sad that the organization they had devoted so much time and energy to was no longer the same CORE. Some resented being excluded racially. A few accepted the necessity and appropriateness of black self-determination and the need for whites to work on white attitudes.

CORE Black Power button from the late 1960s, replacing Freedom Now and Equal Sign buttons of the early 1960s. (Maid Adams personal collection)

In that same March 1968 *Corelator*, Jean Adams placed a "Notice to All White CORE Members and Friends of CORE," acknowledging the change as healthy and stating, "It is neither separatist or racist for black people to want to come together in privacy and . . . work out their own problems." The notice continued, "This leaves whites with the greatest challenge and opportunity of our lives . . . to take action to combat white racism . . . and make a more significant contribution to racial justice than we have made so far." Whites were invited to a meeting on March 28 at the East Madison YMCA. *No one came.*

Jean went on to form Act Now and compiled a list of actions that whites could do to combat racism. She met with a number of university students and individuals in the (white) north end on the same subject. Whites dealing with whites, however, did not seem as exciting as recent civil rights activities. After a few months of slow or nonexistent progress, she abandoned this attempt and turned her attention to other groups such as the peace movement and the United Farmworkers. Other white CORE members turned to volunteering with the antiwar movement, the grape boycott, the women's movement, and the environmental movement. A few joined a short-lived group, the Committee to Defend the Right of the Black Panther Party to Exist!

Various groups, some white, others black, developed spontaneously. Soul

Search, Black and White Concern, We, Grass Roots Committee, CAP-I, Voodoo House, and Join Hands were just a few.

In CORE's final months, various combinations of African Americans met to try to fill the void left from impeaching a chairman, the loss of significant black leadership to local poverty programs, and a general loss of energy due to major changes in direction. In November Ed Russell was elected chairman as part of an all-black slate, but a couple of months later he resigned. One longstanding black CORE member who tried to bridge this transition was Barbara Davis Robertson. She remembers well-intentioned but inexperienced people who, she felt, did not know enough to pull the collapsing CORE together. It was a shell of an organization by that time, with fewer members, a lack of projects to focus on, a shortage of money, and the competition of other, more viable and exciting organizations. Most attempts to revive CORE were made by people just entering the organization, who were not familiar with the realities at the time. Mike Ross proposed a voter registration campaign—a worthy project—but was unable to get enough members to carry it out. CORE was in debt, yet the new treasurer proposed an unrealistic annual budget of more that $7,850, which would include renting an office and hiring a secretary. Seattle CORE had never had that kind of money at any time in its existence! So even though some people stepped up to revive CORE, none had the burning desire or the experience to resurrect the dying organization. Like Barbara, they left for other efforts on newer and more effective paths.[10]

The last *Corelator*, April 1968, announced the election of Mike Ross as chairman of Seattle CORE and included a plea for additional active members.[11] It announced that Floyd McKissick, national director, would speak at Garfield High School on April 17 "to discuss Blackness and the struggle for liberation." A fundraiser reception would follow at the home of Carla Chotzen, a white CORE member. With our history of working together, CORE members saw no contradiction in this interracial gathering of longtime fellow activists. Barbara Davis Robertson, a member of the all-black interim committee, remembers being at the Chotzens' that evening. She recalls, "Nobody was angry. We liked, respected and appreciated those whites who had worked so hard and done so much. But we wanted to be all black to control our destiny."[12]

In their history of National CORE, Meier and Rudwick state that Seattle CORE was one of the few chapters during the transition to Black Power that "did not witness attacks upon their white members."[13] While there were intense verbal disagreements on policy, these were never physical and did not become personal. It is not surprising, then, that a number of these early interracial relationships continued with genuine and sustained friendships for decades.

One analyst of the era put it this way: "As is often the case in social movements, especially radical movements, one generation of activists often gives way to another. Parties or organizations change as members rethink their position on fundamental political questions and re-strategize their approach for social change."[14] In Seattle too, changing times required a different relevancy. CORE faded away sometime in 1968 due to lack of continuity of leadership, money, and participants and also due to the powerful, changing times. Activists were attracted to new organizations that were doing things in new ways. CORE's ending marked the passing of an era and the birth of a new one.

EPILOGUE · LEGACY AND CHALLENGES

S alman Rushdie, internationally famous novelist, quoting an unidentified history professor, tells us, "You should never write history until you can hear the people speak . . . After all, if you can't hear them speak, you don't know enough about them, and can't tell their story."[1]

The four authors of the book you are now reading are the speakers. Through the preceding material we speak. We also made decisions, produced studies, walked on picket lines, organized boycotts, sang songs, and sat-in. We convey all the reality of 1960s civil rights history in Seattle to today's readers. In doing this we not only recount the events of which we were a part but also offer an analysis of what our activities meant at the time and our contribution to an ongoing process and a look ahead to the challenges still facing us. You hear us tell our own story.

In the first area of focus, employment, the Congress of Racial Equality achieved two goals. Our conscious intention was to secure jobs for African Americans in all sectors of the economy—as clerks in supermarkets and department stores, office workers (not only janitors), restaurant workers (not only dishwashers), taxi and truck drivers, municipal employees, workers in the trades, and members in unions. It took many years to achieve these modest goals, and sometimes the real numbers achieved were small compared with the need. But today the population born after 1960 can hardly imagine the all-white or very segregated employment scene in Seattle before CORE took to the streets.

The second goal was in some part a by-product of the first but may have been more important. That is, CORE made Seattle more aware of discrimination in employment and other areas. CORE studies of employment, with their hard numbers and facts, forced the broader population to see that Seattle was part of a discriminatory society different only in degree from places with less savory reputations. Seattle is known for process. CORE's employment activities were the beginning of a process of self-knowledge about race relations.

The employment battle CORE began in the 1960s was largely successful. As early as August 1963, through successful negotiations and direct action, Seattle CORE had produced over 250 jobs for African Americans, more in that period than any federal, state, or city agency concerned with racial discrimination. Most of these represented breakthroughs in job categories and better wages for black workers, particularly in the mercantile and service sectors. Through our efforts, we were able to prove to employers and personnel departments that hiring minorities would not deter business.[2]

Now the battle for gainful employment has shifted, and the importance of education has grown. Economic success and job growth are in the areas of technology and entrepreneurship. African Americans in the early twenty-first century are largely absent from this technological society. As job demands become more complicated, the challenge is to recognize that race, education, and poverty are intricately interwoven and need to be dealt with simultaneously if we are to level the playing field and become a more just society.

CORE's second area of concern was "open" housing—making housing available to anyone of any race anywhere a person could afford to buy. Legally, the freedom of African Americans and other minorities to buy housing outside the Central District has been achieved thanks to the efforts of CORE and others—the Fair Housing Listing Service, the NAACP, state and municipal legislation, and most decisively by the national Civil Rights Act of 1968. Racial discrimination in the selling of housing has been outlawed. Nevertheless, Seattle, like most American cities, remains largely segregated in its housing patterns. Economic forces remain primary. As the *Seattle Times* noted in 2001, "gentrification, the price paid last decade for high property values, has dispersed blacks away from Seattle's Central Area and toward South King County."[3] Dr. Henry McGee pointed out "a massive shift in the racial landscape . . . In 1990 there were about three times as many black residents as whites in the Central Area," but by 2006 "the once 'black' community is now more than fifty percent Euro American, and probably . . . less than thirty percent African American."[4] Today's patterns are affected by earlier "white flight" to the suburbs and by the current return of an economic elite back into the central city. Today's gentrification presents a stark contrast to earlier times, with great wealth now required to buy million-dollar homes in a neighborhood that has become increasingly white as black families move to more affordable housing in the south end. The African American ghetto of the 1960s, the Central Area, is now a majority white area.[5]

Income has become the decisive issue for people of any race who work in the city but cannot afford to live near their jobs. Those with no jobs or minimum-wage jobs often can afford no housing at all. This growing homeless population is disproportionately African American. Providing shelter, social services, training, and work has become a major problem for American society. What is needed is not in question, but whether we as a society have the will to make the all-out effort necessary to resolve the structural problems fueling homelessness seems increasingly unlikely.

CORE's emphasis on racial integration in housing lives on in some federal programs such as Hope VI, which is helping public-housing authorities to build racially and economically integrated communities, including Seattle's NewHolly, Rainier Vista, and Highpoint. These developments represent the early stages of experimentation. Will they succeed? We may not know for decades.

Without racially and economically integrated communities, Seattle's more than fifty-year history of segregated schools will continue. Fifty-four years after the nation's Supreme Court outlawed segregation in the nation's schools, a series in the *Seattle Times* was headlined "The Resegregation of Seattle's Schools."[6]

CORE, the NAACP, and the Urban League all recognized Seattle schools as segregated and inadequate in the 1960s. CORE analyzed the situation and presented a detailed proposal for integration, as did the other organizations. Anthropologists, social workers, planners, and other university faculty joined community people to urge the Seattle School Board to deal early and decisively with school integration in Seattle, within the first decade following the Supreme Court mandate. Proposals for integration relied on redistricting, some subsidized housing, building new schools to serve integrated populations, and shifting integrated populations of students en masse from school to school through the system. CORE organized a school boycott and Freedom Schools to bring the issue to the broader community and to make African American parents aware of what the Court said their children deserved.

The school board moved slowly from its position that there was "no problem" to one that called for African American parents to voluntarily integrate their children at the family's expense. In 1966 the school district moved to pay for transportation and gradually tried other programs. It was not until 1978, a decade after Seattle CORE ceased to exist and almost twenty-five years after the Supreme Court desegregation decision, that the school board instituted a mandatory, citywide busing plan.

CORE's activities to end segregated schools in the 1960s led to training teachers in diversity, to black history in the curriculum, and to an increase of African Americans in school district administrative positions. It did not achieve integration in the Seattle schools. The recent *Seattle Times* special series on Seattle schools quotes the American Education Research Association as follows: "Studies clearly show that diverse schools contribute to improved cross-racial understanding, a reduction in prejudice and a willingness to live and work in diverse settings."[7] The challenge now is how to achieve this desirable goal. Education affects income, income affects housing, and race affects education, income, and housing. All these factors are intertwined. As Michael DeBell, vice president of the school board, asked, "How can we continue to move forward with the same limited resources, with the same segregated city, the same poverty?"[8]

The Congress of Racial Equality investigated, negotiated, and acted, often successfully, on these issues in the 1960s. CORE activists speak in this book about the people, activities, goals, and spirit of an important movement, a part of the process of making Seattle a more integrated and just society. We hope that this book will not only tell how we were and what we did to become who we are but also inspire all of us to work toward what we could still be—a world of equality.

APPENDIX 1

Seattle's Freedom Patrol • *by Sue D. Gottfried*

=====================================

Seattle CORE and civil rights activists worked on a number of problems in addition to employment, housing, schools, and support for activists in the South. One regular challenge—among the first concerns CORE had considered undertaking—was police brutality. The black community had to deal with hostile police behavior repeatedly. How could CORE confront and end such violence? This article by CORE member Sue D. Gottfried, published in 1965, describes an attempt to address the problem.[1]

A new kind of walk for freedom was born in Seattle recently: walking a policeman's beat.

On July 24, [1965] police on the night beat in five Seattle areas began to be trailed by well-identified shadows. The shadows—in male-female teams of two—wore large cardboard badges labeled "Freedom Patrol." After the night's "tour of duty," Freedom Patrol members trudged the stairs to the offices of Seattle's Congress of Racial Equality (CORE), host and service-arm to the project but not its sponsor, to make written reports on police conduct.

The immediate provocation that led to the formation of the Freedom Patrol was the fatal shooting of a Negro, Robert L. Reese, by off-duty Seattle policeman Harold J. Larsen in a tavern brawl on June 20. Because the killing was allegedly a racial incident, raising serious questions about police practices, the Washington chapter of the American Civil Liberties Union urged a grand jury investigation. In a public statement, the chairman of Seattle CORE called for establishment of a permanent police review board.

Public officials did not respond to these suggestions. After a coroner's inquest made a finding of "excusable homicide," Larsen, and Patrolman Franklyn Junell, also involved in the brawl, were suspended for thirty days by Police Chief Frank C. Ramon for their "failure . . . to handle a police action in accordance with their training, experience, and departmental procedures." Chief Ramon also announced that he was acceding to the jury's recommendation that policemen not be armed when engaged in off-duty social activities.

That, presumably, was that.

But this disposition of the case aroused outraged feelings in the Negro community and among whites concerned with social justice. Their distrust of the Seattle police and frustration with the deafness of public officials to appeals for corrective measures had been ripening over at least a decade. As long ago as 1956, a citizens' investigating committee appointed by the mayor had recommended establishment of a civilian police review board. This recommendation was never acted upon. As recently as early 1965, when a series of public hearings produced abundant testimony alleging police brutality, the mayor and the city council were still unmoved to take any action whatever.

On July 10, a few days after the coroner's inquest, Seattle's Central Area Council on Civil Rights—a nine-man team of civil rights leaders—called a public meeting to plan protest action. The meeting organized itself into a "Citizens Committee on Police Practices." Goals of the group—to be sought on the legal front as well as through direct action—included investigation of the Reese case by a Federal or county grand jury, and the calling in of a high-level outside agency for study and analysis of police training and performance.

It was at this meeting that the concept of the Freedom Patrol was first broached, to an audience of about 500 Negroes and Caucasians. The purpose of the Freedom Patrol was described as that of documenting police misconduct through observation of police on their beats, and a check on bookings and charges at the city jail, in an effort to bring about official action to correct discriminatory practices.

The Freedom Patrol idea was received with excitement and enthusiasm by those present, although it was evident at this early stage that the exact mode of operation for these "walking citizen review boards" was still far from clear.

Over the ensuing two weeks, a steering committee worked with civil rights leaders and advisers to plan for the effective use and control of the Freedom Patrol. A legal memorandum relating to citizen police-surveillance and records-investigation was drawn up by the ACLU; careful procedures for screening Patrol applicants were worked out; a strict nonviolent discipline was developed; and training sessions were planned.

These preparations were, of necessity, experimental, and more hurried than some of the planners would have wished. The first patrol to hit the streets was a highly selective group, including such figures as the ministers of the two leading Negro congregations, one of them the chairman of the Central Area Council on Civil Rights; the president of Seattle NAACP; the vice president of Seattle CORE; the executive secretary of Seattle Urban League; and the executive minister of the Greater Seattle Council of Churches.

Behind the scene were other volunteers: a director, two assistant directors, a training staff, office staff, attorneys on call, telephone monitors, roving automobile patrols, and captains of the evening. Freedom Patrol members had been instructed to keep police within full view, but not to interfere with police operations. They had been asked not only to avoid "attitudes showing malice" toward police, but even to avoid getting into conversations with them. However, on the first Freedom Patrol tour, the *Seattle Times* reported that "the patrolling officers chatted frequently and in friendly fashion" with Freedom Patrol members.

Although conversations dwindled after the first night, the surface evenness of Patrol-police relations has continued. Freedom Patrollers have reported incidents of policemen attempting to give them the slip, and of being led by police through such extraordinary terrain as unlighted construction sites; but they have not reported overt challenge by police.

It is estimated that ninety-five per cent of Seattle's Negro population is concentrated in the areas covered by the Freedom Patrol. Other races are also represented in these areas. Many of the people, of whatever race, are down-and-outers—unemployed, vagrants, alcoholics, drug addicts, petty traffickers in illegal commodities. Some uneasiness about this population was confessed by the predominantly middle-class Negroes and whites of the Freedom Patrol, as they first ventured into such territories as "skid row." But the one impression Freedom Patrollers have come to agree upon is the tolerant-to-friendly-to-warm attitude of the "civilians"—most of whom appear to be well informed of the Patrol's mission.

On August 18, four Negro men, who with the deceased Robert Reese had been involved in the June 20 tavern fight, were convicted of assault. The following week, Patrolman Junell was found innocent by a Justice Court of the charge that he provoked the assault by using such derogatory expressions as "nigger." In the course of this trial, it came to light that Assistant Police Chief Charles Rouse and a police sergeant had withheld the names and statements of four witnesses to the tavern altercation. The only results of this disclosure were that the police sergeant was moved to another detail, and Rouse was moved down a notch to the job of deputy chief. No further fuss about the suppression of evidence was made by anyone in public authority. While policemen Larsen, Junell and Rouse settled back into the routine of their ordinary lives, the four convicted Negroes drew sentences which will keep them under alternate incarceration and observation over the coming year.

As may be supposed, these developments failed to reassure critics that justice reigns triumphant in the city of Seattle. The Citizens Committee on Police Practices has intensified its efforts to bring outside pressure to bear, concentrating on signed petitions to the United States Civil Rights Commission to hold hearings.

Complaints of police misconduct, also for forwarding to the U.S. Civil Rights Commission, come mainly through letters, telephone calls, and personal interviews initiated by alleged victims. The Freedom Patrol itself has observed no clear-cut incidents of police misbehavior. Somewhat to the contrary. "They assist the drunks ever so gently into the wagons, then look over their shoulders at us as if to say, 'See? This is how we act all the time,'" said a Patrol member with a wry grin. An attorney who is a member of the Freedom Patrol has remarked that the openness of the Patrols is "not good investigatory technique."

But if its *modus operandi* does not lend itself to evidence-gathering, the Patrol's open presence may be having other good effects. A police department employee recently told a Freedom Patrol acquaintance that for the first time in his near-decade of service, he had heard a police captain cautioning police about abusive language and behavior toward minority-race citizens. There are reports that arrests have declined in neighborhoods watched by Freedom Patrollers; there are rumors that alleged police-protected illegal business operators have been told to "cool it for a while," with a consequent falling-off in such trades.

The Freedom Patrol is without clear precedent in the annals of nonviolent direct action. In its form, as well as in its ethnic self-consciousness, it bears some resemblance to the "Peace Patrol" of the East Harlem Action Committee, which during the 1964 summer riots in New York succeeded in preventing clashes between helmeted police and Puerto Rican residents. It bears a still fainter resemblance to the voluntary patrols which sought to protect Jewish residents of Brooklyn from hoodlum violence. Perhaps more closely related ancestors of the Freedom Patrol were the "haunting" squads which came into being in the Gandhian movement. The Indian nonviolent campaigners developed a system of following public officials wherever they went, to remind them of the immorality and injustice of their behavior.

Indirectly "haunted," Seattle's Mayor J. D. Braman was moved in mid-September to set up a "human relations division" within the police department, for the express purpose of bettering relations between police and minority groups. The mayor's action was the first tacit admission by any city official that police practices could stand improvement.

Although the strength of the Freedom Patrol—originally numbering some fifty-five trained "regulars"—has been roughly halved by familiar processes of erosion, a hard core of volunteers continues to appear on the streets two or three nights a week. Meanwhile the organization of Freedom Patrols in Los Angeles and New Orleans has been reported. The life of this new version of "haunting squads" may only have begun.

Authors' Note: This article ends optimistically. Despite significant improvements in police procedures over the years, however, excessive force by police officers still angers the black community. In the summer of 2008, for example, the NAACP held hearings in its project "People's Panel on Police Accountability." On May 20, 2008, the Seattle Post-Intelligencer reported, "Blacks were eight times more likely than whites to be arrested for obstruction, and . . . about half of the cases were dismissed by the City Attorney's Office before trial." On July 2, 2008, the Seattle Times reported that a Seattle City Council panel recommended strengthening the civilian review board that oversees police accountability. Unfortunately, police brutality remains a recurrent issue.

APPENDIX 2

Memories of a Freedom Rider • *by Ray Cooper*

===

We authors faced challenges finding people who were active in Seattle CORE more than four decades ago, but thanks to today's technology, we located Seattle's first Freedom Rider, Ray Cooper, in North Carolina. In December 2006 Ray put into words his experiences forty-six years earlier, to help us understand what he, along with other Freedom Riders, went through. Here in his letter, are his exact words.[1]

In the spring of 1961 a Greyhound bus was bombed and burned in Anniston, Alabama while the police watched. Passengers were attacked, pulled from the bus and beaten. They were Freedom Riders from the National Congress of Racial Equality. James Farmer, the director, had America's attention when he called for a continuation not a retreat. The image of the burning bus on television made a clear case for a strategy of sending bus after bus into Jackson, Mississippi until the jails became full and the state would be forced to desegregate inter-state travel facilities. And that is what happened. It was the law of the land. The Supreme Court had established it.

The appeal produced Riders from across America. While friends began organizing a Seattle chapter of CORE with the goal to raise funds for airfare to Los Angeles, I volunteered to join the California group. Within two weeks of the Anniston bombing I was on a bus bound for New Orleans. The CORE chapter in New Orleans was conducting training classes in the practice of nonviolent civil disobedience.

Gathering in New Orleans, we were getting to know one another, bonding to find the courage to act together. There was a wave of volunteers and we had the moral advantage. I could not have continued past New Orleans if there had been a meager turn out. Strength in numbers. Was I frightened? Yes. But like the others I was calm and focused. I was nineteen and was about to do something meaningful for the first time in my life. I had resolved not to participate with the U.S. military adventure in Vietnam. The battle at home was my choice. I was testing myself, challenging my country to actually "free the slaves" not just talk about it. Do it now.

I had read about Gandhi in high school. He stood against the British Empire. People listened to him and won. I admired that. Martin Luther King Jr. quoted him. I respected that. I believed that nonviolent resistance would also work in America where people professed belief in democracy. It was a gamble but was a rather "strong hand." We won.

Now in my mid sixties, I live in the South. The South has changed. America has changed since 1961. It was not the Freedom Riders that produced that transformation. The Freedom Ride's victory was the set up for the voter registration campaign. It was that victory which changed America. If you can vote you are a citizen. The truly brave people in the struggle were local folks who went to the voter registration offices and then returned home and faced the consequences. There were young people from Jackson, black and white, who walked into the segregated Greyhound station, joined us, went to prison and when released returned home in Jackson. These Freedom Riders were the courageous ones.

We finally headed for Jackson. We sang freedom songs from the long struggle, crafting new words to suit our campaign. There were non-freedom riders on this Greyhound bus also. Greyhound maintained a business as usual schedule throughout the summer, treating us well.

We arrived in Jackson in June. Police and their vans surrounded the terminal. They watched passively as we walked into the whites only waiting room. Once inside we sat on available benches together with arms locked. The police ordered us out. We declined. Threatened with arrest we went limp and were dragged from the Greyhound station by our feet and were loaded into paddy wagons. (The Black Mariah, we later called it.) Arrested and booked for unlawful assembly, we entered the jails of Jackson City and County. We were, of course, segregated by race and sex. Our fear was not of police mistreatment, but of the uncertainty of being housed with criminal prisoners. At no point during the summer did this occur. The standard length of incarceration was forty-five days, first in Jackson and ultimately at Parchman Farm Mississippi State Penitentiary. All summer long the buses kept arriving with more Freedom Riders. Our plan to max out the jail facilities was working. What a relief!

At the Parchman Farm, some distance north of Jackson, we first were housed in maximum security cells, three men in a two man cell. We alternated by sleeping on the floor . . . cement. The summer heat was intense, the food was poor and time stood still. We sang but that quickly enraged the jailer. They threatened to put us out in the farm's cotton fields as forced labor. We refused. It was not the work we feared but the danger of isolation out in the fields with chance of bodily harm. As a group we decided to be beaten together inside, rather than alone in the fields. We remained indoors, unbeaten, until moved to a large communal housing where we met Freedom Riders from across the nation for the first time.

The routine was dull. Summer just crawls in the Mississippi heat. We made chess men from Wonder bread, practiced yoga, took cooling showers (cold water). The Broadway musical West Side Story was a hit in 1961. Some New Yorkers had seen it and did a mangled yet entertaining re-creation. There was nothing to read. I slept a lot. On Sundays a rabbi from Jackson visited us for service. Of course, we were all Jews. The guards laughed and said they expected that we were. The rabbi did an inter-denomination service interjecting relevant news concerning world and national events, as well as related to our legal situation. This he did against regulations. Our lawyers were able to communicate, somewhat, with us through the rabbi. The news that buses were still arriving in Jackson encouraged us greatly.

Wonder bread, pork 'n beans, grits, and greens, corn bread and an egg now and then with thin coffee made with chicory and most amazingly a scraping of blackened fried grease . . . forty seven days in Hell's Kitchen.

Uncertain about when we would be released, kept ignorant until the hour of our departure, we were transported back to Jackson in a motley fleet of small pickups with camper backs. We saw the cotton fields recede behind us. Yazoo City and other cross road towns looked as timeless and god forsaken as anything we had ever seen.

In Jackson, we were hosted by a church. Supper in the basement dining hall. Ham!! Salad!! Green beans!! Mashed potatoes, PIE!! Coffee and iced tea. Smiling black mothers saying "have another piece of pie, son?" Shaking our hands. Smiling, Smiling. It only occurs to me now, that this reception was for them, to be repeated daily until all the Freedom Riders were eventually released. Weeks on end of pies and hams and smiles. God bless them, we were home and safe. A dance at the Negro community social center followed—an integrated event in Jackson, Miss. in 1961! A police guard with patrol cars out front kept order as we rocked on indoors to the hit of the summer, Ray Charles "Hit The Road Jack." This same summer Ray Charles refused to play a segregated concert hall in Atlanta. The wall was coming down. Dixie was cracking up. Gandhi and Martin Luther King Jr. were right: challenge people with love and nonviolence and they have a chance to behave well. Change them in their hearts with love.

There were rough days ahead for others but our group was treated well. Except for greasy grits.

Contributions to our legal defense funds were generous, and provided bus fare home with pocket money, to eat as we traveled. We promised to return to Jackson for arraignment and then for trial. I made two trips from Seattle to Jackson, first arrest, then arraignment. Then Mississippi capitulated, all charges dropped. No trial.

At home from prison I toured Washington State with CORE's Freedom Ride film, receiving contributions for ongoing legal expenses. We were ready to return to prison believing that was likely and then Mississippi folded. I spoke at churches and colleges, showing the film. I was briefly famous in my home state, remaining active in the civil rights movement for a time. Having no particular political skills and needing to gain an education, I turned my attention to art school in California.

From the Freedom Rides I learned to face the world with confidence. Along the way I met Martin Luther King Jr., shook his hand and thanked him for his good leadership. His call for justice in America has been key to who I am, what I have become. The Montgomery bus boycott, the lunch counter sit-ins, the integration of public schools, the Freedom Rides . . . I had stood with these courageous people and found myself.

I did not participate in the Voter Registration drive. I went to college, then traveled in the world, became an artist and a father. I live in the South now. I love it here. Is it perfect? No place is . . . yet.

APPENDIX 3

Biographical Sketches of Selected CORE Activists

These people were all friends and colleagues of the authors. Our memories and CORE history as documented in this book form the basis of these sketches, supplemented in many cases by interviews and documents as noted.

Jean Adams, later *Maid Adams*, and her husband, despite excellent credit, experienced long delays in approval of a mortgage for buying a house in Madrona. She realized that African American buyers could not know if similar delays were due to their race, and so was motivated to activism. After joining CORE in 1962 at the recommendation of Wing Luke, she served as coordinator of negotiation teams for grocery and department stores and helped publish and distribute the booklet on Negro pioneer George Washington Bush. She was coprincipal of the First AME Freedom School. Maid accepted the need for black self-determination in CORE's last days and moved on to volunteer with the United Farmworkers Union grape boycott. She returned to the University of Washington to get her master's degree in education and then served as an instructor and program director at Green River Community College for twenty years. She continues to teach and participate in community activities.

Reginald Alleyne (1932–2004), known as Reggie, came to Seattle from Boston and Washington, D.C., where he had graduated from Howard University Law School and begun his career in the law. He filled various offices for Seattle CORE, serving as chairman in the pivotal year of 1963. After passage of the civil rights acts, he was among the first federal employees appointed as contract compliance officers to enforce a new concept—affirmative action. In 1969, having earned his LLM from Columbia University, he joined the faculty of the law school at UCLA as its first African American professor. There he spent the remaining twenty-five years of his distinguished career. His specialty in labor law led him to the field of labor arbitration; he later served as vice president of the National Academy of Arbitrators.[1]

Daisy Boyetta (1924–2007), daughter of Sarah Lynch and mother of Infanta Spence (both activists themselves in CORE), was a stalwart member of CORE. Daisy was raised in Seattle and attended St. George's Catholic School. She worked as a domestic, then in the dietician department of the University of Washington Hospital, and finally as the owner of the [Marcus] Garvey Bookstore on Twenty-Third near Madison with her mother. Strong and vocal on every subject concerning segregation and discrimination, Daisy was a constant on the picket lines and at demonstrations and marches. She served on CORE's Emergency Committee for several years and was an active member of the negotiating team. She also participated in many Community Action Programs as part of her involvement in the War on Poverty. She helped start the Central Area Chamber of Commerce. Daisy went on to work for the state of Washington, addressing the needs of abused children.[2]

John C. Cannon (1923–) moved from Louisiana to Los Angeles for high school. He enlisted in the United States Army in 1942, served for a while in the all-black 555th Parachute Infantry Battalion ("Triple Nickels"), but served mostly in the Medical Service Corps. An army major while in CORE, he served on CORE's Emergency Committee until ordered to Korea. After twenty-four years' service, he retired as a lieutenant colonel, returning to Seattle in 1966. He worked in Seattle's Division of Urban Renewal until his appointment, in 1970, as the first administrator of Odessa Brown Children's Clinic. Thereafter he became executive director of the Ecumenical Metropolitan Ministry and, from 1980 to 1988, executive director of the Central Area Senior Center. He served on boards of directors of many organizations, including the Seattle Public Library. He retired to West Virginia to be near his son, a retired army officer. The Cannon House, an assisted-living facility in Seattle on Twenty-Third Avenue South near Yesler Street is named to honor his many contributions to Seattle.[3]

Carla Anette Chotzen (1924–) fled Nazi Germany with her family as a young girl. She graduated from the University of Rochester. As assistant to a professional photographer, she learned the skills needed to become an outstanding portrait photographer of children. While raising her family of eight children, she joined CORE in 1963 and launched a campaign to raise funds to pay transportation costs for children in the Voluntary Racial Transfer Program. She cochaired the school boycott Freedom School project, which, due to her organizational skills, was one of CORE's most successful campaigns. Her daily life was not complete without a morning run and then a swim in Lake Washington—365 days a year—rain or shine. Retired and in her late eighties, she is still committed to a healthy life style.[4]

John Cornethan (1925–99), the son of Alabama sharecroppers, served as a private in the United States Army and moved to Seattle in the 1950s. He was the first African American to hold the position of lineman's helper for Seattle City Light. Despite his knowledge and skills as an electrician, John was denied the promotions he sought for many years due to the racial practices of City Light at that time. John found his way to CORE through the University Unitarian Church. He was an early participant in all CORE's projects and a constant on the picket lines. Father of three sons, he was a big man with a quiet voice—a person you could count on to always be there when needed. John held the offices of vice chairman and then chairman in 1966–67. After thirty-five years of employment, he retired from his "day job" at City Light but continued to be active in the peace movement and other causes championed by the Unitarians for Social Justice.[5]

Barbara Davis, later *Folayan Oni-Robertson* (1941–), joined CORE because she believed in CORE causes—equality for minorities to obtain jobs, to purchase homes without discrimination, and to be treated as equals by the police. Barbara taught at the Freedom School, was a constant at Picture

Floor Plans demonstrations, walked Seattle's police beat as a member of the Freedom Patrol, and often carried her picket sign on Seattle buses, as she did not own a car. Folayan was the last secretary of Seattle CORE. She later worked with Head Start in King County as a health education coordinator. Interested in African American art, she wrote books for children about African Americans and instilled an appreciation for African American culture in at least two generations of children.[6]

Jean Durning (1934–) and her husband moved to Seattle in 1959. She led CORE's campaign to integrate the Bon Marché under Reverend Mance Jackson, helped organize the Seattle demonstration to coincide with the great March on Washington, and served on the CORE Emergency Committee. Thereafter, she was active in political campaigns, taught junior high school, and, at the Human Environment Foundation in Washington, D.C., coordinated studies on minority students entering environmental and natural resource careers. From 1981 to 1993 she served as northwest director of The Wilderness Society during the height of controversy over ancient forests, helping coordinate volunteers of many environmental organizations, lobbying Congress, and dealing regularly with government agencies and with press and broadcast reporters.

Judith (Judy) Esparza (1932–) moved to West Seattle in 1958 with her daughter and husband, Gilbert, who started work at Boeing while she completed her studies for her doctorate in political science and public administration at the University of Washington. Upon their move to Bellevue in 1961, Judy became an active member of the East Shore Unitarian Church, helping to launch the church's involvement with the Fair Housing Listing Service. Both Judy and Gil Esparza were active members of CORE. In 1964 Judy assumed the chairmanship of the Housing Committee and launched Seattle CORE's first sit-ins at Picture Floor Plans. The family lived in Washington, D.C., in 1968–70, returned to the Seattle area for five years, and then went back to D.C. They returned permanently to Seattle in 2001. Unfortunately, Judy's employment and role as an activist were cut short by debilitating illness.[7]

Sue Gottfried, later *Sue Davidson* (1925–), is a socially and politically active author and advocate on behalf of peace and justice issues. Sue cochaired the school boycott and Freedom Schools project as part of her CORE activities in 1966. In that same year her book *What Do You Mean, Nonviolence? The Story of Wars with Peaceful Weapons* was published. Her commitment to nonviolence made her an obvious choice to work with the American Friends Service Committee's campaign to bring about an end to the war in Vietnam. Sue was an observer on the Freedom Patrol, a CORE project she describes in appendix 1. After her work with CORE, she became a "citizen participation planner" for the Seattle Model Cities Program. In the mid-1970s, Sue was the text editor for works published by the Feminist Press. When recently interviewed she was surrounded by many of the multicultural articles and pamphlets she wrote before, during, and after her work with Seattle CORE.[8]

Esther Hall, later *Esther Hall Mumford* (1941–), came to Seattle from Louisiana in 1961 to attend the University of Washington, where she majored in political science. She was active in both the campus Civil Rights Action Group and Seattle CORE. Esther was the first black office worker at the Carnation Milk Company after CORE broke the color barrier there. She and her husband, Don, are the parents of Donald Jr. and Zola. In 1989, as part of Washington State's centennial celebration, Esther was named a "Washington Living Treasure" based in part on her six publications about African Americans in the Northwest, including *Seattle's Black Victorians*, *Seven Stars and Orion*, and *Calabash*. Esther was a founding member of the Black Heritage Society. In 2004 Esther joined other former CORE members in Florida to participate in the Election Protection Coalition to ensure fair voting practices on election day.[9]

Walter Hundley (1929–2002), who started life in a rough Philadelphia neighborhood, went on to Yale Divinity School and then earned degrees in social work from the University of British Columbia and the University of Washington. In Seattle CORE he led negotiations with employers, served as vice chairman in 1964 and chairman in 1965, and was its representative on the Central Area Civil Rights Committee. Under the federal War on Poverty, he became director of the Central Area Motivation Program (CAMP), then director of the Seattle Model Cities Program, after which he became director of the city's Office of Management and Budget. From 1977 until ill health overtook him in 1988, he was superintendent of the Seattle Parks and Recreation Department.[10]

Reverend Mance Jackson (1930–2007) moved from Los Angeles to serve as pastor at Seattle's Bethel CME Church on Twenty-Third Avenue. Amazed and angry to find Seattle apathetic about racial injustices, he joined Seattle civil rights efforts through NAACP and CORE and cofounded the Methodist Episcopal Ministers Alliance. In Seattle CORE he served on the Negotiating and Emergency committees and led the campaign for equal employment at the Bon Marché. In late 1963, after his house had twice been firebombed, he moved to Atlanta to attend seminary "and to go to school in civil rights activity." Seminary study was followed by three years as pastor of a church in Berkeley, California. He then returned to Atlanta, teaching while earning his doctorate in theology from New York Seminary. For thirty years he was a member of the faculty of the Interdenominational Theological Center of Atlanta Universities.[11]

Norman O. Johnson (1934–), son of a large family in Philadelphia, left home after discovering Seattle in 1959 while serving in the military. He worked as a draftsman at Boeing, then attended Seattle Community College and the University of Washington, receiving his master's degree in social work in 1973. The victim of police harassment himself while attending the university, Norman became one of the founders of CORE and the first treasurer of the group. In addition to picketing, he often served as a monitor at large demonstrations and marches. His skill at fundraising for civil rights carried over into the work he does now as the executive director of Therapeutic Health Services (THS), a position he has held for the past three-and-a-half decades. This agency, with numerous branch offices, addresses addiction and mental health problems for citizen of all races and colors from all over western Washington. Norman has traveled extensively, including trips to many countries in Africa. He is not ready to retire.[12]

Wallace L. Johnson (1932–), the son of Arkansas farmworkers, spent four years in the U.S. Air Force. He attended AM&N College (later renamed University of Arkansas at Pine Bluff) on the GI Bill and graduated in business administration while also working as the only black office machine salesman in the state of Arkansas. He moved to Seattle in 1959 and completed his MBA at the University of Washington. In Seattle CORE in 1961–62 he developed a training program for supermarket cashiers that led to many African Americans being hired. Vice Chairman of CORE in 1962, he also helped with negotiation, fundraising, and training of new CORE members. As a loaned executive from the Boeing Company, he helped start the Seattle Opportunities Industrialization Center (SOIC; now Seattle Vocational Institute). He attended Stanford University's Executive Program and later became director of administration and finance for the City of Seattle's Department of Community Development. He later worked for and retired from the Port of Seattle.[13]

John (David) Lamb (1935–), father of two and a musical instrument teacher for the Seattle public schools, joined CORE in 1963. Having mastered silk screening, he set up a print shop in his basement and produced picket signs and CORE posters. As picket captain for the demonstrations against A&P, he not only organized and led the group but composed a song to highlight the bigoted attitude of A&P's management, "We've Got No Problem Here." David gave time and leadership to the school boycott in 1966. He continued his commitment to social causes, protesting the war in Vietnam. He has retired from teaching. His musical compositions can be heard on recordings by the Kronos Quartet and saxophonist Paul Cohen. He also composed a children's opera, *King Midas*, which was performed in Seattle in 1966.[14]

Ethel Lightfoot (1904–95) was born in the same small town as President Eisenhower—Denison, Texas. After high school she attended Prairie View State College, a black college established in 1876 and opened to women in 1879. Without completing her degree, she and her husband left Texas for Seattle in 1926. Using their savings as a down payment, they bought an apartment building at Twenty-Fourth and Madison that they owned for many years. In 1961 she responded to our appeal for applicants to work at Safeway and soon joined CORE. A small, determined woman committed to ending discrimination, she walked picket lines, phoned others to join in, and frequently served as a negotiator. The November 1967 *Corelator* commends her as "one of the hardest working members" of CORE's Employment Committee. She was a regular at her church and was an active member of the Central Community Club and Neighborhood Unity Club.[15]

Sarah Lynch (1896–1994) moved to Seattle from Jamaica as a young woman. She later married Joseph Lynch, from the island of St. Vincent, who was a follower of Marcus Garvey and the Universal Negro Improvement Association (UNIA). Together they raised five children and instilled in them the values of the UNIA and the Garvey movement. Joining CORE at age sixty-six, Mrs. Lynch committed much of her energy to opening job opportunities for African Americans, often serving as a "one woman" negotiating team. She chaired the Employment Committee late in CORE's existence. She received awards from the Catholic Archdiocese of Seattle for her help in caring for neglected and abused children. She helped found the Central Area Chamber of Commerce. A believer in lifelong learning, she enrolled in classes at Seattle Community College at the age of seventy. Prior to her death at age ninety-eight she often acted as spokesperson for the Central Area Senior Center. Including Mrs. Lynch herself, five members of her family were active in CORE.[16]

Harold (Tim) Martin (1930–2002), father of four children and veteran of the Korean War, served on the executive board of Seattle NAACP and became chairman of Seattle CORE in 1964. He not only chaired the James Baldwin fundraiser but designed the posters and publicity for this and many other CORE events. Tim was not an aggressive person but was firm in his determination not to be ruled by a discriminatory society. He worked as a technical illustrator at Boeing and was the first African American to move into Lake Hills on the Eastside—in 1959 with his interracial family. Along with his wife, Georgia, he spent countless hours in the effort to break the segregated housing pattern in the Seattle area. Tim, soft-spoken but resolute, contributed greatly to CORE's image as respectable and deserving.[17]

Don Matson (1929–2004), a carpet layer and father of four, joined CORE within months of the formation of the group. Don was an important liaison with the University Unitarian Church. He published the monthly Corelator on a mimeograph machine in the basement of his home. The Fair Housing Listing Service came into being through the efforts of Don and members of the Unitarians for Social Justice. His efforts to break the color line in the trade unions continued into the remaining days of CORE. He was an advocate for women's rights, abortion rights, and prison reforms. For his work and commitment to these causes addressed by his church, he was elected to the National Executive Board of the Unitarians for Social Justice. He continued to work on social issues until failing health ended his physical involvement in 2004.[18]

Earl V. Miller (1923–2005), born and educated in the South, with advanced training in Iowa, was the first black urologist in Seattle when he moved here in 1959 with his wife, Dr. Rosalie Miller, and their children. He became active in both the NAACP and CORE and served on the board of the integrated housing enterprise, Harmony Homes. On behalf of both the NAACP and CORE, he negotiated with employers to increase minority hiring. His leadership in efforts to integrate the Seattle school system led to his appointment by the school administration to its first citizens' group on segregation problems, the Equal Education Opportunity Committee. Dr. Miller's distinguished career in urology included contributing papers to professional medical journals and appointment as clinical associate professor at the University of Washington Medical School.[19]

Ernestine (Ernie) Rogers, later Sadikifu Akina-James (1945–), traveled on a Greyhound bus from a small segregated town in Louisiana in 1962, the year she graduated from high school, and arrived in Seattle hoping to enter the University of Washington. She joined CORE shortly after arriving and became active in any and all projects that might bring an end to segregation policies in the North. Ernie was a teacher in the Freedom School, a positive force in CORE, and became secretary in 1965. After CORE she worked with the Atlantic Street Center project on middle schools and community awareness programs through CAMP. She received her degree in social work in 1969. Sadikifu served as manager of the King County Veterans and Human Services Levy, continuing an eighteen-year career with county government.[20]

Edward (Ed) Russell (1927–2007) found his way to Seattle from Tusca-loosa, Alabama, via Port Huron, Michigan, where he graduated from high school. He attended the University of Washington and earned his master's degree in urban planning. He was an active member of the NAACP and Seattle Urban League. Ed, father of three, joined Seattle CORE in 1963 and contributed to projects and demonstrations to end discrimination in Seattle. He was elected chairman of Seattle CORE in December 1967, during the transition to Black Power. Continuing his commitment to ending segregation in employment, he supported Tyree Scott and the United Construction Workers Association in their attempt to break the color line in the construction trades. He worked for the U.S. Army Corp of Engineers and retired in 1997. His other community commitments included participation with the YMCA and St. Vincent de Paul Society.[21]

Edward (Ed) Singler (1931–), a lawyer and one of the founders of Seattle CORE, held the office of vice chairman and chairman, the only white person in that office in the seven-year history of Seattle CORE. As vice chairman, Ed conducted the orientation and training sessions for new members. He also provided legal counsel for Seattle CORE. His efforts to end discrimination led to working in San Francisco in late 1965 as a field representative for the states of Washington and Alaska in the Johnson administration's War on Poverty program. Returning to Seattle in 1967, Ed became the director of Seattle's Department of Human Resources, followed by years as regional administrator for the federal Office of Health and Human Services for Region 10. At the same time he was actively involved in the opposition to the war in Vietnam. In retirement he became a member of the Pike Place Market Historical Commission, served for six years as Washington State president of the AARP, and served on the governors' committee investigating electronic health records.

Joan Singler (1934–), a college student and mother-to-be in 1961, was also a founder of Seattle CORE. Along with raising her daughters she served as CORE secretary and chaired the Housing Committee. After moving to San Francisco in 1965, Joan led the San Francisco Women for Peace in a boycott against the Dow Chemical Company, producer of napalm used in the Vietnam War. Upon returning to Seattle, she completed her work for a bachelor's degree in psychology and a teaching certificate in early childhood education. Along with her studies she spent time working on behalf of the Farm Workers Union in their fight for better working conditions and wages. In the 1970s Joan was a key leader in the campaign to elect Marvin Durning as governor of Washington and in his subsequent run for the U.S. Congress. While later working as a travel consultant, Joan also volunteered on behalf of victims of domestic violence. Presently she serves on the State Executive Council of AARP.

Bettylou (Burleigh) Valentine (1937–), a national board member of the NAACP, came to Seattle for graduate school at the University of Washington in 1959. In Seattle she became active in CORE and served as secretary in 1964. She helped organize the campus Civil Rights Action Group (CRAG) after the university administration refused to allow an NAACP chapter on campus. After graduation she and her husband, Val, moved to Washington University in St. Louis and became active in the CORE chapter there. They next moved to an urban American ghetto for several years, living, teaching, and doing research and writing, an experience that became the basis for her PhD thesis in anthropology and her subsequent book *Hustling and Other Hard Work*. For fifteen years thereafter the Valentines taught, researched, and wrote in and about Suriname, Papua New Guinea, and China. In the sixteen years before she retired, Bettylou was the director of a youth and family service organization in the Central Area of Seattle, where she had done her original CORE work.

Charles A. (Val) Valentine (1929–90) came to the University of Washington as a faculty member in anthropology after holding positions at the University of Pittsburgh and the University of Kansas (where in the late 1950s he had worked to integrate the municipal swimming pool). He became active in Seattle CORE in the early 1960s, combining his activist approach with academic skills to do much of the research for Seattle CORE. Val helped to organize CRAG and encouraged fellow faculty members to join CRAG and CORE. His book *Culture and Poverty: Critique and Counterproposal* (University of Chicago Press, 1968) earned him a place in *Who's Who in America*. For Val's midlife activities, see Bettylou Valentine's entry above. Always determined to bring about change and improve the lives of oppressed people, he died within twenty-four hours of spending the day on a picket line in front of the federal building in Seattle.[22]

James Washington Jr. (1911–2000), one of six children of a Baptist minister, was born in Gloster, Mississippi. With his wife, Janie Rogella Washington, he moved to the Northwest in 1944, first as a journeyman electrician at Bremerton Naval Base and then as a shoe repairman at Fort Lawton in Seattle (now Discovery Park). By the mid-1950s this self-taught artist was able to support his family by painting and, first and foremost, by carving beautiful works in stone and marble. He became active in both the NAACP and CORE. He joined CORE in September 1961 and hand-painted some of CORE's early picket signs. He served on many CORE negotiating teams and was a regular on the picket line. In 1964 he represented CORE on the Central Area Civil Rights Coordinating Committee. Mr. Washington represented the NAACP on the Education Committee for the school boycott and taught at the Freedom School. He was an artist, a lecturer, and a poet. His sculptures can be seen in banks, hotels, schools, churches, and parks in the Northwest, at the Washington State Capitol, and in museums throughout the world.[23]

Frances White, later *Karimu White* (1915–2003), was an active CORE member until the group dissolved. She helped lead several fundraising events. A member of CORE's Education Committee, she initiated and taught the first Negro history classes. Karimu was instrumental in publishing the booklet on Negro pioneer George Washington Bush, which she sold in front of grocery stores, and she led students on an inspirational field trip to Olympia and Bush Prairie, where this pioneer had settled. She later embraced pan-Africanism, attending national conferences, and became a respected elder consulted by the Black Student Union and sought out by scholars and activists when they came to town. A woman of elegant unpretentious taste, she collected African art and books, learned Swahili, and maintained her dedication to the cause all her life.[24]

APPENDIX 4

Seattle CORE Members and Active Supporters

===================================

This list has been compiled from Seattle CORE membership records (only available for some of the years) and other documents, mainly issues of *Corelator*, and the authors' memories. It may be incomplete. Listed in italics are nonmembers who cooperated on projects, including Freedom Schools, walked multiple picket lines, donated money, or offered professional support (such as attorneys on call).

Ackley, Blaine
Ackley, Representative Norman
Ackley, Mrs. Norman
Adalist, Joyce
Adalist, Lloyd
Adalist, Lynn
Adam, Frenchie
Adam, Barry
Adams, David
Adams, Jean (later Maid Adams)
Adams, Reverend John
Adams, Mrs. John

Adkins, Selma
Alexander, Lewis
Alice, Lawrence
Allen, Beverly
Allen, John
Allen, Wiley
Alleyne, Delores
Alleyne, Reggie
Anderson, Carl
Anderson, R. E.
Andrews, Clifford B. T.
Arbaugh, Reverend William

Arkley, Al

Atkins, Ralph

Atkinson, Gilbert

Baker, Jolly Sue

Baker, William

Balliet, Robert

Banks, Ed

Banks, Mrs. Ed

Barash, Daniel

Barrett, Barbara

Barrett, Richard

Barton, Mary

Bash, Leola

Beachner, Charles

Beaty, Mr.

Beatty, Yvonne

Beckwith, Christine

Beeman, Reverend Paul

Beer, Larry

Bergman, John

Berry, Overton

Beyer, Rich

Biggard, Terril

Bilancia, Philip

Birn, Elaine

Bissett, Diane

Bissett, Gordon

Blaine, John H.

Blanke, Arthur

Blum, Stanton

Bodin, Aaron

Bodin, Iris

Boler, John F.

Borden, Oliver

Bosserman, Charles

Bosserman, Charlotte

Boyd, Mrs.

Boyetta, Daisy

Bower, Diana

Bower, Ted

Bray, Keve

Brooks, Violet

Brose, Tom

Brown, Frank

Brown, Dr. Walter Scott

Brown, Reverend William

Buckingham, Shirley

Buckley, Marion

Bullitt, Kay

Bundy, John

Bundy, Mattie

Burn, Stephanie

Burns, Don

Burns, Penny

Burns, Robert M.

Burton, Phil

Byrd, Roberta (later Roberta Byrd Barr)

Cannon, Dorothy

Cannon, Major (later Lieutenant
   Colonel) John C.

Capezzuto, Joe

Carlson, JoEllen

Carrington, Cordell

Carrington, Ralph

Carrington, Regina

Carrington, William

Carrington, William, Jr.

Carson, Ron

Carter, Carolyn
Carter, Oliver
Carter, Randolph
Chaback, Bobbe Jean
Chotzen, Carla
Chotzen, Yvonne
Christensen, Louise
Clark, Charles
Clark, George
Clayton, Stanley
Clinton, Reverend Donald A.
Coe, Mary
Colbert, Mr.
Colby, Bob
Cole, Ernestine
Cole, Flora
Cole, George
Cole, Richard
Coney, Bryon
Connor, Gene
Connor, Edna
Connolly, Archbishop Thomas
Cooper, Alan
Cooper, Margaret
Cooper, Ray
Cornethan, Charles
Cornethan, John
Cornethan, Lucille
Corr, Cecelia
Corr, John
Corr, Linda
Costigan, Giovanni
Costigan, Mrs. Giovanni
Cottrell, Nick
Crawford, Reverend Edd

Crawford, Lee
Crawford, Odie
Crawford, Willie
Crocker, Margaret
Crisman, Marie
Crisman, William
Crofton, Eugene
Crow, Ginny (later Ginny Nicarthy)
Crowley, Louise
Cuevas, Aura
Curtis, Russell
Curtis, Mrs. Russell

Daniels, E.
Daniels, Mrs. Magnolia
Darling, Althea
Darrah, John
Davenport, Bob
Davenport, Pat
Davis, Barbara (later Barbara
    Robertson, later Folayan
    Oni-Robertson)
Daye, Carolyn
Dean, Georgia Lee
Dean, Yvonne
DeBerry, Clyde
DeBerry, Helen
DeCoster, Dorothy
DeCoster, Larry
Denkinger, Rudolf
Dennen, Margaret
Dickinson, Gloria
Diebert, Claudia
Doerflein, Mary
Dogge, Pearl

Dougall, Lucy
Dougherty, Reah
Dowzard, Patricia
Duncan, Don S.
Duncan, Georgia
Dunn, Clarence
Dunn, Cordelia
Dunn, E. H.
Durning, Jean
Durning, Marvin

Eason, Doris
Eaton, Eula
Edmon, John
Elder, L. Scott
Elfalan, Jose
Elliot, C. Elizabeth
Elliott, Mildred
Emmons, James
Erickson, Alice
Erickson, Reverend Walfred
Esparza, Gilbert
Esparza, Judy
Estep, Landon
Evans, Leandrin
Evans, Rachel

Farris, Jerry
Fawcett, Ellen
Fawcett, John
Fawcett, Ruth
Fay, Jim
Felchner, David
Fiedler, Beth
Fiedler, John

Fields, Bob
Finrow, --
Fischer, Kathleen
Fischer, Sharon
Fisher, Myrna
Fogerty, Ann Snyder
Forbes, Lady Willie
Fox, Jim
Fraiser, Sam
Franklin, Harold
Franklin, Mamie
Fusco, Elizabeth (Liz)

Gallant, Barbara
Gallant, Dr. Jonathan
Gandy, Pat
Gates, Isabelle M.
Gayton, Gary
Gearin, David
Geary, Kenneth
Gefer, Elizabeth
Gellerman, Mildred
George, Earl
George, Vivian
Gerber, Anne
Gerber, Sid
Gibson, Mary
Gilbert, Jill
Gilbert, John
Giles, Barbara
Givens, Cecilia
Givens, David
Givens, Mrs. David
Givens, Eddie
Givens, Gladys

Givens, Louise
Givens, Margaret
Givens, Stella
Goldberg, Dr. Irving A.
Goldenberg, Dr. Samuel
Goldenberg, Mrs. Samuel
Gordon, Diane
Gordon, Kathy
Gottfried, Alex
Gottfried, Sue Davidson
Graham, Darlene
Grantham, George
Grazette, Lincoln
Green, Susie
Griffith, Dr.
Griffiths, W. M.
Grinds, Esther
Gross, Alice
Grove, Mrs. William

Hahn, Sally
Haley, Donald
Haley, Margaret
Hall, DeWayne
Hall, Esther (later Esther Hall
    Mumford)
Hall, Reverend Henry
Hanawalt, Frank
Hanawalt, Mrs. Frank
Hanserr, Evelyn
Hardin, Kathleen
Hardin, Linda
Harris, Calvin
Harris, DeWitt
Harris, Herb

Harris, Roger
Harris, Rufus
Harris, William K.
Harvey, David D.
Hatfield, Glenn
Haun, Sally
Hawes, Anne
Hawkins, Lucy Mae
Hawthorne, Ruth
Hayes, Elaine
Hearde, Esther
Hearde, Oscar
Heatlie, David K
Hebert, Tom
Heide, William H.
Henderson, Charles
Henderson, Mrs. Charles
Hendricks, Shirley
Henry, Billy
Henry, Flo
Henry, Jackie
Henry, William
Hews, Janet
Hill, Duna
Hill, Ed C.
Hill, Mrs. Edward
Hilliard, Hartz
Hills, Gordon
Hirsh, Rabbi Norman
Hirsh, Peggy
Hodges, Chuck
Hogenauer, Irwin
Holiday, Ann
Holland, Mrs. Dorothy
Hollingsworth, Eddie

Hood, Don
Hood, Joanne
Hopperstad, Shari
Horn, Ronald
Howard, Mona
Howlett, Charles
Howlett, Elinore
Howlett, Jessie
Hubbard, Beverly
Hubbard, Lynn
Hubbard, Walt
Huber, Tom
Hudson, Beatrice
Humes, Hascal
Hundley, Felisa
Hundley, Walt
Huttman, Beth
Huttman, John

Illg, Paul
Illg, Ruth
Isaacs, Walter
Isaacs, Mrs. Walter

Jackins, Chris
Jackins, Dorothy
Jackins, Gordon
Jackins, Harvey
Jackins, Sarah
Jackins, Tim
Jackson, Beatrice
Jackson, John A.
Jackson, Reverend Mance
Jacobson, Anne
Jacobson, Fred

Jacobson, Paul
Joffe, Anna
Johansen, Karen
Johnson, Ann
Johnson, Mrs. Carl
Johnson, Charles V.
Johnson, Gerri
Johnson, Gladys
Johnson, Joyce
Johnson, Mrs. Narvell
Johnson, Norman O.
Johnson, Rafe
Johnson, Wallace
Johnson, Wesley
Jollie, Liz
Jones, Dorothy
Jones, Jean
Jones, Larry
Jones, Ray
Jones, Rex
Jones, Robert B.
Jones, Mrs. Robert B.
Jones, Robert L.
Jones, Susan
Jones, Theodore
Jones, Venita

Kalbey, Steve
Kanner, Elliott E.
Kaplan, Sarah
Kaplan, Seymour (Sy)
Kashiwagi, Mary
Katagiri, Reverend Mineo
Kennedy, Laura
Kennedy, Willie

Kimbrough, James

Kimbrough, Marjorie

King, Ivan

Kirkpatrick, Betty Jane

Kirkpatrick, Ken

Klee, Frenchie

Klee, Carl

Klinger, Reverend Daniel

Klyn, Joan

Kobler, Arthur L.

Koebler, Mrs.

Konick, Joyce

Konick, Willis

Koppel, Anci

Krushner, Mrs.

Laband, Dr. M.

Lamb, John David

Lamb, Mary

Lamb, Tommie

Laners, Barbara

Langness, Leslie

LaNore, George

Lavandier, Mike

Lavrinec, Rudy

Lee, To-shun

Lewis, James

Lichter, Alan

Lightfoot, Ethel

Lindsey, Bonnie

Little, Ruth

Livingston, Mrs. Goodhue

Locke, Merlene

Lord, Barbara

Lowe, Freddie

Lueders, Marge

Luce, Dr. Ralph

Lund, Janet

Lyle, Ed

Lynch, Father John D.

Lynch, Mattie

Lynch, Mrs. Sarah

Lynch, William (Bill)

MacDonald, Ken

Manning, Duane

Markey, Anita

Marking, K.

Marks, John

Martin, Florence

Martin, Georgia

Martin, Harold "Tim"

Martinsen, Betty

Masek, Lois

Matson, Don

Matson, Donna

McDaniel, Verta

McDuffie, Larry

McGibbons, John

McIntosh, Lester

McKinney, Reverend Samuel

Meacham, Stewart

Mead, Jane

Mercer, Lyle

Meriwether, Gertrude

Mero, Reverend Ralph

Mesher, Shirley

Metzon, Martin

Metzon, Ruth

Miller, Dr. Earl V

Milne, Margaret
Miracle, Hugh
Miracle, Joan
Mitchell, Frank
Moore, Arvelle
Moore, Diane
Moore, Jeanie
Moore, Mary
Moore, Ray
Morgan, Clarence
Morgan, Karen
Morrill, Margaret
Morrill, Richard
Morrow, Alice
Morrow, John
Moulton, Joyce
Murano, Nina
Murphy, Alice
Murphy, Dorothy
Murphy, Shelley
Murphy, Vivian
Murray, Lena

Nash, David
Newman, Cara (later Cara
  Newoman)
Newman, Harold
Noe, Billie
Noe, Cyrus
Nordli, Eric
Northwood, Larry
Northwood, Olga
Norton, Nancy
Nugent, Alice
Nylung, Barbara

Oakes, Ira
O'Keefe, Ed
O'Keefe, Kitty
Oliver, Charles
Oliver, Isaac
Oliver, Jim
Olson, J.
Orians, Dr. (Gordon?)
Orth, Bonnie
Ottenberg, Phoebe
Ottenberg, Simon

Page, Lionel
Parker, Thomas
Parry, Naomi
Patton, Dixie
Patton, Elizabeth
Patton, William
Paul, David
Pedersen, Jerry
Pennell, Paul
Petersen, Reverend Lemuel
Phillips, Alice
Phillips, Margaret
Pierce, Garnet
Pierce, Ralph
Pierini, Elizabeth
Pierre, Tomme
Polack, Mary Jane
Porter, Reverend Paree
Pratt, Edwin
Provo, Fred
Provo, Mary
Pruet, M.
Putnam, Betsy

Quainstrom, Judy
Quinn, Kate

Rabbitt, Patti
Rabbitt, Terry
Rae, Reverend James
Raible, Reverend Peter
Reardon, Susan
Red, Alfred
Redwine, Bob
Reese, Katherine
Rehwinkel, Jeanne
Reid, Letealia
Reid, Rosemary
Rice, Paul
Rice, Mrs. Paul
Richard, Dorothy
Richards, Lorna
Richman, Carol
Richman, Kathy
Ricker, Judy
Rigert, Janice
Rigert, Joseph
Riggins, J. J.
Riggins, Margie
Robel, Thorum
Robinson, Richard
Rocz, Ronald
Rogers, Albie
Rogers, Ernestine (Ernie)
   (later Ernie James, later
   Sadikifu Akina-James)
Rose, Ken
Rosen, Michael
Rosenbaum, Dr. Harold B.

Rosenfeld, Dan
Ross, Reverend John
Ross, Mrs. John
Ross, Michael
Rousseve, Ron
Rowe, Joyce
Rude, Reverend Loren
Russell, Bill
Russell, David
Russell, Ed
Russell, Florence

Sadler, Dr. Russell
Sale, Roger
Salvus, Nora
Sanders, Albert
Sandsted, Margaret
Sarcozo, Leon
Scattergood, Charles
Schaefer, Jon
Schafer, Jackie
Scheffer, Beth
Schira, Cynthia
Schroeter, Len
Schwartz, Carl
Scott, Donald
Seney, Don
Shannon, Augusta
Shelton, Robert
Shower, Ralph T., Jr.
Siegel, Shirley
Siegl, Henry
Simms, Dorothy
Singer, Rabbi Jacob
Singler, Edward

Singler, Joan

Smith, Albert

Smith, Reverend C. E.

Smith, Carole Dianne

Smith, Claude

Smith, E. June

Smith, Erv

Smith, Jennifer

Smith, Joan

Smith, Leon

Smith, Mrs. M. H

Smith, Payton

Smith, Sam

Sobel, Mrs. Raymond

Solemslie, M.

Sorenson, Soren

Sparks, William O.

Spellman, Paula

Spence, Infanta

Spencer, Mrs. Judson

Spring, Reverend Chad

Spurlock, Mary Lou

Spurlock, Shirley

Stallworth, Mary

Stein, Joan

Stein, Roger

Steinbrueck, Elaine

Stokes, Robert

Stone, Gerard

Studen, Bob

Studen, Jocelyn

Sullivan, John

Summerrise, Hellyne

Summers, Lee

Swerdloff, Mona

Swerdloff, Ron

Tamarin, Adele

Taylor, Carl

Taylor, Donald

Taylor, Mrs. Donald S.

Taylor, George

Taylor, Mrs. George

Thalberg, Irving

Thalberg, Suzanne

Thomas, Anthony

Thompson, Dr. Alvin

Thompson, Fred E.

Thompson, Frenchie

Thompson, Laurence C.

Timmes, Elbert

Tinsley, A. W. (Bud)

Tinsley, Hazel

Tobin, Carol

Tomlinson, Barbara

Trigg, Mrs. Edward

Tuell, Dean

Turner, Cecil

Tyler, James M.

Vahey, Reverend Robert

Valentine, Bettylou

Valentine, Charles (Val)

Van Wagener, Mrs.

Verhuel, Phyliss

Vincett, Dale

Von Dassow, Corinne

Von Dassow, Dick

Wadsworth, Columbus
Walkinshaw, Jean
Ware, Flo
Ware, Jeri
Warner, Dick
Warner, Tom
Washington, James, Jr.
Waters, Gladys
Watson, Mrs. David
Watson, George
Watson, Walter B.
Weaver, Paul
Weschler, Linda
Wessels, Leonard
West, Calvin
West, Marion
West, Ray
Westberg, Alfred J.
Westerlund, Dorothy
Westman, Doris
White, Ed
White, Eddie
White, Frances (later Karimu White)
White, Mrs. Fred
White, Joe
White, Patty
Whittenbaugh, John
Wiersema, Harry
Wild, A.W. (Bill)
Wiley, James
Wiley, Ruby
Wilkerson, Zayman
Williams, Reverend C. E.
Williams, Ford

Williams, Freddie
Williams, Heide
Williams, Ida
Williams, Imogine
Williams, J. R.
Williams, Ray
Williams, Robert
Williams, Roosevelt
Willis, Janice
Willman, Ken
Wilson, Evan
Wilson, Roye
Winsor, Bob
Winston, Roy
Withrow, Howard O.
Wolman, Blanche
Womack, William
Wood, Ted
Woods, Ernest
Woodson, Fred
Wright, Raymond

Yarborough, Letcher
Yates, Elizabeth
Yearly, Bonnie
Young, Bianca
Young, Dan
Young, Eva
Young, Landon
Young, Marqui
Young, Richard (Dick)

Zeh, Judith
Zietlow, Edward

NOTES

Recollections of the four authors pervade this book but are cited only for unexpected facts or for quotations. These memories are not written elsewhere, but some are included in audiotaped oral history interviews at the Museum of History and Industry, Seattle. Video interviews of Maid Adams, Bettylou Valentine, and Joan Singler are at the University of Washington's Seattle Civil Rights and Labor History Project. Extensive excerpts of the video interviews can be seen at www.civilrights.Washington.edu.

Don Matson's extensive file of Seattle CORE documents (referred to in the notes as CORE, Matson Collection) are being donated to the University of Washington Libraries, Special Collections Division, by Don's family and thus will be available to the public.

Seattle CORE's newsletter, the *Corelator* (using the same name as National CORE's newsletter and initially spelled *CORElator*), provides a month-by-month description of virtually all Seattle CORE activities. It is a major source for this book. Copies are available at Congress of Racial Equality, Seattle Collection, 1563, box 2, Special Collections Division, University of Washington Libraries. In the notes the location Congress of Racial Equality, Seattle Collection, 1563, Special Collections Division, University of Washington Libraries will be referred to simply as Seattle Collection (plus box number and folder identification where relevant). Joan Singler's summaries of all *Corelators* plus a few other sources can be found at http://depts.washington.edu/civilr/CORE_timeline.htm.

Major civil rights events in the South are well documented, including in Taylor Branch's three-volume *America in the King Years*, other books listed in the bibliography, and various websites. They are not further identified here.

PREFACE

1 See Edward P. Morgan, "At the Center of Public Memory: Martin Luther King Jr. as Icon," in *Civil Rights Movement in American Memory*, ed. Romano and Raiford, 140–41. See also Sugrue, *Sweet Land of Liberty*, xvi–xvii.

2 Meier and Rudwick, *CORE: A Study in the Civil Rights Movement*, xv.

3 Memoirs of civil rights activity in the South include those by Daisy Bates, Melba Patillo Beals, Clarice Campbell, Fanny Lou Hamer, Elizabeth Huckaby, Mary Elizabeth King, James Meredith, Cleveland Sellers, as well as those listed in the bibliography.

4 Sugrue, *Sweet Land of Liberty*, 165.

5 Bell, *CORE and the Strategy of Nonviolence*, 29.

INTRODUCTION

1 Decennial Population, City of Seattle, 1900–2000, City of Seattle Strategic Planning Office. See also Taylor, *Forging of a Black Community*, 192.

2 Sale, *Seattle Past to Present*, 246–47.

3 Sugrue, *Sweet Land of Liberty*, xxii.

1 · THE FORMATION OF SEATTLE CORE

1 Norm Johnson, interview by Joan Singler, April 8, 2006; Ray Cooper, phone interview by Singler, April 2006; Cooper email to Singler, February 5, 2009.

2 Ray Williams, phone interview by Joan Singler, June 22, 2006; Ivan King, interview by Singler and Bettylou Valentine, May 6, 2006; Ivan King, interview by Trevor Griffey, Activist Oral Histories, www.civilrights.washington.edu.

3 Elaine Hayes, interviews by Joan Singler, May 9, 2006, and February 1, 2009; Hopper and Gipson, *Frontier of the Spirit*.

4 "Unitarians for Social Justice Annual Report, 1961–'62 by Integration Committee, May 7, 1962," University Unitarian Church library archive, Seattle.

5 Ray Cooper, communications with Joan Singler, April and December 2006 and February 5, 2009, see Appendix 2; "U.W. Student: 'Freedom Rider' Pleased with Results of Trip," *Seattle Times*, September 3, 1961; "Newlywed Reluctant to Go to Prison," *Seattle Times*, February 9, 1962, front page.

6 Jon Schaefer, letters to Don and Donna Matson, August 12, 1962, through January 16, 1963, CORE, Matson Collection.

7 Joan Singler, "Report on Action Project & Selective Buying Campaign, January 15, 1962," CORE, Matson Collection.

8   Henry, "Burton, Philip," essay 321, www.HistoryLink.org.

9   For NAACP leader profiles, see Charles V. Johnson, interview by Trevor Griffey and Brooke Clarke, www.civilrights.washington.edu; Henry, "Burton, Philip," essay 321, www.HistoryLink.org; Henry, "Smith, E. June" www.BlackPast.org; Sidney Gerber Papers, 503/584/968, Special Collections Division, University of Washington Libraries. See also box 1, NAACP Papers, 465–001, Special Collections Division, University of Washington Libraries.

10 "U.W. Student: 'Freedom Rider' Pleased with Results of Trip," *Seattle Times*, September 3, 1961. Before adoption of the chapter constitution, members were not differentiated between "active" and "supporting." The *Seattle Post-Intelligencer*, December 20, 1961, reported that CORE had twenty-three active members, but that number was increased substantially in March 1962 by awarding active status to those members who had been deeply involved prior to adoption of the constitution.

11 Walt Hubbard, interview by Trevor Griffey, www.civilrights.washington.edu, Activist Oral Histories; "Annual Report of the Catholic Interracial Council, 1965–1966," box 1, folders 32–33, Walter T. Hubbard Papers, 5330–001, Special Collections Division, University of Washington Libraries.

12 Archbishop Connolly letter to Walter Hubbard and the Catholic Interracial Council, August 15, 1967, box 1, folder 33, Hubbard Papers, 5330–001, Special Collections Division, University of Washington Libraries.

13 "Task Force on Urban Problems," vol. 1, no. 5, May–June 1969, 6–7, box 1, folder 32, Hubbard Papers, 5330–001, Special Collections Division, University of Washington Libraries.

14 Joan Singler, "Report on Action Project & Selective Buying Campaign, January 15, 1962," CORE, Matson Collection; "CORE Business Meeting November 8 . . . Report from CORE Meeting, Nov. 1, 1961," box 2, *Corelators* folder, Seattle Collection (donated to University of Washington Libraries by Maid Adams and Frances [Karimu] White).

15 Wallace Johnson, emails to Joan Singler and to Jean Durning, May 8, 2008, and following; "Constitution of the Seattle Chapter of the Congress of Racial Equality—CORE November 1961," box 1, Seattle Collection.

16 Summaries of nearly eight years of *Corelators* give a sense of the multiplicity of activities happening simultaneously over the life of Seattle CORE. See the "Timeline" section for CORE at www.civilrights.Washington.edu. The direct URL for the timeline is http://depts.washington.edu/civilr/CORE_timeline.htm.

17 James Farmer's early life as a brilliant young debater is captured in the recent film *The Great Debaters*, starring Denzel Washington and produced by Oprah Winfrey.

18 Singler, "Report on Action Project & Selective Buying Campaign, January 15, 1962," CORE, Matson Collection.

19 Norm Johnson, interview by Joan Singler, April 8, 2006; box 2, Financial Records, Membership Lists, Seattle Collection; Ray Cooper thanks to Sid Gerber, box 1, general correspondence, Seattle Collection.

20 [National CORE], "This Is CORE" and "CORE Rules for Action," CORE, Matson Collection.

21 Organization chart and meeting agenda for December 13, 1962, attached to *Corelator*, December 1962, box 2, Seattle Collection.

22 Charles V. Johnson, interview by Joan Singler, spring 2008.

23 "Pastor New Chief of Rights Group," newspaper clipping [August 1963], box 2, Clippings folder, Seattle Collection.

24 Jean Durning to family, February 19, 1962, Durning personal papers; *People's World*, February 24, 1962, quoted in FBI file on Seattle Congress of Racial Equality (100–25362), April 26, 1962; sign-up sheet of film sponsors, box 2, Seattle Collection.

25 Flier, "Congress of Racial Equality Presents 'Freedom Ride,'" CORE, Matson Collection.

2 · SEATTLE CORE'S EMPLOYMENT ACTION

1 William Yardley, "Seattle Takes Steps to Recognize Minorities' Role in Shaping Region," *New York Times*, February 6, 2008. Dr. Gregory holds the Harry Bridges Endowed Chair of Labor Studies at the University of Washington.

2 "CORE Rules for Action," CORE, Matson Collection.

3 Joan Singler, "Report on Action Project," January 15, 1962, CORE, Matson Collection (hereafter Singler, "Report on Action Project").

4 Ibid.

5 Richard Morrill, interview by Jean Durning, spring 2009; Morrill, interview by Joan Singler, August 8, 2009.

6 Flier, "Don't Shop Where You Can't Work," CORE, Matson Collection.

7 Wallace Johnson, interview by Joan Singler, August 23, 2006; Johnson emails to Singler, May 8, 2008, and following.

8 Singler, "Report on Action Project"; [John and Beth Huttman], "Safeway's Policy of Racial Discrimination," [October 1961], CORE, Matson Collection (hereafter, Huttman Report).

9 Huttman Report.

10 Singler, "Report on Action Project"; typed document with handwritten notation "Copy of news item to Retail Clerks," no date, CORE, Matson Collection; King County Labor Council COPE, *People's World*, November 25, 1961, 3, as cited in FBI file SE 100–25362.

11 "Seattle Congress of Racial Equality Picket Rules," CORE, Matson Collection.

12 Congress of Racial Equality Western Regional Office files, microfilm A8104, reel III, Special Collections Division, University of Washington Libraries. (Western Regional Office original files are at the Wisconsin Historical Society.)

13 Singler, "Report on Action Project"; box 8, Safeway folder, Seattle Collection.

14 Singler, "Report on Action Project"; "Group Pickets Store Here," *Seattle Post-Intelligencer*, October 28, 1961; "Pickets Taken from 2 Stores," *Seattle Post-Intelligencer*, November 2, 1961.

15 "Status Report on Selective Buying Campaign," box 8, Seattle Collection.

16 Wallace Johnson, interview by Joan Singler; Johnson emails to Singler and to Jean Durning, May 8, 2008, and following; Ed Singler recollections.

17 Box 8, Safeway Stores folders, Seattle Collection. See also Jean Adams, "Project in the Area of Employment," January 1964, CORE, Matson Collection (hereafter Adams, "Project in Employment").

18 Adams, "Project in Employment."

19 Edward S. Singler to Manager, Lucky Food Store, October 30, 1963, box 8, Employment Correspondence folder, Seattle Collection.

20 "Survey of Seattle Lucky and Foodland Stores," August 19, 1963, box 8, Seattle Collection; Ed and Joan Singler and Jean Durning recollections.

21 Walt Hundley, interview by Mary Henry for Black Heritage Society, June 6, 1999, excerpt reprinted by Museum of History and Industry, Seattle.

22 Adams, "Project in Employment."

23 Jean Durning recollection; Adams, "Project in Employment."

24 Adams, "Project in Employment."

25 James Washington Jr., "Report to the Labor and Industry Committee—NAACP," March 10, 1965, James Washington Jr. Civil Rights folders, James and Janie Rogella Washington Foundation, 1816 Twenty-Sixth Avenue, Seattle, WA 98122; Ed and Joan Singler recollections.

26 Reginald Alleyne letter to "Dear Friends," September 18, 1963, CORE, Matson Collection.

27 Maid Adams recollection.

28 David Lamb email to Joan Singler, January 22, 2007.

29 "Operation Turkey," box 7, A&P Tea Company folders, Seattle Collection.

30 Box 2, Lists, and box 12 card file, Seattle Collection.

31 CRAG membership list, Bettylou Valentine personal papers.

32 CORE, Matson Collection. Dave Lamb wrote additional verses when the A&P campaign progressed to a shop-in.

33 Gordon Jackins, interview by Joan Singler, August 15, 2006; David and Mary Lamb, interview by Singler, June 12, 2006; Cara Newoman, interview by Singler and Jean Durning, March 9, 2009; Carole Dianne Smith, interviews by Singler, April 28, 2006, and February 9, 2009; Rob Monahan, "'Shop-In' Comes to Seattle: CORE Renews Demonstrations at A. & P.," *Seattle Times*,

March 22, 1964; "'Shop-Ins' Are Staged at 2 Stores in Seattle," *Seattle Times*, March 22, 1964.

34 David Lamb, interview by Joan Singler, June 12, 2006.

35 Anne Heckler, "CORE to Keep Up Job Pressure, Nordstrom's, A&P, Hit," *Argus*, September 8, 1964.

36 Negotiators report, September 3, 1963; "Negotiation Report, Carnation Milk Co. Visit #3," May 27, 1964; Reginald Alleyne to Mr. Henry C. Weber, June 21, 1964; all in box 7, Seattle Collection.

37 Harold T. Martin to The President's Committee on Equal Employment Opportunity, June 10, 1964, box 7, Seattle Collection.

38 Esther Hall Mumford, interview by Bettylou Valentine, October 28, 2006; Esther Hall Mumford, phone interview by Joan Singler, June 2006.

39 "Statement of the Honorable Ross E. Barnett, Governor of the State of Mississippi," July 12, 1963, Senate Commerce Committee Report, S1732, *To Eliminate Discrimination in Public Accommodations Affecting Interstate Commerce*, 359, 367; "Barnett Blasts Kennedys and Reds," *Seattle Times*, July 12, 1963.

3 · EMPLOYMENT DOWNTOWN

1 Jean Adams, "Project in the Area of Employment," January 1964, CORE, Matson Collection; authors' memories.

2 *Corelator*, April 1962–May 1963; Rhodes negotiation minutes, June 14, 1963, James Washington Jr. Civil Rights folders, James and Janie Rogella Washington Foundation, 1816 Twenty-Sixth Avenue, Seattle, WA 98122.

3 "Bon Marche Survey," December 1, 1962, box 7, Seattle Collection; Joan Singler, "Negotiation with Mr. Uhrich of the Bon Marche Feb 28 (4th visit)," CORE, Matson Collection; Mance Jackson, phone interviews by Jean Durning, March 21 and April 4, 2006.

4 Turning in charge cards was a tactic students in Atlanta had used against Rich's Department Store two years earlier (Branch, *Parting the Waters*, 346), but our Bon committee was unaware of that. Reginald Alleyne to Dear Friend, May 10, 1963, and pledge card, CORE, Matson Collection.

5 Reverend Mance Jackson to Dear Pastor, [late May, 1963] (note at bottom margin in Durning's handwriting), box 7, Seattle Collection; printed leaflet "CORE/NAACP Join Freedom March" and mimeographed flier "Join the Freedom Marchers," both in CORE, Matson Collection; Seattle CORE/Thomas H. Brose, "For Immediate Release," June 9, 1963, box 7, Seattle Collection.

6 Quoted by Reginald Alleyne, "Interim Report on CORE/NAACP Bon Marche Project," July 12, 1963, box 7, Seattle Collection.

7 Jean Durning to Grandad, June 8, 1963, Jean Durning's personal collection.

8   Alleyne to Victor Uhrich, June 8, 1963, Seattle Collection; Joan Singler, "Negotiators Report of Meeting on June 11, 1963, 1:30 p.m. at the Bon Marche Store," CORE, Matson Collection; [Joan Singler, recorder], "Second Meeting with the Bon Marche as Follow-up on June 14, 1963," box 7, Seattle Collection.

9   "No picket at Bon . . . Today," box 6, Employment Ephemera folder, Seattle Collection.

10 "700 March in Racial Protest," *Seattle Times*, June 15, 1963. News reports of crowd size ranged from seven hundred to thirteen hundred demonstrators.

11 Jean Durning remembers telling a researcher that she expected America to achieve full equality of opportunity within about five years. The researcher, a California CORE member and graduate student, who stayed overnight in the Durnings' house, undoubtedly was Inge Powell Bell.

12 "700 March in Racial Protest," *Seattle Times*, June 15, 1963; Charles Dunsire, "Black Leaders Here Launch Fight for Equality," *Seattle Post-Intelligencer*, June 16, 1963; Reggie Alleyne, "Interim Report on CORE/NAACP Bon Marche Project," July 12, 1963, Seattle Collection.

13 Reginald Alleyne, "Interim Report on CORE/NAACP Bon Marche Project," July 12, 1963, Seattle Collection.

14 Jean and Marvin Durning and Joan and Ed Singler clearly recall Tom Brose's call to KING radio. None of us is sure which figure Brose used, but all remember how authoritatively he announced an exact number (slightly under twelve hundred) "by actual head count" and that the radio repeated that number.

15 Bon Marche negotiation reports, June 14 and 27 and October 3, 1963, and January 16, 1964, box 7, Seattle Collection; "Clerks' Union Hits 'Reverse' Discrimination," *Seattle Times*, August 6, 1963; Don Page, "Store, Union in Accord on 'Seniority' of New Employees," *Seattle Post-Intelligencer*, August 7, 1963.

16 Jean Adams, recorder, "Frederick and Nelson Negotiation Report," July 3, 1963, James Washington Jr. Civil Rights folders, James and Janie Rogella Washington Foundation, Seattle; no elevator operators, Maid Adams and Jean Durning recollections. See also Jean Adams, "Summaries of Reports on Past and Current Negotiations," January 1964, CORE, Matson Collection.

17 Durning recollection. See also "Negotiation Report, Best's Apparel, 17 April 65," CORE, Matson Collection.

18 Dr. Infanta Spence-Lewis, interview by Joan Singler, November 14, 2006.

19 Newman emails to Joan Singler, March and September 8, 2009.

20 Val Valentine, "Plan for Action, 15 May 1964," box 8, Nordstrom-Best folder, Seattle Collection; "CORE 'Action' at Store Is Averted," *Seattle Times*, May 16, 1964; "CORE, Shoe Firm Agree on Job Program," *Seattle Times*, May 26, 1964.

21 Anne Heckler, "CORE to Keep Up Job Pressure, Nordstrom's, A&P, Hit," *Argus*, September 18, 1964 (emphasis in original).

22 Charles Valentine, "DEEDS: Background and Basis" (hereafter DEEDS

Report), paper version, CORE, Matson Collection; electronic version, http://
depts.washington.edu/labpics/repository/v/core/deeds/valentine_report_
ocr_op.pdf.html. Also see typed list beginning "1. This listing is only of man-
ufacturers. Other businesses in Seattle may hire as many or more employees," [research for DEEDS Report], CORE, Matson Collection.

23 DEEDS Report, 51.

24 DEEDS Report, 57, table 2, "Private Office Employment"; Lane Smith, "Civil
Rights Groups Indorse CORE Jobs Drive, but Not Boycott," *Seattle Times*,
October 25, 1964.

25 "Potential for Negro Employment Downtown," DEEDS Report, 69, appendix
5, table 1.

26 "Growth of Employment in Downtown Seattle," DEEDS Report, 38, data
from Central Association of Seattle.

27 Lane Smith, "Civil Rights Groups Indorse CORE Jobs Drive, but Not Boycott,"
Seattle Times, October 25, 1964.

28 "C.O.R.E. Slates Demonstrations," *Seattle Post-Intelligencer*, October 24, 1964;
"Fact Sheet on Downtown Employment," August 1964, CORE, Matson Collection; Tim Martin to Friends of Civil Rights, August 26, 1964, CORE, Matson Collection; Martin to Friends of Civil Rights, October 28, 1964, CORE,
Matson Collection; fliers "Jobs Rally," "Jobs for Negroes Now!" "DEEDS Special Call to Action!" "DEEDS Project Goes Ahead," "Who? *You, Your Children, Friends," all in CORE, Matson Collection.

4 · TAXI COMPANIES AND UNIONS

1 Jean Adams, "Taxi-cab Appointments: 8/27/64," CORE, Matson Collection;
see also *Corelator*, March, August, and September 1964.

2 Washington State Board against Discrimination, "Findings and Recommendations in Taxicab Hearing," [summer 1964], CORE, Matson Collection.

3 Ibid.

4 "Taxi Stands" list, box 8, Taxi Survey folder, Seattle Collection; "Taxi Picket"
sign-up sheet, box 8, Seattle Collection; Tim Martin, press release, "Operation Pogo Stick," box 8, Seattle Collection; Harold "Tim" Martin to Dear
Friend, no date, CORE, Matson Collection; fliers "Are You Being Taken for a
Ride?" and "Taxi Information for Operation Pogo Stick," CORE, Matson Collection.

5 Anne Hecker, "CORE to Keep Up Job Pressure," *Argus*, September 18, 1964.

6   "10–5–64 Mr. Lancaster . . . ," note in Don Matson's handwriting, box 8, Taxi Survey folder, Seattle Collection.

7   Brock to Hosking, box 8, Taxi Survey, correspondence folder, Seattle Collection.

8   See Patrick McRoberts, "Seattle General Strike Begins on February 6, 1919," essay 5372, www.HistoryLink.org; Ross Reider and Walt Crowley, "West Coast Waterfront Strike of 1934," essay 1391, www.HistoryLink.org; and other entries at www.HistoryLink.org.

9   Ed Singler recollection; FBI file SE 100–25362, citing *People's World*, November 25, 1961, 3 (which identified the speakers only as one white and one Negro).

10 *Seattle Post-Intelligencer*, July 19, 1963.

11 [Dick Cole], "A Proposal for Union Co-operation," May 1964, CORE, Matson Collection.

12 Hundley to Director, General Services Administration, September 2, 1965, CORE, Matson Collection.

13 Washington State Board against Discrimination, "Agenda, Meeting on Apprenticeship and Training Programs," February 25, 1966; [Washington State Board against Discrimination], "Outline—Union Investigation" with attached tables, "Non-white Participation in the Building Trade Unions—Seattle—October/November 1965"; Washington State Board against Discrimination, "Building Trades Crafts Unions: Conclusions," no date, after November 1965; all in CORE, Matson Collection.

14 "Task Force on Urban Problems," vol. 1, no. 5, May–June 1969, 6–7, box 1, folder 32, Walter T. Hubbard Papers, 32–33, 5330–001, Special Collections Division, University of Washington Libraries.

15 "Governor's Executive Order Pertaining to Fair Practices by State Agencies," August 2, 1966, CORE, Matson Collection.

16 Washington State Board against Discrimination, "No. 4: Policy Statement: Affirmative Action in Minority Group Employment," September 15, 1966, CORE, Matson Collection.

17 Seattle CORE [Don Matson], "Labor Unions, a Report on the Seattle Area," November 9, 1966, CORE, Matson Collection.

18 Flier announcing Herb Hill address at First AME Church, sent to CORE mailing list, CORE, Matson Collection.

19 *Corelator*, April 24, 1967, box 2, Seattle Collection.

20 Kayomi Wada, "Central Contractors Association," www.BlackPast.org.

21 The report by Trevor Griffey is available at www.civilrights.washington.edu.

1   Legislative Committee, Apartment Operators Association, to Fellow Apartment Operators, January 31, 1963, box 9, Housing Incoming Correspondence folder, Seattle Collection.

2   Reginald Alleyne, "Fear of Pressure," letter to editor, *Seattle Post-Intelligencer*, March 8, 1964.

3   Robert C. Weaver, "Chicago: A City of Covenants," *Crisis*, July 1946, 76, as quoted by Sugrue, *Sweet Land of Liberty*, 201.

4   Taylor, *Forging of a Black Community*, 194.

5   "Digest of Process in Developing a Clearing Service on Minority Housing Undertaken by the Greater Seattle Housing Council, Seattle, Washington," July 6, 1961, CORE, Matson Collection.

6   Gordon Jackins, interview by Joan Singler, August 15, 2006.

7   Contributing members of Harmony Homes: Sid and Anne Gerber, Stimson and Kay Bullitt (through the Bullitt Foundation), Stanley Arkley, Doctors Earl and Rosalie Miller, Alice Phillips, Edward Stern, Robert Winsor, Harold "Tim" Martin, and Ed Pratt (Seattle Urban League executive director), box 14, Harmony Homes folders, Sidney Gerber Papers, 503, 584, 968, Special Collections Division, University of Washington Libraries.

8   Box 14, Harmony Homes folders, Sidney Gerber Papers, 503, 584, 968, Special Collections Division, University of Washington Libraries; James and Marjorie Kimbrough, interview by Joan Singler, February 13, 2007.

9   Sid Gerber to "Hello Fellow Brokers," March 16, 1960, and other papers, box 14, folder 5, Sidney Gerber Papers, 503, 584, 968, Special Collections Division, University of Washington Libraries.

10 Gerber loans, box 5, Sidney Gerber Papers, 503, 584, 968, Special Collections Division, University of Washington Libraries.

11 Robert Winsor, interview by Joan Singler, March 14, 2007.

12 Elaine Hayes, interview by Joan Singler, May 9, 2006, and February 1, 2009; Don Matson, untitled report of Unitarians' involvement and history with the Fair Housing Listing Service, [about June 1962], CORE, Matson Collection; "Integration Committee Annual Report to Unitarians for Social Justice, 1962–1963," University Unitarian Church Library Archives, Seattle.

13 *Mercer Island Reporter*, January 24, 1962.

14 "In the Market for a Home" and FHLS leaflet, "A New Home in Your Future?" CORE, Matson Collection.

15 Harold (Tim) Martin and Georgia Martin, untitled six-page report [to mayor's Citizens' Advisory Committee on Minority Housing], August 15, 1962, CORE, Matson Collection; Tim Martin oral history, February 18, 1992, Eastside Heritage Center, excerpts reproduced in "My name is Tim Martin," a "first person

flier" for distribution at an exhibit at the Museum of History and Industry, Seattle.

16 "Fair Housing Listing Service Inventory," winter 1963, CORE, Matson Collection; "'Fair Housing' List Service Formed, Seeks Buyers, Sellers," *Aero Mechanic*, January 14, 1963; press release, "Seattle Fair Housing Listing Service," May 20, 1964, box 14, folder 14, Sidney Gerber Papers, 503, 584, 968, Special Collections Division, University of Washington Libraries.

17 CORE Housing Committee, "Report of Housing Discrimination by Real Estate Industry," [October 1963], CORE, Matson Collection.

18 Ibid.; Realtors' postcards ("You can decide . . ."), CORE, Matson Collection.

19 CORE chapters in other cities used the name "Operation Windowshop" earlier, but Seattle's project was designed differently. See Meier and Rudwick, *CORE: A Study in the Civil Rights Movement*, 184.

20 "CORE invites you to join Operation Windowshop," CORE, Matson Collection.

21 "'Imported Agitators' Reported; CORE Denies It," *Seattle Times*, July 28, 1963; "Nonwhites Will Repeat Realty Search," *Seattle Times*, July 29, 1963.

22 CORE Housing Committee, "Report of Housing Discrimination by Real Estate Industry," [October 1963], CORE, Matson Collection.

23 Marshal Wilson, "Plans Mapped for Second 'Windowshop,'" *Seattle Post-Intelligencer*, July 31, 1963.

24 "'Windowshop' for Houses Continues," no date, box 9, *Windowshop clippings* folder, Seattle Collection; notice of meeting August 19, 1963, box 9, *Housing Outgoing* folder, *Seattle Collection*.

25 Tom Brose to City Councilman Floyd Miller requesting proclamation of August 28, 1963, as Civil Rights Day in Seattle, box 1, Correspondence 1963 folder; Brose to Chief of Police (telegram) and Brose to City Engineer (telegram) requesting parade permit, box 1, Correspondence 1963 folder; Acting Mayor Floyd Miller to Brose, official proclamation of Civil Rights Day, August 28th, 1963, in observance of the March on Washington for Jobs and Freedom; all in Seattle Collection.

26 Affidavit of Reverend Lemuel Petersen, June 18, 1964, *Seattle Real Estate Board and Picture Floor Plans, Inc. v. Seattle Congress of Racial Equality*, no. 621098, Superior Court of the State of Washington.

27 In addition to civil rights campaign leaders Reverend John Adams, Reverend Samuel McKinney, and Reverend Paree Porter, these clergy were Reverend William Arbaugh, St. Stephen's Lutheran Church; Reverend Paul Beeman, Magnolia Methodist; Reverend William Brown and Reverend Mineo Katagiri, University Congregational; Reverend Edd Crawford, Madrona Community Presbyterian; Reverend Walfred Erickson, Clyde Hill Baptist; Rabbi Norman Hirsh, Temple Beth Am; Reverend Daniel Klinger, Mercer Island

Presbyterian; Reverend Lemuel Petersen, University Baptist; Reverend James Rae, Mount Baker Park Presbyterian; Reverend Peter Raible, University Unitarian; Reverend Loren Rude, the Lutheran Student Foundation; Reverend Chad Spring, East Shore Unitarian; Rabbi Jacob Singer, Temple de Hirsch; Reverend Robert Vahey, Grace Methodist; and Reverend C. E. Williams, New Hope Baptist.

28 Joan Singler, telegram to Governor Rosellini, September 12, 1963, box 1, General Correspondence folder; Singler and Reggie Alleyne to Governor Rosellini, September 16, 1963, box 9, Outgoing Correspondence folder; press release, box 9, News Releases folder; excerpts from Governor Rosellini's address to National Conference of Commissions against Discrimination, July 23, 1962, box 9, Housing Ephemera folder; all in Seattle Collection.

29 Newspaper article, [September 16?], 1963, "Rosellini Hit for Praise of Realtors," box 9, Clippings folder, Seattle Collection.

30 Don Matson to Citizens' Advisory Committee on Minority Housing, August 16, 1962; "Report of the Citizens' Advisory Committee on Minority Housing," [December 1962]; both in CORE, Matson Collection.

31 Alleyne to Mayor Clinton, December 28, 1962, box 1, General Correspondence folder, Seattle Collection; "Statement on the Need for a Seattle Anti-discrimination Housing Law," [May 1963], written and signed by Reginald Alleyne for CORE, also signed by Charles V. Johnson, NAACP; Reverend Mance Jackson, Bethel CME Church; Reverend Samuel B. McKinney, Mount Zion Baptist Church; Reverend C. E. Williams, New Hope Baptist Church; and State Representative Sam Smith (mimeographed), CORE, Matson Collection,

32 "Negro Leader Urges Housing Law" and Douglas Willix, "Council Influenced by Spokesmen for Open-Housing Ordinance," both Seattle Times, July 2, 1963.

33 Lane Smith, "City Council Stalls on Housing, Negroes Charge," Seattle Times, July 2, 1963.

34 "Negro Girls Lead Sit-in at City Hall," Seattle Times, July 22, 1963; "Group Continues Sit-in at City Hall," Seattle Times, July 23, 1963; "Racial Flare-up at City Hall," Seattle Times, July 25, 1963.

35 Alfred J. Westberg to the Honorable Gordon S. Clinton, August 29, 1963, enclosing ordinance, box 1, Correspondence, Misc. folder, Seattle Collection.

36 Seattle CORE untitled press release, January 28, 1964; leaflets, "Racial Discrimination Hurts Seattle"; both in CORE, Matson Collection.

37 CURE newsletter, box 9, Housing Ephemera folder, Seattle Collection.

38 "Archbishop Calls for Total Commitment on Racial Justice," Catholic Northwest Progress, March 6, 1964.

39 E. M. Sterling, "County Law Would Ban Bias in Housing Sales," Seattle Times, February 23, 1964; "Archbishop Calls for Total Commitment on Racial Justice," Catholic Northwest Progress, March 6, 1964. See also Forrest Williams,

"By 2 King Co. Commissioners: 'Housing' Bill Signed despite Legal Cloud," *Seattle Post-Intelligencer*, March 10, 1964.

40 Seattle Real Estate Board leaflet, "Before You Vote . . . What about Forced Housing?" CORE, Matson Collection; Apartment Operators Association ad, "Your Rights Are at Stake," Campaign Literature, Spring 1964, call number R324.79 C152, Seattle Public Library (and *Seattle Times*, March 9, 1964); Apartment Operators Association flier, "Attention Renters," Campaign Literature, Spring 1964, call number R324.79 C152, Seattle Public Library.

41 Kenneth Coleman, Chairman, Citizens Committee for Open Housing, to Dear Friends, March 24, 1964, CORE, Matson Collection.

6 · DIRECT ACTION TO END SEGREGATED HOUSING

1 Mrs. G. L. [Judy] Esparza, "A Report on Seattle CORE's First Sit-in Demonstration at a Real Estate Office," [March 1964], CORE, Matson Collection.

2 [Judy Esparza], "A Statement of Principles by Seattle Congress of Racial Equality," March 22, 1964, CORE, Matson Collection.

3 Mrs. G. L. [Judy] Esparza, "A Report on Seattle CORE's First Sit-in Demonstration at a Real Estate Office," [March 1964], CORE, Matson Collection; "C.O.R.E. Members Picket, Sit-in at Realty Firm," *Seattle Post-Intelligencer*, March 23, 1964; "Picketing: CORE to Continue Realty-Firm Sit-ins," *Seattle Times*, March 23, 1964.

4 "Suggested Provisions for a Written Agreement between Seattle CORE and Any Realtor Practicing Racial Discrimination," CORE, Matson Collection.

5 [Judy Esparza], "A Report on Seattle CORE's Direct Action Housing Project Protesting Racial Discrimination Practices at Picture Floor Plans, Inc., a Real Estate Office," [after May 12, 1963] (hereafter "Report on Direct Action at PFP"), CORE, Matson Collection; Ernie Rogers (Sadikifu Akina-James) and Barbara Davis (Folayan Oni-Robertson), joint interview by Bettylou Valentine, May 5, 2007.

6 "Report on Direct Action at PFP."

7 Ibid.; Joan Singler recollection.

8 "Report on Direct Action at PFP."

9 Martin to The Honorable J. D. Braman, April 18, 1964, box 9, Seattle Collection; "Report on Direct Action at PFP."

10 F. C. Ramon, Chief of Police, "Intra-departmental Communication of the Seattle Police Department," April 13 and 14, 1964, box 6, Police Department folder, Seattle Human Rights Commission, 1958–65, 976–001, Special Collections Division, University of Washington Libraries.

11   William Ames, "Seattle Mayor Accents 'Rights,'" *Christian Science Monitor*, June 8, 1964, as reported in *Seattle Observer*, June 24, 1964.

12   "Report on Direct Action at PFP"; Martin to Chief F. C. Ramon, April 22, 1964, and Ramon to Martin, April 23, 1964, both in box 6, Seattle Collection. For fifty-one police photos of CORE demonstrators at Picture Floor Plans, see City of Seattle, City Clerk's Online Information, Municipal Archives photograph index, at www.clerk.ci.seattle.wa.us.

13   "Report on Direct Action at PFP."

14   [Esparza], "A Statement of Principles by Seattle Congress of Racial Equality," March 22, 1964, CORE, Matson Collection.

15   "Report on Direct Action at PFP."

16   Ibid.; *Corelator*, June 1964.

17   *Seattle Real Estate Board and Picture Floor Plans, Inc. v. Seattle Congress of Racial Equality*, no. 621098, Superior Court of the State of Washington.

18   Ibid.

19   "Burton Scathes State Discrimination Board," *Seattle Observer*, June 17, 1964.

20   "Intra-department Communications, Seattle Police Department," June 13, 1964, box 6, Police Department folder, Seattle Human Rights Commission, 1958–65, 976–001, Special Collections Division, University of Washington Libraries.

21   Fair Housing Listing Service, Sidney Gerber Papers, 503/584/968, Special Collections Division, University of Washington Libraries.

22   RCW Title 64, Real Property and Conveyances—Section 64.38.028 Removal of discriminatory provisions in governing documents, Finding—Intent—2006c58.

7 · SEATTLE'S SEGREGATED SCHOOLS

1   Pieroth, "Desegregating the Public Schools," 132–36.

2   "24-Hour Vigil Begun in Seattle," *Seattle Times*, June 26, 1964.

3   Charles Valentine, "Segregation and Integration in Seattle's Public Schools: An Analysis and Plan Offered by Seattle CORE," box 5, Seattle Collection.

4   *Corelator*, August 1964.

5   Box 5, Seattle Collection.

6   *Corelator*, January 1965.

7   Pieroth, "Desegregating the Public Schools," 283–84; "Suit to Halt Racial Imbalance in Seattle Schools Is Filed," *Seattle Times*, March 18, 1966.

8   "A Proposal for Re-organization of the Elementary Division of the Seattle Public Schools," CORE, Matson Collection.

9   "CORE-NAACP Statement," *Corelator*, May 20, 1965.

10 Seattle School Board minutes, May 12, 1965, Seattle Public School Archives, Record 61, pp. 302–5, Seattle Public Schools, 2445 Third Avenue South, Seattle.

11 Cornethan and Smith, "CORE-NAACP News Release, 5/13/65," box 5, News Releases, Seattle Collection.

12 Chotzen to Barth, October 1, 1965, box 5, Outgoing Correspondence, Seattle Collection; Chotzen to Morrill, October 1, 1965, Seattle Collection.

13 Sue Davidson, interview by Joan Singler, Bettylou Valentine, and Maid Adams, April 15, 2007.

14 "Seattle Clergy Ask U.S. Action in Alabama," *Seattle Post-Intelligencer*, March 13, 1965; "1,000 State Marchers Protest Slaying of Minister in Selma, Ala.," *Seattle Post-Intelligencer*, March 14, 1965; Lane Smith, "Martyrdom Honored: Dozens Keep All-Night Vigil Here for Mr. Reeb" and "Service to End Vigil Here for Slain Cleric," *Seattle Times*, March 14, 1965; "One Career Marine Officer," *Corelator*, March 1965.

15 "Persons volunteering for committee on schools, June 8, 1965," Sue Davidson personal papers.

16 *Corelator*, June 9, 1965; flier "All Seattle Children Need . . . ," CORE, Matson Collection; four leafleteers' maps, box 3, Misc., Maps of Central Area folder, Seattle Collection; *Corelator*, June 9, 1965.

17 First AME Church, Volunteers for Home Meetings (sign-up sheet), box 6, Home Visits folder, Seattle Collection.

18 "Suit to Halt Racial Imbalance in Seattle Schools Is Filed," *Seattle Times*, March 18, 1966; Pieroth, "Desegregating the Public Schools," 283–84.

19 Lane Smith, "School Board Issues Racial-Policy Statement," *Seattle Times*, March 18, 1966; Seattle Schools, "Education for Understanding: A Report on Intergroup Education in the Seattle Public Schools," [March 1966], Schools scrapbook, CORE, Matson Collection.

20 Walt Hundley, interview by Mary Henry, June 6, 1999, taped Oral History, Black History Heritage Society, Museum of History and Industry, Seattle.

8 · BOYCOTT AND FREEDOM SCHOOLS

1 *Corelator*, February 20, 1966

2 Cornethan, Smith, and Adams to school officials, reprint, no date, Schools scrapbook, CORE, Matson Collection.

3 *Corelator*, March 21, 1966.

4 [Jean Adams], "Impressions of First AME Freedom School as Seen by the Vice Principal," [early May 1965], Maid Adams personal files; Maid Adams recollection; box 5, Freedom Schools 1966 Financial Records folder, Seattle Collection.

5   Seattle School Integration Committee minutes, March 25, 1966, box 5, Seattle Collection.

6   Lane Smith, "Churchmen Back School Boycott," *Seattle Times*, March 17, 1966.

7   "Presbytery Encourages Boycott," *Seattle Times*, March 17, 1966.

8   Charles Russell, "15 Ministers Lash School Boycott," *Seattle Post-Intelligencer*, March 19, 1966, front page.

9   Lane Smith, "Downtown Pastors Object: School-Boycott Controversy among Clergy Cuts Deeper," *Seattle Times*, March 19, 1966.

10   "Freedom Pupils Hear Attack on Compulsory School Law," *Seattle Times*, March 31, 1966.

11   Peter Raible, "'De Facto School Segregation'—a Pulpit Editorial Given by the Reverend Peter Spilman Raible, Minister, at University Unitarian Church of Seattle on March 23 and 27, 1966," Schools scrapbook, CORE, Matson Collection; "Unitarians Adopt Boycott Resolution," *Seattle Times*, March 29, 1966; Lane Smith, "Morality of Boycott: Clergy Has Mixed Feelings," *Seattle Times*, March 25, 1966.

12   Lane Smith, "Archbishop Backs School Boycott," *Seattle Times*, March 22, 1966; Herb Robinson column, "'Boycott' Has Legal Undertones," *Seattle Times*, March 23, 1996.

13   Lane Smith, "Morality of Boycott: Clergy Has Mixed Feelings," *Seattle Times*, March 25, 1966; Bill Sieverling, "The School Boycott: A Crisis of Conscience," *Seattle Post-Intelligencer*, March 27, 1966; Peter Raible, "'De Facto School Segregation'—a Pulpit Editorial. . . ," Schools scrapbook, CORE, Matson Collection.

14   Lane Smith, "Rabbi Proposes Parley on School Racial Issues," *Seattle Times*, March 25, 1966, front page.

15   Herb Robinson column, "Reaction to Boycott Surprises Backers," *Seattle Times*, March 20, 1966.

16   Bottomly to Fred Breit (memorandum), March 2, 1966; Bottomly to Armand Colang (memorandum), March 2, 1966; Bottomly to Joseph L. Thimm, March 8, 1966; Bottomly to Fred Breit and Robert Bass, March 21, 1966; Bottomly to Fred Breit, March 30, 1966; all in box 1, folder 8, Seattle Public Schools, 2153, Special Collections Division, University of Washington Libraries.

17   Lane Smith, "Central Area Pupils Show Big Response to Boycott," *Seattle Times*, March 31, 1966; Tom Read, "School Boycott Bells Ring Out," *Seattle Post-Intelligencer*, April 1, 1966.

18   Maid Adams recollection.

19   [Jean Adams], "Impressions of First AME Freedom School as Seen by the Vice Principal," [early May 1965], Maid Adams personal files.

20   Ibid.

21   Trudy Weckworth, "North End Pastor Reports on Freedom School Group,"

undated clipping, Schools scrapbook, CORE, Matson Collection; "Elementary Freedom Schools—Class Schedules, Day 1 and 2," and "Atlantic Street Center—Senior High School Schedule," box 5, Freedom School, 1966 folders, Seattle Collection; "Jr. High Freedom School Mount Zion Baptist Church, Schedule of Classes," Schools scrapbook, CORE, Matson Collection; *Corelator*, April 25, 1966.

22 "Our Staff [First AME Freedom School]" and "Prince Hall Freedom High School Staff, March 31, April 1 and Special Interest People," box 5, Freedom School, 1966 folders, Seattle Collection; Marshall Wilson, "Freedom Schools Have Varied Staffs," *Seattle Times*, March 31, 1966.

23 [Jean Adams], "Impressions of First AME Freedom School," [early May 1965], Maid Adams personal files.

24 Ibid.

25 Marshall Wilson, "Ballard Teacher Puts His Civic Principles above Pay," *Seattle Times*, April 1, 1966.

26 Steve Kent, "Raible Family Split by Boycott," *Seattle Post-Intelligencer*, April 1, 1966.

27 "Absentee Count Up in Boycott," *Seattle Post-Intelligencer*, April 1, 1966; Lane Smith, "School Absenteeism Is Up as Two Day Boycott Ends," *Seattle Times*, April 1, 1966; Tom Read, "School Boycott Bells Ring Out," *Seattle Post-Intelligencer*, April 1, 1966.

28 "Presbytery Encourages Boycott," *Seattle Times*, March 17, 1966; "Catholic Group 'Strongly' for School Boycott," *Seattle Times*, March 20, 1966; Lane Smith, "Archbishop Backs School Boycott," *Seattle Times*, March 22, 1966; "Teachers Endorse Boycott," *Seattle Times*, March 28, 1966; "Union Women Back Seattle School Boycott," *Seattle Times*, March 20, 1966; Lane Smith, "Morality of Boycott: Clergy Has Mixed Feelings," *Seattle Times*, March 25, 1966; "Churchmen Back School Boycott," *Seattle Times*, March 17, 1966; *Corelator*, April 25, 1966.

29 Marty Loken, "Teen Gauge: Freedom School Pupils Discuss the Boycott," *Seattle Times*, April 2, 1966.

30 Cal Harris and Les McIntosh, "Meeting of the Education Committee, C.O.R.E., Tuesday, 26 April, 1966, Resolution on School Integration Campaign," CORE, Matson Collection.

31 School Integration Rally announcement, box 5, Education Reports, Seattle Collection; *Corelator*, May 23, 1966.

32 Pieroth, "Desegregating the Public Schools," 287–88.

33 Ibid.; Adams, Hundley, McKinney, Pratt, Smith, Cornethan, and Johnson to Parents, July 6, 1966, CORE, Matson Collection.

34 Felisa Hundley, interview by Joan Singler, April 30, 2007; authors' recollections.

35 Sadikifu Akina-James (Ernie Rogers) and Folayan Oni-Robertson (Barbara Davis), interview by Joan Singler and Bettylou Valentine, May 5, 2007; "10 Seattleites at Institute on Desegregation," *Seattle Times*, July 2, 1966; *Corelator*, June 20, 1966, August 23, 1966.

36 "Negro History Class," *Corelator*, February 20, 1967; "Archdiocese Buys 500 Copies of 'George Washington Bush,'" box 4, Seattle Collection.

37 Sadikifu Akina-James (Ernie Rogers) and Folayan Oni-Robertson (Barbara Davis), interview by Singler and Valentine, May 5, 2007.

38 "CAMP Won't Aid Student-Transfer Plan," *Seattle Times*, May 9, 1967.

9 · MAINTAINING THE ORGANIZATION

1 Maid Adams recollection.

2 Minutes of membership meeting, August 23, 1964, box 2, Seattle Collection.

3 Meier and Rudwick, *CORE: A Study in the Civil Rights Movement*, 226.

4 Ibid., 201.

5 "At Picture Floor Plans . . . ," "During the Tradewell shop-in . . . ," and "Malicious and vulgar slogans . . ." quotations from Val and Bettylou Valentine, "Violations of the CORE Rules for Action," [August 1964], box 3, Ad Hoc Committee folder, Seattle Collection.

6 "Last Saturday afternoon . . . ," "They also share an attitude . . . ," and "With one or two exceptions . . ." quotations from Jean Adams, three-page untitled document beginning "I would like to state my concern. . . ," [August] 1964, Maid Adams personal files (partial copy at Seattle Collection).

7 Hall, recorded by Valentine, untitled list beginning "The following information. . . ," [August 1964], box 3, Ad Hoc Committee folder, Seattle Collection.

8 Executive Board meeting minutes, May 11, 1964, box 2, Seattle Collection.

9 Tim Martin, Walt Hundley, Bettylou Valentine, and John Cornethan to Active Member, "Special Meeting—Monday, August 24," box 2, *Corelators* folder, Seattle Collection.

10 Joan Singler remembers Donna frequently telling this story.

11 Norm Johnson, interview by Joan Singler, April 8, 2006.

12 Joan Singler's FBI file is number 100–40694. We also received the FBI files of Ed Singler, John Cornethan, and Reggie Alleyne.

13 "Intra-department Communication, Seattle Police Department," April 6, 1964, Human Rights Commission, 976–001, Special Collections Division, University of Washington Libraries; "Intra-department Communication," to M. E. Cook, Deputy Chief, Seattle Police Department, April 24, 1964.

14 FBI file 100–25362, summary, November 29, 1966.

15 Donner, *Age of Surveillance.*

16 Durning to her parents, August 1963, Durning personal files.

17 Cara Newoman, interview by Joan Singler and Jean Durning, May 9, 2009.

18 Financial Records, box 2, Seattle Collection; ledgers, cash book, box 12, Seattle Collection.

19 Inflation factor based on ranges in U.S. Bureau of Labor Statistics, Consumer Price Index, Seattle 1961 to February 2010, as follows: all urban consumers, 7.72%; wage earners and clerical workers, 7.3%. See www.Seattle.gov/financedepartment/CPI/historical.htm (accessed May 10, 2010).

20 "Comedian Finds No Race Bias at Fair," *Seattle Times,* June 25, 1962.

21 Joan Singler recollection.

22 Jean Durning recollection.

23 Louis Guzzo, "Words and Music: Gregory Zeroes In on Prejudice," *Seattle Times,* June 25, 1962; John Voorhees, "Look and Listen: Negro Comic's Wit Is a Hit—Barbed, Yes, but Never Bitter," *Seattle Post-Intelligencer,* June 25, 1962; Norm Johnson, interview by Joan Singler, April 8, 2006; *Corelator,* May and July 1962.

24 "Accounting of Dick Gregory Show," box 2, Financial Records folder, Seattle Collection.

25 Baldwin spoke at Denver, Seattle, Eugene, San Francisco, Sacramento, and Los Angeles. Reel I, CORE Western Regional Office files, microfilm A8104, Special Collections Division, University of Washington Libraries.

26 Maid Adams recollection.

27 *Corelator,* February–April 1963; program of Baldwin lecture, including list of patrons, CORE, Matson Collection.

28 Jean Durning recollection.

29 Carole Dianne Smith, emails to Joan Singler, April 28 and August 24, 2009.

30 David Laskin, review of *The Fire Next Time,* Amazon.com.

31 *Corelator,* May 1963.

32 *Corelator,* October–December 1965.

33 *Corelator,* October–November 1964, January and September 1965, November–December 1967; flier "Look! Holiday Specials from CORE," CORE, Matson Collection; "CORE Committee to Adopt a Civil Rights Worker," CORE, Matson Collection.

34 *Corelator,* July 1964, March and July–September 1965, April–May 1966.

35 *Corelator,* July 1966; authors' recollections.

36 Direct appeals are in virtually every *Corelator;* Bettylou Valentine to Active CORE Members, [July 1964], box 2, Corelators folder, Seattle Collection; pledge cards, membership cards, CORE, Matson Collection.

1 "'Black Power' Not Antiwhite Slogan, Says CORE Unit," *Seattle Times*, July 24, 1966.

2 Jack Shafer, "Back to the '60s," review of *1968*, by Michael T. Kaufman, *New York Times Sunday Book Review*, February 15, 2009.

3 Jean Adams heard and wrote down this comment when McKissick visited Seattle; note (no date) in Maid Adams's personal papers.

4 *Corelator*, July 1967, August 29, 1967; Don Hannula, "CORE Votes for Black-Power Concept," *Seattle Times*, July 28, 1967.

5 "Local CORE to Remain Multiracial," *Seattle Times*, July 19, 1967; "CORE Chairman Defends His Role," *Seattle Times*, August 26, 1967; Lane Smith, "CORE Leader Holds Firm Belief in Militancy—with 'Some Dignity,'" *Seattle Times*, September 10, 1967.

6 Don Hannula, "CORE Votes for Black-Power Concept," *Seattle Times*, July 28, 1967; Walter A. Evans, "What Is Black Power?" *Seattle Post-Intelligencer*, July 29, 1967, front page.

7 Lane Smith, "New CORE Leaders Here Set Meeting on Black-Power Goals," *Seattle Times*, September 14, 1967.

8 "National CORE OK's Recall of Chairman Here," *Seattle Times*, September 13, 1967; "New CORE Leaders Here Set Meeting on Black-Power Goals," *Seattle Times*, September 14, 1967; Hilda Bryant, "Black Power Play Shakes Up C.O.R.E.," *Seattle Post-Intelligencer*, September 15, 1967, front page; *Corelator*, July, August, and October 1967.

9 *Corelator*, October 17 and November 10, 1967.

10 Folayan Oni-Robertson, interview by Joan Singler and Bettylou Valentine, May 5, 2007.

11 We assume the April issue is the last; it is the last we have found in any collection.

12 Folayan Oni-Robertson, personal conversation with Maid Adams, May 6, 2010.

13 Meier and Rudwick, *CORE: A Study in the Civil Rights Movement*, 384–85.

14 Purnell, "A Movement Grows in Brooklyn," 8.

EPILOGUE

1 Andrea Hogue, "Rushdie Turns Up the Heat with a Steamy 16th Century Love Story," *Seattle Post-Intelligencer*, June 6, 2008.

2 "SEATTLE CORE—CORE CONFERENCE, 17 Aug. 1963, Seattle University," text for address to conference, box 2, *Corelators* folder, Seattle Collection.

3   Stuart Eskenazi, "150 Years, Seattle By and By: Familiar Landscape Lured Scandinavians," *Seattle Times*, November 4, 2001.

4   Henry W. McGee Jr., "Seattle's Central District, 1990–2006: Integration or Displacement," *Urban Lawyer* 39, no. 2 (2007): 167, 185.

5   Florangela Davila and Justin Mayo, "The Central Area: Seattle's Changing," *Seattle Times*, July 22, 2001.

6   "The Resegregation of Seattle's Schools," *Seattle Times*, Special Report series, June 1–3, 2008.

7   Linda Shaw, "Schools," *Seattle Times*, June 1, 2008.

8   Jessica Blanchard, "Don't Drop School District's Equity Office Protesters Urge," *Seattle Post-Intelligencer*, June 5, 2008.

APPENDIX 1

1   Originally published in *The Progressive*, December 1965. Reprinted by permission from *The Progressive*, 409 E. Main St., Madison, WI 53703, www.progressive.org.

APPENDIX 2

1   Transcribed from Ray Cooper's handwritten seven-page letter to Joan Singler, which she received on December 28, 2006.

APPENDIX 3

1   Kenneth Karst, "In Memoriam: Reginald H. Alleyne, Professor of Law, Emeritus," University of California, http://www.universityofcalifornia.edu/senate/inmemoriam/reginaldhalleyne.htm.

2   Infanta Spence-Lewis, email to Joan Singler, December 20, 2007; Bill Lynch, interview by Joan Singler, November 2007.

3   The Voices of World War, Education/Research: Transcripts: Europe (Army), John Cannon, http://www.wwiihistoryclass.com/education/transcripts cannon_J_011.pdf and http://www.wwiihistoryclass.com/education/transcripts/Cannon_J_012.pdf; Angelo Bruscas, "Caring for Children for Two Decades: Founders of Central Area Clinic Honored," *Seattle Post-Intelligencer*, October 11, 1991; Elizabeth Rhodes, "Leading the Way," *Seattle Times*, January

20, 1985; African-American Veterans to Participate in WVU Panel Discussion Tuesday," West Virginia University press release, February 11, 2005, excerpt at http://wvutoday.wvu.edu/n/2005/02/11/2958.

4   Loren and Benjamin Chotzen, interview by Joan Singler, November 27, 2007; Yvonne Chotzen emails to Singler, August 2009.

5   Charles Cornethan, telephone interview by Joan Singler, November 28, 2007; Lane Smith, "CORE Leader Holds Firm Belief in Militancy—with 'Some Dignity,'" *Seattle Times*, September 10, 1967.

6   Folayan Oni-Robertson, interview by Joan Singler and Bettylou Valentine, May 5, 2007.

7   Gil Esparza telephone communication with Joan Singler, April 29, 2008, and email May 3, 2008.

8   Sue Gottfried: Sue Davidson, interview by Joan Singler, Bettylou Valentine, and Maid Adams, April 15, 2007; Sue Davidson curriculum vitae, in Davidson personal papers.

9   Esther Hall Mumford, interview by Bettylou Valentine, October 22, 2006.

10 Oral history interview by Mary Henry, June 6, 1999, Black Heritage Society, Museum of History and Industry, Seattle; Mary Henry, "Hundley, Walter R. (1929–2002)," Essay 3173, HistoryLink.org; "Walter Hundley, Unlikely Bureaucrat, Dies at 73," *Seattle Post- Intelligencer*, June 8, 2002.

11 Reverend Mance Jackson, telephone interviews by Jean Durning, March 21 and April 4, 2006.

12 Norman O. Johnson, interview by Joan Singler, April 8, 2006.

13 Wallace L. Johnson, interview by Joan Singler, August 23, 2006, emails May 8, 2008, and subsequent.

14 David and Mary Lamb, interview by Joan Singler, June 12, 2006, and email January 22, 2007.

15 Mrs. Lightfoot's application to CORE regarding supermarket employment, fall 2001, "Application for Employment," box 6, Misc., Applications for Employment folder, Seattle Collection; Infanta Spence-Lewis emails to Joan Singler, April 2006, November 14, 2006, and spring 2007.

16 Infanta Spence-Lewis, email to Joan Singler, December 20, 2007.

17 Harold Martin and Georgia Martin, untitled report [to Citizens' Advisory Committee for Minority Housing], August 15, 1962, CORE, Matson Collection; Tim Martin Oral History, Eastside Heritage Center, February 18, 1992, one-page excerpt by Museum of History and Industry, Seattle; obituary, *Eastside Journal*, July 2, 2002.

18 Laura Matson, interview by Joan Singler, September 2008; Unitarians for Social Justice archives, University Unitarian Church, Seattle.

19 Mary Henry, "Miller, Dr. Earl V. (1923–2005)," Essay 7284, HistoryLink.org; numerous records, NAACP, Seattle, 465–001, Special Collections Division, University of Washington Libraries. For Harmony Homes, see Sidney Gerber Papers, 503/584/968, Special Collections Division, University of Washington Libraries.

20 Sadikifu Akina-James, interview by Joan Singler and Bettylou Valentine, May 5, 2007.

21 Millie Russell response to questionnaire, October 2007; program for Ed Russell memorial service, December 29, 2007.

22 Bettylou Valentine recollection, papers in her personal possession.

23 Deloris Tarzan Ament, "Washington, James Jr. (1911–2000): Art as Holy Land," March 1, 2003, Essay 5328, HistoryLink.org; Susan Noyes Platt, "James W. Washington, Jr. Making a Life/Creating a World," Northwest African American Museum, March 2008; other materials at James and Janie Rogella Washington Foundation, 1816 Twenty-Sixth Avenue, Seattle.

24 Maid Adams recollection; Edward White personal communication with Maid Adams.

BIBLIOGRAPHY

Bell, Inge Powell. *CORE and the Strategy of Nonviolence*. New York: Random House, 1968.

Branch, Taylor. *Parting the Waters: America in the King Years, 1954–63*. New York: Simon and Schuster, 1988.

———. *Pillar of Fire: America in the King Years, 1963–65*. New York: Simon and Schuster, 1998.

———. *At Canaan's Edge: America in the King Years, 1965–68*. New York: Simon and Schuster, 2006.

Cameron, Mindy. "Tradition to Transformation: How Seattle Is Reinventing Its Public Schools." Seattle: Alliance for Education, [2002?].

Chasan, Dan. "All about CORE." Congress of Racial Equality, 38 Park Row, New York, NY, no date.

Clark, Brooke. "Boycott! The Seattle School Boycott of 1966." *Colors Northwest*, February 2006.

CORE. "CORE's Rule for Action." Congress of Racial Equality, 38 Park Row, New York, NY, no date.

———. "This Is CORE." Congress of Racial Equality, 38 Park Row, New York, NY, no date.

Donner, Frank. *The Age of Surveillance: The Aims and Methods of America's Political Intelligence System*. New York: Alfred A. Knopf, 1980.

Droker, Alan. "The Seattle Civic Unity Committee and the Civil Rights Movement." PhD diss., University of Washington, 1974.

Farmer, James. *Lay Bear the Heart: An Autobiography of the Civil Rights Movement.* New York: Arbor House, 1985.

Frantilla, Anne. "The Seattle Open Housing Campaign, 1959–1968." Seattle Municipal Archives, www.seattle.gov/CityArchives/exhibits/ddl.htm.

"Freedom Riders Speak for Themselves." *A News and Letters Pamphlet (8751 Grand River, Detroit, MI)*, November 1961. Civil Rights folders. James and Janie Rogella Washington Foundation, 1816 Twenty-Sixth Ave., Seattle.

Garrow, David J. *Bearing the Cross: Martin Luther King Jr., and the Southern Christian Leadership Conference.* New York: William Morrow, 1978.

Gregory, Dick. *Nigger: An Autobiography.* With Robert Lipsyte. New York: Washington Square Press, 1964.

Hampton, Harry, executive producer. *Eyes on the Prize.* Six-part television series, Public Broadcasting System. Boston: Blackside, Inc., [1987?].

Henry, Mary T. "Barr, Roberta Byrd (1919–1993)." Essay 306, November 9, 1998. www.HistoryLink.org.

———. "Bass, Robert A. (1926–2002)." Essay 7595, December 7, 2002. www.HistoryLink.org.

———. "Burton, Philip (1915–1995)." Essay 321, November 10, 1998. www.HistoryLink.org.

———. "Hubbard, Walter, Jr. (1924–2007)." Essay 8184, June 18, 2007. www.HistoryLink.org.

———. "Hundley, Walter R. (1929–2002)." Essay 3173, www.HistoryLink.org.

———. Walt Hundley oral history interview. June 6, 1999. Black Heritage Society, Museum of History and Industry, Seattle.

———. "Miller, Dr. Earl V. (1923–2005)." Essay 7284, March 27, 2005. www.HistoryLink.org.

———. "Scott, Tyree (1940–2003)." Essay 8222, July 24, 2007. www.HistoryLink.org.

———. "Smith, E. June (1900–1982)." www.BlackPast.org.

Hopper, Mary E., and E. Harriet Gipson. *A Frontier of the Spirit.* Seattle: M. E. Hopper and E. H. Gipson, [1960s].

[Hopperstad, Sherry]. "Washington's Negro Pioneer . . . George Washington Bush." Seattle: Congress of Racial Equality, [1967].

Hult, Ruby El. "The Saga of George W. Bush, Unheralded Pioneer of the Northwest Territory." *Black Digest*, September 1962, 88–96.

Levy, Peter B., ed. *Let Freedom Ring: A Documentary History of the Modern Civil Rights Movement.* New York: Praeger, 1992.

Lewis, John. *Walking with the Wind: A Memoir of the Movement.* With Michael D'Orso. New York: Simon and Schuster, 1998.

McGee, Henry W., Jr. "Seattle's Central District, 1990–2006: Integration or Displacement?" *Urban Lawyer* 39, no. 2 (2007): 167.

Meier, August, and Elliott Rudwick. *CORE: A Study in the Civil Rights Movement, 1942–1968.* New York: Oxford University Press, 1973.

Northwood, L. K., and Ernest A. T. Barth. *Urban Desegregation: Black Pioneers and Their White Neighbors.* Seattle: University of Washington Press, 1965.

Palmer, Douglas. Unfinished biography of Sid Gerber, draft manuscript. Seattle, no date. Sidney Gerber Papers. 503/584/968. Special Collections Division, University of Washington Libraries.

Pieroth, Doris Hinson. "Desegregating the Public Schools, Seattle, Washington, 1954–1968." PhD diss., University of Washington, 1979.

Purnell, Brian. "A Movement Grows in Brooklyn: The Brooklyn Chapter of the Congress of Racial Equality (CORE) and the Northern Civil Rights Movement during the Early 1960s." PhD diss., New York University, 2006.

Rich, Marvin. "The Congress of Racial Equality and Its Strategy." *Annals of the American Academy of Political and Social Science* 357 (January 1965): 113–18.

Richardson, Larry S. "Civil Rights in Seattle: A Rhetorical Analysis of a Social Movement." PhD diss., Washington State University, 1975.

Romano, Renee C., and Leigh Raiford, eds. *The Civil Rights Movement in American Memory.* Athens: University of Georgia Press, 2006.

Sale, Roger. *Seattle Past to Present.* Seattle: University of Washington Press, 1976.

Schmid, Calvin F., and Wayne W. McVey. *Growth and Distribution of Minority Races in Seattle, Washington.* Seattle: Seattle Public Schools, 1964.

Spears, Richard A. *Slang and Euphemism: A Dictionary of Oaths, Curses, Insults, Sexual Slang and Metaphor, Racial Slurs, Drug Talk, Homosexual Lingo, and Related Matters.* Middle Village, NY: Jonathan David Publishers, 1981.

Sugrue, Thomas J. *Sweet Land of Liberty: The Forgotten Struggle for Civil Rights in the North.* New York: Random House, 2008.

Taylor, Quintard. *The Forging of a Black Community: Seattle's Central District from 1870 through the Civil Rights Era.* Seattle: University of Washington Press, 1994.

Valentine, Bettylou. *Hustling and Other Hard Work: Life Styles in the Ghetto.* New York: Free Press, 1978.

Valentine, Charles A. *DEEDS: Background and Basis, a Report on Research Leading to the Drive for Equal Employment in Downtown Seattle.* Seattle: CORE, 1964.

———. "Segregation and Integration in Seattle's Public Schools." Seattle: CORE, August 1964.

Washington State Board against Discrimination. "Non-white Participation in the Building Trade Unions—Seattle—October/November 1965." Report. 1965.

Williams, Juan. *Eyes on the Prize: America's Civil Rights Years, 1954–1965*. New York: Viking, 1987.

Willix, Mary, and Elaine Hayes, eds. *Remembering Ralph Hayes, African American Historian*. Seattle: Creative Forces Publishing, 2008.

DAILY NEWSPAPERS

Daily of the University of Washington
New York Times
Seattle Post-Intelligencer (P-I)
Seattle Times

WEEKLY NEWSPAPERS

Aero Mechanic
Argus
Catholic Northwest Progress
Eastside Journal (Bellevue, WA)
The Facts
Helix
Mercer Island Reporter
Real Change
Seattle Observer (previously *Puget Sound Observer*)

MAJOR ONLINE SOURCES

On-line Encyclopedia of Washington State History. www.HistoryLink.org.
Seattle Civil Rights and Labor History Project. www.civilrights.washington.edu.
Seattle Municipal Archives. www.seattle.gov/CityArchives/exhibits/ddl.htm.
Taylor, Quintard. Online Reference Guide to African American History. www.BlackPast.org.

INDEX

White, Frances, 156, 164, 172, 193–94, 199–200, 231
White, Joe, 96
Whittenbaugh, John, 138
Williams, Rev. C.E., 116
Williams, Ray, 17–18, 24
Wilson, Marshall, 112
Winsor, Robert, 53, 104, 137
women, 184; childcare, 185–87; employment opportunities for, 6; in unions, 96
Wonder Bread, 50

Woodland Park Presbyterian Church, 105, 157
Woolworth, 15, 21
Wright, Eugene, 134

Yellow Cab Co., 83, 86
Young, Andrew, 173
Young, Dan, 95
Young, Tasia, 186

Zackery, Donald, 168

Photo by Walter Bodle

JOAN SINGLER (*top left*) was a founding member of Seattle CORE and served as the CORE secretary and chaired the Housing Committee. She went on to receive a BA in psychology at the University of Washington and a teaching certificate in Early Childhood Development. She most recently worked as a travel consultant and has helped victims of domestic violence. JEAN DURNING (*top right*) joined CORE after moving to Seattle in 1959. Subsequently, she coordinated studies at the Human Environmental Foundation and served as the northwest director of the Wilderness Society from 1981 to 1993, all while teaching junior high school. BETTYLOU VALENTINE (*bottom left*), a national board member of the NAACP, joined Seattle CORE in 1964. She later received her PhD in anthropology from Washington University and is the author of *Hustling and Other Hard Work.* MAID ADAMS (*bottom right*) joined Seattle CORE in 1962. She has an MA in education psychology from the University of Washington and was the program director of the Women's Center at Green River Community College for twenty years. All of the authors have remained active in various political and community issues.

CPSIA information can be obtained
at www.ICGtesting.com
Printed in the USA
LVHW060455291020
670068LV00006B/417